FORCES OF ORDER

David H. Bayley

FORCES
OF ORDER

Police Behavior
in Japan and the
United States

UNIVERSITY OF CALIFORNIA PRESS

Berkeley • Los Angeles • London

University of California Press
Berkeley and Los Angeles, California
University of California Press, Ltd.
London, England
Copyright © 1976, by
The Regents of the University of California
ISBN 0-520-03069-9
Library of Congress Catalog Card Number: 75-17304
Printed in the United States of America

To
W. W. LOCKWOOD —
teacher, friend, and exemplar

Contents

Preface

Americans are often urged to study foreign countries and cultures, the usual reason given being the need to overcome parochialism and to broaden intellectual horizons. These are valuable purposes, to be sure, but they obscure another one which is equally important and often overlooked. Foreign travel is a means of learning about oneself and one's society. What is distinctive in one's own world, too familiar usually to be recognized, becomes obvious by comparison with the lives of others. It is important to discover what differences there are among the peoples of the world; it is no less important to discover what makes these differences alien.

This book is an attempt to learn about the police problems of the United States by studying Japanese police institutions. Japan is a particularly apt comparison with the United States. It is modern and affluent, congested and urbanized. It belongs to the world's "developed" nations. Comparisons between the United States and Japan are not vitiated by disparities in technical capacity, educational levels, wealth, or dominant modes of production. What stands out between the two is culture, not modernity. The thrust of the analysis will be to note differences in institutional practices between the nations' police, then to explain why the practices diverge in characteristic ways. In this way, it should be possible to highlight what in American history, culture, and character shape police performance today.

A study of the police also provides a new vantage point for viewing contemporary Japanese society. Police penetrate society more completely than any other governmental agency, and policemen see things that most private citizens do not. Their perspective, though not representative, is no less authentic than any other. And it may have the advantage of being more extensive. The police are also a part of society. Because society works in them one can learn something about the society by observing them. Borrowing from the anthropologists, the police may be regarded as a village — not the only one but a real one nonetheless.

The book does not provide a complete description of Japanese police institutions; Japanese experience is drawn on selectively in order to illuminate contemporary American police affairs. The topics discussed reflect my own troubled preoccupations — preoccupations I am sure are shared by many others. Moreover, the book focuses on patrol work. This reflects my strong belief that the success or failure of any police force is determined by procedures affecting behavior in encounters, especially face-to-face, between police and citizens. Matters of formal organization, forensic technique, and equipment, which preoccupy so much of the professional literature on the police, will be ignored unless they affect contact-behavior directly. The neglect of patrol work by so many observers, let alone writers of fictional works about the police, is curious in several respects. Patrol activity accounts for the bulk of police manpower; criminal investigation, considered by so many the essence of policing, is a relatively small specialty. Patrol officers provide almost all emergency help; their patrolling is probably the most effective crime prevention measure; and they are the only policemen most people will ever meet. Furthermore, patrol activity is much more open to public gaze than criminal investigation. Because the rights of suspects as well as victims must be protected and because surprise is essential in detection, criminal investigation is largely invisible to outsiders. Paradoxically, then, the public knows least about the police work it is most interested in and cares least about what it can know best. And its interest bears no relation to what most policemen do most of the time.

The following subjects are discussed in the book: the performance record of the police and the incidence of criminality in Japan (chapter 1); police contacts with people and a patrolman's life (chapters 2 and 3); discipline and responsibility (chapter 4); police relations with the community (chapter 5); victimless crime (chapter 6); deviance and authority (chapter 7); violence in society (chapter 8); and the police as an institution (chapter 9).

Policemen in Japan are legally and ostensibly like policemen in the United States. No problems of comparability arise. There is a question, however, whether generalizations can properly be made about police based on national units. Can a characteristic of police operations be fairly called Japanese or American? Are police practices sufficiently homogeneous in each country so such generalizations are intelligent? In Japan they are. Japan has only one police force; its system is not a patchwork of overlapping forces and jurisdictions as in the United States. Though command of operations is decentralized among the country's forty-six prefectures, policies are so standardized that it is proper to refer to the *Japanese* police. In the United States problems of generalization are undoubtedly more acute. I believe it is fair to speak of *American* practices for the following reason: differences along any dimension of comparison are greater between any American force and the Japanese police than between any two American forces. American police forces are more similar to each other than to the Japanese force. This conclusion is subject to testing, and I invite readers to determine from their own knowledge whether features of police activity discussed in the book are more similar within each nation than between them.

The study is based on six months of field research in Japan distributed over two summers. Unable to free myself from the obligations of the academic year, I initially resented the hiatus between the two field experiences. I now believe that dividing field research into separate episodes, as long as they are not too short, has definite advantages provided the interim is used for thorough review and reconsideration. Reflection on an initial research episode allows omissions to be spotted, unfruitful approaches discovered, and tactics reexamined. The second field experience becomes more than a continuation; it is a second study, at some points a restudy.

The research in Japan involved observation of police operations and interviews with hundreds of officers. Because operations are organized for the most part in terms of police stations, I made a selection of police stations located in a variety of socio-economic areas — urban, rural, heavy industrial, upper-class residential, university, new towns, commercial, entertainment, and so forth. The sample was drawn from four prefectures — Tokyo, Aomori, Osaka, and Fukuoka. Generally about five days were spent studying each station. Observation of police operations was carried out mostly at night — the busiest hours for the police. I would accompany officers working in patrol cars or in Japan's unique police boxes (*koban*). Formal interviews were held with the chief of each police station (or his deputy) and with the heads of each major section — patrol, criminal investigation, crime prevention, and administration. Because I was particularly interested in contact-behavior, interviews were held with at least one officer at every rank level within the patrol section of each station. Interviews were also conducted with all ranks of detectives but not necessarily in each station. The police are organized into prefectural commands so it was important to talk to senior officers at prefectural headquarters. This meant the chief of the prefecture and the heads of each functional section. Some specialized operations are organized on a prefectural, as opposed to a station, basis and they required additional study — riot control, traffic regularion, vice surveillance, and some criminal investigation.

Choices about sites to visit and persons to interview were made entirely by me. No attempt was ever made to deny me access to a location, officer, or operation (subject to the legal requirements of confidentiality). Indeed, I often discovered that I was more hesitant to ask to see a particular operation, out of fear of being considered presumptuous, than police officers were to show it to me. I soon sensed that Japanese officers, being experienced professionals, would have thought less well of me if I had not asked to see sensitive situations and talk to critically placed personnel. Altogether, the police were as accessible as I could ask, certainly as accessible as the canons of scholarship require. I am deeply grateful to the Japanese police for the trust in me which this openness represented.

Travelling and working with the police provides an extraordinarily varied and intimate view of any society. In Japan I have accompanied the police at all hour into bars, jails, dancehalls, fish markets, striptease shows, security posts, schools, movie theaters, private homes, pedestrian malls, Mah-Jong parlors, apartments, restaurants, pawn shops, public baths, shops, entertainment arcades, temples, and gangster offices. This book is about the human events that occurred in those settings and the way in which the police related to them. As varied as the settings, the events had one quality in common — they were real. They were not staged or contrived or acted out for the tourist. Some events were dramatic — a lost child or the hospitalization of an alcoholic husband. Some incidents were hilarious, as when an elderly woman asked my patrolmen companions to have me — referred to as the *gaijin* (foreigner) — eat her four-year-old grandson because he was misbehaving. Many events were acutely embarrassing to the people involved — teenagers who had been caught breaking into a high school, a businessman helplessly drunk, homosexuals arrested in a public place. And some were poignant. I remember particularly a distinguished chief of police who, retiring after thirty-three years of service, acknowledged my presence among the audience — some of whom were in tears — when he gave his farewell address to his men. For an outsider to be allowed to be part of such human events is a great privilege. Time and again I asked myself what right I had to intrude into the lives of so many people. Scholarly observation often seemed like an act of trespass. Yet the Japanese people — police and private persons alike — not only permitted me to enter their lives as they lived them, they consistently pretended that I was inconspicuous. For such generosity and consideration, any expressions of gratitude are inadequate.

Though access to police operations and personnel was faultless, there are still important questions to be raised about the veracity of my findings. To what extent can a scholar, and a foreigner to boot, expect to be told the truth by policeman about police matters? It would be naive to think that Japanese policemen were not apprehensive that I would portray them in an unfavorable light. They were concerned about the reputation of their organization and their reactions to me were instinctively cautious. This is true of policemen everywhere, whether in Bombay, New York, or Stockholm. At the same time, police institutions are not impenetrable to scholarship and I did not find that wariness on the part of the police was peculiarly acute in Japan. Policemen in most countries want their point of view to be presented. If they find a researcher sympathetic and willing to listen, they seize the opportunity to present life as they see it and live it. This is precisely what the researcher wants, for it allows dialogue to begin that can lead to the building of trust. In the Japanese case, my being a foreign professor aided this process in some respects. Japanese policemen think that their own scholars insufficiently appreciate the job of the police and habitually approach the police with strong ideological biases. My interest, therefore, was subtly flattering, according them the serious academic attention they thought they deserved. Moreover, they were impressed by the fact that I wanted to find out about daily operating procedures, rather than simply about certain highly publicized events or aspects of police work. Being an American helped as well. Japanese policemen are proud of their accomplishments and want foreigners to know about them. To show these to an American, whose police system they believe to be in serious trouble, was especially attractive. This is not to suggest that they were completely forthcoming about their own defects. Of course they tried to show themselves to best advantage. For a researcher, however, unwillingness to communicate is a far more serious obstacle than desire to impress. Handling bias and building rapport are what interviewing is all about; without ready communication the researcher cannot begin to employ the skills of his craft. Japanese policemen were anxious to talk, and because they felt they had nothing to hide—a point that will be discussed in chapter 1—they were far less defensive than many American policemen I have interviewed.

One method of building rapport is to demonstrate shared expertise. People in most occupations like nothing better than to talk about their work to interested and informed outsiders. Prior to going to Japan I had spent two years in India and several in the United States studying police operations. The police institution was not new to me. By referring to police practices elsewhere with appropriate detail, I could convince Japanese officers that I was a serious student of their work. As my knowledge of Japanese procedures grew, I could compel more frank exchanges by citing specific observations and facts. On several occasions when a pointed question of mine had been met with vague generalities, I responded by noting gently but frankly that I actually had seen the contrary. Rather than being affronted, my informants consistently paused, laughed, and complimented me on the unusual penetration of my research. They would then go on to supply additional information. Their readiness to reply to contradictory fact with forthright candor is an admirable trait.

Finally, the process of building rapport is something the Japanese understand explicitly. One of the words Japanese use to discuss interpersonal relations is *ninjo*. The other is *giri*, and both will be discussed in detail later. *Ninjo* refers to sympathy, warmth, empathic identification between two persons. Where only social scientists talk much about rapport in the United States, every Japanese can recognize and discuss the amount of *ninjo* in a relationship. *Ninjo* enhances rapport; in some ways it is rapport. Policemen were willing, therefore, to shape their response to me according to whatever subtle links of warmth and sympathy our meeting generated. They were not locked into a posture of reaction by my formal attributes; they were open to the creation of personal bonds that transcended official roles. This did not happen in every case, but it was a possibility that increased the likelihood of obtaining candid responses.

In summary, Japanese policemen were as quick as American policemen to perceive the thrust of my questions, to determine potential embarrassment. Because, however, they were proud of what they were doing, admired expertise, and were open to the interplay of personality, frank exchanges with Japanese police officers were not usually difficult to obtain.

The most serious handicap from which this study suffers is my inability to speak Japanese. I was forced to work entirely through an interpreter. How much I missed as a result I cannot begin to estimate. The costs were greater in conducting field observations than formal interviews. Indeed, there are advantages to using an interpreter in an interview. Translation, though it prolongs interviews, provides moment of respite during which the researcher can make notes and organize thoughts before plunging into another question. Control is easier to maintain, though nuances are undoubtedly missed that should affect the course of the conversation. In field observation there are no advantages at all, apart from having an extra pair of eyes. There is so much that might be important, yet winnowing decisions have to be made. At a street altercation, for example, what should the researcher tell his interpreter to tell him: what is each person saying, what are the identities of each speaker, how much respect is being shown, what is the issue, who is trying to mediate, what seems to be the emotion behind the words of each speaker, and so forth? A great deal can be learned by simply watching, listening for tones of voice, and observing gestures and facial expressions. But inferences based exclusively on observation are apt to be misleading; the researcher can be wholly wrong and never know it. The longer a researcher and his interpreter work together, the more sensitive they become to each other's needs. The interpreter understands more fully what the researcher is interested in; the researcher learns when he must be quiet and allow the interpreter to listen uninhibitedly. Enormous patience is required on both sides.

To the extent that it was possible to minimize the disadvantages of working in a language I did not understand, I was able to do so through the ability, sensitivity, and intelligence of Nozomu Nakagawa, who served throughout the project as my interpreter. "Naka-san," as he allowed me to call him, began by being my interpreter, became a colleague, and ended as a friend. Not only was he a faithful voice and keen ear, he contributed original insights to the research and often prompted me about matters that I would have neglected to explore. Having lived for several years in the United States, he understood which aspects of Japanese culture an American would misperceive or overlook. With infinite care he explained the subtleties of many situations until he was sure I understood. Because he was with me throughout the project, he came to understand the purposes of the research and to anticipate my needs for information.

It often seemed to me that our relationship was the reenactment of a famous comradeship from literature: that of Don Quixote and Sancho Panza. Like Don Quixote I was the taller, thinner, older of the two. I possessed a set of objectives intelligible fully only to myself. Like Sancho Panza, Naka-san had to mediate between my driving vision and the reality of life in Japan. Often I stood mutely amid a host of attentive Japanese, like an abstracted statue, as Naka-san tried to fit my desires to the possibilities of the social setting. He had to watch as I strove with false impressions, waiting for the appropriate moment to teach me that what I perceived were really windmills. And he felt Sancho Panza's anxiety that his Don might suddenly say or do something totally out of keeping with propriety.

I am very grateful to the encouragement and intellectual support provided my many American experts on Japan. As a group, they proved to be most unclannish, not at all resentful of an India scholar poaching in their preserve. They introduced me to friends, gave invaluable advice about tactics, and shared their knowledge and insights. Most important of all, they reassured me that the study was both useful and feasible. I hope that after reading this book they still believe so. I am particularly indebted to Lawrence W. Beer, Joyce C. Lebra, Chalmers Johnson, W.W. Lockwood, Marius B. Jansen, and Rodney W. Armstrong. Mikio Kato and the staff of the International House of Japan, Tokyo, provided crucial technical assistance, wise counsel, and a friendly home away from home. Sayako Hirose and Takeko Sakakura diligently translated many documents. The manuscript was typed by Sue Hemphill. The study was made possible by grant No. G5-33052 from the National Science Foundation. I am very grateful for their support.

My greatest debt is owed to countless police officers throughout Japan who generously gave their time, experience, and hospitality. Many of them have become personal friends. I hope that what I have written justifies in some measure the faith they have had in me. The Japanese have done their best to help me understand their country and its police system. If I have failed to do so, the fault is mine.

1. Heaven for a Cop

Japan is a long way from the United States. With respect to law enforcement it is a different world.

Ask a senior police officer anywhere in Japan—a station chief, riot-troop commander, or head of a detective section—what kind of misconduct by subordinate officers causes him the greatest concern and he will invariably cite off-duty traffic accidents, drunkenness, and indiscretions with women. Almost as an aside he may mention that policemen are sometimes careless with their pistols, discharging them accidentally or having them stolen. One listens in vain for concern about the disciplinary problems that trouble commanders in the United States—brutality, rudeness, corruption. Even off-the-record, when rapport has been built through hours of technical talk, shared patrol experiences, and innumerable cups of green tea, Japanese officers steadily maintain that the major discipline problems involve off-duty behavior, especially driving, drinking, and womanizing.

To an American this kind of testimony is incredible. American officers, though hardly forthcoming on this topic, would not be nearly as bland and disingenuous. So the suspicion grows that Japanese officers are not being candid. They may be reluctant to tell an outsider, especially a foreigner, the true state of affairs. Or, alternately, perhaps they themselves do not know what is really going on. Rather than dissembling, they are simply ill-informed.

If they are not being candid, the fault is systematic. What they report privately is exactly what they tell their public, and both are supported by official statistics. In 1972, for instance, there were approximately 182,000 police officers in Japan.[1] Only 45 of them were discharged for misbehavior. Departmental punishments—meaning temporary suspension, reduction in pay, and formal reprimands—were given to another 524 officers.[2] Compared to the incidence of police misconduct in the United States, this is a drop in

1. National Police Agency, *The Police of Japan* (Tokyo: The National Police Agency, 1974), p. 45. These figures are for authorized strength; actual strength is somewhat less.
2. Data provided by the National Police Agency. These figures include officers found guilty by courts.

the bucket. The New York City police department, which has 35,000 men, punished 216 officers in 1972, not quite half the total for all Japan. Even a moderate-sized force like the one in Denver, Colorado, with about 1,300 officers, either fired or pressured into resigning 12 policemen in 1972, almost one-third the Japanese total. Lesser punishments were awarded to 233 other officers.[3] The reasons for punishing officers in Japan were indeed trivial. The most common reason for punishing a policeman, including firing, was involvement in a traffic accident, private as well as on-duty incidents.[4] The next most important reasons were loss of the police handbook (13 percent) and improper drinking behavior (10.5 percent).

The official view, unbelievable as it seems, is supported by outside observers. Police reporters and defense attorneys, who have a vested interest in finding out what is really going on, all say that corruption is almost nonexistent and brutality extremely rare. Nor do they think it likely that supervisory officers are being misled or careless. They do not believe that Japan is sitting on the brink of major police scandals.

In a representative year only five officers are punished in connection with corruption.[5] Observers, as well as policemen, dismiss out of hand the notion of group corruption through a network of payoffs from criminal operatives such as gamblers, prostitutes, or narcotics peddlers. Japanese officers are fascinated by the organization of such systems in the United States. So much so that an American observer sometimes feels like a corrupter of the innocent as he explains to a rapt audience the details of American ingenuity. Brutality — unnecessary physical force — occurs sometimes in the handling of disorderly drunks, as the police themselves admit, but hardly ever in the course of criminal investigations. Defense lawyers and police reporters also call attention to the rough handling of student demonstrators; the majority of complaints as well as proven charges, they say, arise in this connection. Defense attorneys deny that standards of police propriety in handling suspects are affected by social class. They do not believe that lack of wealth makes suspects more vulnerable to abuse by the police. Theft and extortion by policemen are as rare as other forms of misconduct, and again never seem to involve groups of officers. In 1972

3. Data provided by the police departments of New York City and Denver, Colorado.
4. 48 percent of all officers fired and 43 percent of officers punished for other reasons.
5. Data provided by National Police Agency.

nine officers were punished for theft, fraud, and embezzlement together.

Another piece of evidence that discipline in the police is as good as police officers say is that there is no movement among the public for the creation of new mechanisms of supervision and investigation of misconduct. There is already a form of civilian review outside the police. This is the Human Rights Bureau of the Ministry of Justice, established in 1948. There are human rights offices in every major city plus 10,000 volunteer counsellors throughout the country. They receive complaints about violations of rights at the hands of government servants as well as private citizens. Amazing as it may seem, the number of complaints against the police brought to the Human Rights Bureau has been falling every year. In 1972 only 123 complaints were received in all Japan.[6]

The skeptic may argue that a low number of complaints indicates that people are simply not sensitive to police misconduct, not that behavior is uniformly good. This is plausible, but it is not the case in Japan. Police officers complain with considerable justification that newspapers are delighted to publicize the misdeeds of policemen. It is especially irritating to them when the press identifies an offender as an "ex-police officer," making a point of a former affiliation. Police and crime stories are big news. Police reporting is one of the largest areas of specialization in every daily newspaper. Yomiuri Shimbun, for example, assigns twenty-four reporters to police reporting in Tokyo alone.[7] Reporters cultivate personal contacts within the force so that they are not dependent on official versions of events. Furthermore, the Japanese public has had considerable experience with police misconduct in the recent past. There are still vivid memories of prewar investigative practices which relied heavily on harassment and third-degree. During the immediate postwar years corruption was common as black-marketeers and gangsters tried to subvert whole police departments.[8] The Japanese people

6. Information provided by the Human Rights Bureau, Ministry of Justice, Tokyo, 1973.
7. Twelve reporters are assigned to the headquarters of the Metropolitan Police Department and twelve more to the headquarters of the eight police districts into which Tokyo is divided. Personal interview, 1973.
8. Perhaps the most widely publicized scandal occurred in Honjo, Saitama Prefecture, in 1948. An Ashahi newspaper reporter was assaulted on the street for revealing systematic pay-offs to local politicians and the police by gangsters involved in black-market operations. Asahi Shimbun, *The Pacific Rivals* (New York: Weatherhill-Asahi, 1972), p. 143, and Supreme Commander for the Allied Powers, "Police and Public Safety," *History of the Nonmilitary Activities for the Occupation of Japan*, Historical Monograph Number 55, pp. 102-105.

have ample reason for knowing what an unwatched and unregulated police can do.

The fact is that a transformation has occurred in police behavior in Japan within twenty-five years, a relatively short period of time. It is associated with democratization and is one of the most prized developments of the postwar period. Japan's contemporary record of excellence with respect to police behavior is striking, then, not only in relation to the United States but in relation to its own past.[9]

In sum, if generality of agreement among people in a country is the mark of truth, then Japanese police behavior is astonishingly good. The incidence of misconduct is slight and the faults trivial by American standards. Though a cynical American may always wonder if enough is known about the conduct of individual officers — whether by himself or by insiders — he must begin to consider the disturbing possibility that police conduct need not inevitably, recurrently, require substantial improvement.

Japanese police operations are not conducted in an atmosphere of crisis and declining public confidence. There has been no spate of special investigations or national commissions. Surveys show that the public believes that police performance has been steadily improving. A poll taken in 1972, for instance, showed that 80 percent of the people who think the police have changed in the last five years believe it is for the better. There are some pockets of hostility, mostly among ideologies of the left. University students in particular are antagonistic to the police, especially during organized political demonstrations.

The Japanese police display a pride in themselves that is quite remarkable. They are supremely self-confident, not doubting the worth of the police role in society or the public's support of it. The 1973 *White Paper on the Police* betrays no deep-seated anxiety about the position of the police in modern Japan. Policemen are neither defensive nor alienated. Though they have a strong sense of belonging to a distinct occupational community, solidarity has been self-imposed. They have not been driven in upon themselves by a critical public, isolated among their own kind. There has been no "blue power" movement in Japan, no organized effort among policemen to fend off threats to police autonomy. Officers do not feel victimized in pay or benefits, though they can cite improvements they would like in working conditions. Strikes by policemen are unheard of and the regulations banning formation of police unions are unquestioned. Recruitment of new officers is relatively

9. American experts on Japan that I have talked to, some of whom lived in Japan during the Occupation, are unanimous in the opinion that police behavior has changed radically for the better in the last two decades.

easy, the number of applicants running at six times the number of vacancies.[10]

American policemen view other agencies in the criminal justice system as uncertain allies in the fight against crime. Resentment is particularly bitter against the courts, which they claim have unduly restricted the activities of policemen or are being too lenient with arrested offenders. Japanese detectives, by contrast, are more outspoken about their own shortcomings than those of others. Getting them to evaluate the effect of judicial decisions on police performance or criminality is like pulling teeth. They seem to have given the matter very little thought. They certainly do not feel that they have been insufficiently supported or frequently criticized unfairly.

Even more striking is the absence of heroism in the posture of Japanese policemen. They do not think of themselves as society's last defense against moral decay. Correspondingly, there is no self-pity among them; they do not feel embattled against the unappreciative and the hostile. Police offices are not decorated with signs saying "Even pigs need friends" or "When you're in trouble, call a hippie" or posters showing a policeman giving mouth-to-mouth resuscitation, with the caption, "Some call him pig."

The primary purpose of any police force is to protect people from crime. The crime rate in Japan is so low in comparison with that of the United States that Japanese policemen seem hardly to be challenged at all. This accounts, to some extent, for their self-confidence. There were four-and-a-half times as many murders per person in the United States in 1973 as in Japan—1.9 compared with 9.3 for every 100,000 people.[11] The New York metropolitan area alone, with a population of just under 12 million, had 1,739 murders in 1973—three-fourths as many as Japan, which has a population of 107 million.[12] Tokyo, which, like New York, has a population of 12 million, had only 196 murders.[13] The incidence of

10. Information provided by the National Police Agency.
11. Computed from data in U.S. Department of Justice, Federal Bureau of Investigation, *Crime in the United States: Uniform Crime Reports—1973* (Washington: Government Printing Office, 1973), and Japan, Ministry of Justice (information furnished privately, 1975). All figures that follow dealing with crime are from the same sources except where noted.
12. Two thousand fourteen homicides were known to the police in Japan in 1973.
13. It might be objected that using crime figures from New York City biases the sample of American criminality. This is not so. With respect to the F.B.I.'s index of serious crimes, at least forty-nine metropolitan areas in the United States had higher crime rates than New York in 1973. The rate for index crimes in the New York metropolitan area in 1973 was 5,457 per 100,000 persons. F.B.I., *Uniform Crime Reports—1973*, Table 5.

rape is five times higher in the United States than Japan.[14] In the New York metropolitan area, a woman is ten times more likely to be raped than in Tokyo. The most mind-boggling statistic has to do with robbery—taking property with force or threat of force. The rate is over one hundred five times higher in the United States than in Japan. In 1973, for example, there were 1,876 robberies in Japan against 382,680 in the United States, with 361 in Tokyo against 74,381 in New York City.[15] The reason for this enormous discrepancy has to do with the prevalence of guns in the United States. A drawn gun is a palpable threat. Japan, however, is a totally disarmed society; criminals hardly ever carry firearms. Theft is therefore less dangerous to its victims in Japan than in the United States because thieves are less able, perhaps less willing, to injure people.[16]

The Federal Bureau of Investigation in the United States analyzes trends in crime according to an index composed of the seven most serious crimes: murder, forcible rape, robbery, aggravated assault, burglary, larceny over fifty dollars and auto theft. To underscore just how different Japan is from the United States with respect to crime, consider this fact: there are four times as many serious crimes committed per person in the United States as there are crimes of all sorts, even the most petty, in Japan.[17] In 1973, for example, there were 8,638,400 serious crimes in the United States; in Japan, there were 1,190,549 crimes of all sorts.[18]

14. 5.1 per 100,000 persons versus 24.3 per 100,000 persons.
15. The Japanese penal code distinguishes two kinds of robbery: first, "simple robbery," Article 236—depriving a person of property through violence; and second, "Robbery involving homicide, injury, or rape," Articles 240 and 241— where the victim is killed or injured as a result of the commission of robbery. To come to a total robbery figure for Japan, I have added together the figures for both kinds. The statistics available on robbery for Tokyo do not make this distinction. It is possible, therefore, that the Tokyo figure is underreported by as much as half. The contrast with New York is clearly substantial.
16. The legal definition of robbery is the same in both countries as are the criteria for classifying robberies, according to police officials responsible for collecting crime data in both countries. One possible source of confusion comes in distinguishing robbery from extortion. In Japan, a person deprived of property because he could not resist is a victim of robbery; a person deprived of property because of fear of assault is a victim of extortion. In 1972, there were 13,197 cases of extortion in Japan. If all these were classified as robberies, the total for robbery would still be substantially lower than in the United States.
17. Referring in Japan to crimes under the Penal Code, but excluding negligence cases.
18. The rates respectively are 4,116 per 100,000 for serious crime in the United States and 1,110 per 100,000 for Penal Code offenses, excluding negligence, in Japan.

Yearly increases in the crime rate in the United States are as inevitable as death and taxes; they have ceased to be news. It is hard to believe, therefore, that in Japan there were actually fewer crimes in 1973 than in 1946, despite an increase in population. The crime rate — the incidence of crime per person — has fallen by almost half in the past twenty-five years. Since 1967, the rate for serious crime has risen by about 60 percent in the United States; in Japan, it has fallen by 2 percent.

Narcotics addiction and drug abuse, which have so baffled and alarmed the American public, have steadily declined in Japan. There were one-fourth as many violations of the drug laws in Japan in 1973 as in 1959. In 1973, in all of Japan, only 591 persons were sent by the police for prosecution for offenses involving hard drugs.[19] In Tokyo, the world's largest city, only about thirty persons are arrested each year for violation of hard drug laws.[20] Contrast this with New York City where addicts are estimated at a quarter of a million and 23,000 arrests were made in 1972 for sale and possession.[21] Marijuana and amphetamine use has been rising in Japan but their incidence is still miniscule compared with the United States — in 1973, 617 cases involving marijuana and 8,301 involving amphetamines.

Can these figures on the incidence of crime in Japan be accepted at face value? Are there any reasons for believing that they may be less reliable than American figures? In making an assessment of the reliability of crime statistics, two problems must be distinguished: underreporting — the failure of victims to bring offenses to the attention of the police — and falsification — the failure of the police to report accurately what they know.

Studies of underreporting by victims to the police have been done in both countries. They show that the rate of underreporting is higher in the United States than in Japan. The National Police Agency in Japan compared survey results from both countries for similar kinds of crime and found that the true incidence of theft was 82 percent higher than reported figures in Japan and 122 percent higher in the United States.[22] For aggravated assault, the true rate

19. Information provided by the National Police Agency.
20. Offenses under the Narcotics Control Law.
21. U.S. Department of Justice, Drug Enforcement Administration, *Drug Enforcement Statistical Report* (statistics complete through 1973), p. 37.
22. National Police Aency, *Study of Unreported Crime* (1970), Table 16. The results of this confidential study, printed only in Japanese, were made available to me by the National Police Agency. The N.P.A. study compares survey results from Japan against the National Opinion Research Corporation survey in the United States which was sponsored by the President's Commission on Law Enforcement

was 42 percent higher in Japan and 105 percent higher in the United States.[23] More recent polls support the conclusion that underreporting is greater in the United States than in Japan. A 1972 public opinion survey in Japan found that 40 percent of people who had been victims of crime failed to report them to the police.[24] Studies by the United States government in 1972 discovered that in the country's thirteen largest cities twice as many crimes were committed as were reported to the police.[25] Differences in crime rates between the United States and Japan cannot be discounted, therefore, on the basis of differences in the willingness of people to report crime to the police.

Inaccurate reporting by police officials is a more difficult problem to analyze because it is hard to construct an independent check of what police officers know apart from what they say. Notorious cases of distorted reporting have come to light sufficiently often in the United States to make most observers skeptical about official figures. To take one example, the crime rate in New Haven, Connecticut, rose 150 percent when a new police chief insisted on accurate reporting.[26] The fact that the ratio of unreported crime to reported crime in Philadelphia in 1972 was 5.1 to 1 has been attributed to falsification of official statistics as well as underreporting by victims.[27] There have been no revelations or even accusations of this kind in Japan. Procedures for collecting information about crime are identical in all police jurisdictions and reports are sent routinely to a central statistical office. Senior police officers serve short tours of duty in any jurisdiction, so they identify with a national police community rather than a local one. It is not especially in their interest to make a particular locality look good

and Administration of Justice. See *The Challenge of Crime in a Free Society* (Washington: Government Printing Office, 1967). The comparison between the United States and Japan is charitable to the United States. Theft in the U.S. refers to any property stolen whose value is in excess of $50; theft in Japan refers to any stolen property, regardless of value. Presumably the greater the value of property stolen, the more willing people are to report it to the police. These figures show, therefore, that Americans fail to report serious thefts more often than Japanese fail to report any theft.

23. *Ibid.*
24. Survey sponsored by the Office of Prime Minister and reported in *Public Opinion* (December 1972). This is a Japanese journal.
25. Survey carried out by the U.S. Bureau of the Census for the Law Enforcement Assistance Administration. Results reported in the *New York Times*, 15 April 1974, p. 1. The average ratio of unreported crime to reported crime in the thirteen cities was 2.5 to 1.0.
26. James F. Ahern, *Police in Trouble* (New York: Hawthorne Books Inc., 1972), p. 152.
27. *New York Times*, 15 April 1972, p. 1.

with respect to crime. Furthermore, routine rotation of personnel—usually every two years—makes it difficult to shape procedures to produce results that would be helpful to a particular officer's career. Since senior officers come and go, routine becomes compelling. And there would always be the danger that a subsequent supervisor, secure in his reputation, would unmask willful tampering.

Official figures on crime in Japan should be accepted as evidence of a profound difference in the incidence of criminality between Japan and the United States. This conclusion need not be based exclusively on statistics; it is supported by quite obvious differences in the quality of life. The streets of Japan are safe. Americans who live for a while in Japan soon begin to experience a liberating sense of freedom; they forget to be afraid. They learn to walk through city streets by night as well as day and not fear the sound of a following step, the sight of a lounging group of teenagers, or the query of a stranger for directions. Vandalism is rare; even graffiti is unobtrusive, at most pencilled mustaches on subway billboards. Public telephones show no signs of tampering and bus drivers make change. Every foreign visitor has a story of surprising acts of individual honesty—money left untouched in hotel rooms, lost purses returned, currency found again in the pocket of a suit brought back from the cleaners. In commuting to police operations I have walked at all hours through neighborhoods of every conceivable social condition and I have never experienced the slightest apprehension. Only twice did the police warn me about areas that should be avoided at night—the Sanya section of Tokyo and the Airin area of Nishinari ward in Osaka. These are Japan's "Skid Rows."

While the safety of Japanese cities cannot be overemphasized, representing as it does a qualitative difference in civility, Japan is not quite paradise. It has criminal problems—violence, gangsters, extortion, infanticide, bestiality, and rape. It has the pathologies of any society. Reducing crime is an important part of Japanese police work, one that the public appreciates. Subjective concern with crime is not directly proportional to objective incidence.

The Japanese record should convince thoughtful Americans to reassess two popular explanations about rising crime rates. First, crime is often attributed to urbanization, the clustering of people more densely into compact areas. Japan's population is about half that of the United States, yet it is crowded into a land area no bigger than California.[28] If forested land is excluded from calculations of

28. Japan, Office of the Prime Minister, Bureau of Statistics, *Statistical Handbook of Japan, 1972* (Tokyo: Japan Statistical Association, 1972), Chap. 3.

respective land areas, there are 2,326 people per square mile in Japan and 83 per square mile in the United States.[29] Almost two-thirds of Japan's 107 million people live concentrated around three metropolitan areas — Tokyo, Nagoya, and Osaka. Population density in Tokyo is 40,000 per square mile compared with 26,300 per square mile in New York City.[30] Almost one-fourth of all Japanese live within thirty-seven miles of downtown Tokyo — 25 million people.[31] What would Americans do to one another, one wonders, if half of them lived in a space no larger than California? Would crime rates fall, as they are doing in Japan?

Second, Americans often explain criminality in terms of their history, especially the frontier tradition of individual self-assertion, violence, rough-hewn justice, and handguns. Americans accept the recently coined aphorism that violence is as American as apple pie; they believe that their unique tradition underlies contemporary lawlessness. Yet Japan's history has also been marked by blood, creating a legacy that touches contemporary culture. Political assassinations, for instance, have been much more common there than in the United States. Martial arts have always played a large role in popular culture. Japanese glorify the sword-wielding samurai every bit as much as Americans do the straight-shooting cowboy. Violent samurai dramas saturate Japanese television as monotonously as westerns do American television. Japan made a virtue at one time of unquestioning loyalty to the Emperor and, by extension, to military discipline. It has openly fought to create an overseas empire and has committed acts of brutal oppression. If Japanese

29. Statistics from the United Nations by the Boston Consulting Group, *A Perspective on Japan* (1972), p. 5. United Nations, *Demographic Yearbook, 1971*, Table 2, gives the density of the Japanese population at 283 per square kilometer (all land included) and of the United States at 22 per square kilometer.

30. The calculation of comparable density figures for Tokyo and New York City is not straightforward. The area of the Tokyo metropolitan government is coincidental with Tokyo Prefecture, but to compare Tokyo Prefecture with New York is misleading because the prefecture is like "Greater New York," the New York City metropolitan area. The calculations presented above are based on figures for the five boroughs of New York City and the twenty-three special wards of Tokyo. In 1970, the population of Tokyo's twenty-three wards was 8,840,942, occupying 220 square miles. United Nations, *Demographic Yearbook, 1971*, Table 9; *Japan Almanac, 1972* (Tokyo: Mainichi Newspapers, 1972), p. 650; Tokyo Prefecture — "Greater Tokyo" — had a population of 11,513,028, covering 792 square miles (Japan Almanac, 1972, p. 101). My calculation of density figures for Tokyo agrees with statistics in the *Statistical Handbook of Japan, 1972*, pp. 21-22. The density of Tokyo-to (Tokyo Prefecture) is given as 13,800 per square mile and of Tokyo-ku (Tokyo City) is given as 39,850 per square mile.

31. *Collier's Encyclopedia* (1971 edition), Vol. 22, p. 348.

social relations are tranquil today, it is not because their national experience is a tale for children.

These two theories may be so beguiling to Americans because they not only seem to explain, they also excuse. Urbanization is a fact of life; it has occurred and there is little that can be done about it. The past, similarly, is beyond the reach of social engineering. Therefore, crime is inevitable. Nothing can be done. The appropriate response is not collective action and self-appraisal but individual acts of self-protection—stronger locks, guns in the bedside table, migration to suburbs, large dogs, and avoidance of streets at nighttime. These theories allow the face in the mirror to escape responsibility.

Police work in Japan is not only less demanding than in the United States, it is also vastly less dangerous. Guns play a very small part in crime. In 1970, for instance, only 137 crimes involved the use of pistols, and arrests were made of persons armed with handguns only 457 times. Out of 82,431 cases of murder, non-negligent manslaughter, robbery, forcible rape, burglary, and assault in Tokyo in 1970, only 16 involved the use of handguns.[32] The unexpected in police work is much less threatening than in the United States. Policemen are not haunted by fear of the sharpshooting assassin, the armed motorist, or panicky criminal. The most dangerous weapon a policeman encounters is a knife or, occasionally, a sword. Since policemen carry nightsticks and .38 caliber revolvers, and are rigorously trained in hand-to-hand combat, the odds are solidly in their favor. They do not go in armed convoys, as has happened in American cities, and it would be considered outlandish for an officer to carry an auxilliary small-caliber pistol concealed in his pocket, as some American policemen do. During 1969-1973 only 16 policemen were killed on duty as a result of a felonious act in Japan, and only 3 of those by firearms.[33] In 1973 alone, 127 American policemen were killed by felons, 125 by firearms.[34]

From an American point of view, contemporary Japanese society is an anomaly. It is affluent, mobile, congested, technologically innovative, and penetrated by mass communications. In outward appearance, it is so like the West as to lack intrinsic interest; it is neither exotic nor traditional, as less developed countries are. Yet this country, with all the attributes Americans consider modern, has

32. Yorihiko Kumasaka, Robert J. Smith, and Hitoshi Aiba, "Crimes in New York and Tokyo: Sociological Perspectives" (Unpublished paper, 1972), pp. 4-5.
33. These figures, provided by the National Police Agency, cover 1969-1973.
34. *Uniform Crime Reports, 1972*, pp. 37-39.

a crime rate that is low and declining. Streets are safe and narcotics addiction infinitesimal. Law enforcement is conducted virtually without stress. Policemen are proud rather than defensive. They perceive the public as supportive, the political environment benign. The ordinary citizen expects exemplary behavior from policemen and has been given few reasons for believing this unrealistic. How has this remarkable combination of modernity and tranquility been achieved? How can it have happened that a country so similar to the United States can be heaven for a cop?

2. Koban

Police operations in Japan are based on a unique system of fixed police posts. There are two kinds: *kobans* in cities and *chuzaisho* in rural areas. Personnel of kobans change each shift; they report for duty at a police station and fan out to the kobans. A chuzaisho is a residential post, manned around the clock by a single officer—occasionally two—who lives with his family in attached quarters. The number of personnel in a koban varies considerably depending on the area, from as few as four to as many as ten or twelve in a single shift. In physical appearance hardly any two kobans are the same. A koban may be a narrow two-story structure stuck like a chip in crevice between two tall office buildings. Or it may be a detached circular one-story building located beside a busy intersection. A koban may be a small house on the bank of a canal or one among a row of glass-fronted shops in the arcade of a railway station. Some share structures with other enterprises. One, for example, has a restaurant above it and a bar in the basement below. Kobans are stuck on traffic islands, in converted cafes, and under railway underpasses. They fit wherever they can, making do with space available. The only features common to all are a round red light globe hung over the front door that glows at night, posters of wanted men pasted to a bulletin board on the front wall, and walls painted a dull gray. Chuzaisho look like ordinary but nontraditional homes. Some in northern Japan have recently been built to resemble alpine cottages with sharply peaked roofs. Because farm homes are not dispersed in single units over the countryside but cluster in communities, chuzaisho are usually located in moderate-sized villages, each on its own small plot of land.

There are about 5,800 kobans in Japan and just over 10,000 chuzaisho. Though chuzaisho outnumber kobans about two to one, kobans are the more important posts because almost four-fifths of the population lives in urban areas. Kobans serve small, very densely populated areas. In metropolitan Tokyo, for instance, where there are approximately 1,000 kobans, the average area covered in about 0.22 square miles containing a population of 11,500 people. In a rural prefecture such as Aomori at the northern tip of Honshu, each chuzaisho covers about 19.2 square miles and 7,890 persons.[1]

Unlike the United States, police operations in Japan have not been organized in terms of the patrol car. Fixed posts outnumber patrol cars — "*patr'o* cars," the Japanese say, rather than "p'*trol*'" cars — almost five times.[2] Osaka, Japan's second largest city, is representative of the urban distribution of personnel between cars and kobans: one-sixth of all patrolmen work in cars, five-sixths in kobans.[3] In recent years the relative importance of patrol cars to kobans has been a matter of lively debate in police circles. Mobility is not as important a consideration for the Japanese police as for American. A smaller proportion of land is devoted to streets than in the United States: only 14 percent of the land area of Tokyo, for example, is composed of streets compared with 35 percent in New York and 43 percent in Washington, D.C.[4] Still, since larger areas could be covered with fewer personnel, some economies might be made by substituting cars for kobans. During the past eight years there has been a shift in favor of patrol cars. The number of kobans and chuzaisho has declined by 20 percent while the number of patrol cars has increased by 57 percent.[5] The reduction in fixed posts is largely accounted for by chuzaisho rather than kobans: 25 percent in chuzaisho, 7 percent in kobans. Since most of the additional patrol cars went into traffic operations, it can be concluded that police administrators are reluctant to shift the mode of patrol operations significantly, especially in urban areas. They know, for one thing, that the public is adamantly opposed to the abolition of kobans.[6] And they recognize the enormous value of maintaining close contact with neighborhoods and not mechanizing the relationship between police and citizen. Most senior officers believe that equilibrium between cars and fixed posts has been

1. In 1972, the number of *chuzaisho* in Aomori was 181. Information furnished by the Aomori Prefecture police. In 1971 the population of Aomori Prefecture was 1,428,000 and land area was 8.998 square kilometers. *Statistical Handbook of Japan, 1972,* p. 21.
2. In 1973 there were 3,690 police cars in Japan: 1,092 assigned to traffic and 2,598 to patrol. There were 17,322 fixed posts of all kinds: 1,210 police stations, 5,891 kobans, and 10,291 *chuzaisho.* Data furnished by the National Police Agency.
3. Data furnished by the Osaka Prefecture police, 1973.
4. As of April 1973. Information furnished by the Tokyo Metropolitan Police Department.
5. Information provided by the National Police Agency.
6. Results of a public opinion survey, National Police Agency, Committee on Comprehensive Countermeasures, *Interim Report* (Tokyo: National Police Agency, 1970), Chap. 3. Available only in Japanese.

reached and that the existing system of deployment will remain stable for some time. In fact, because new towns are springing up on the periphery of metropolitan areas, the number of kobans will probably increase.

Patrol car operations are integratred closely with koban activity. A patrol car's chief function is to increase the number of men on the street actively patrolling, since koban personnel patrol intermittently. Because cities are highly congested and a koban's area of jurisdiction is small, patrol cars do not possess an advantage in response time. Koban personnel, on foot or bicycles, frequently arrive first in response to calls for assistance. Patrol cars provide transportation between kobans and the police station, carrying prisoners to the station for processing and detention and policemen for consultations. To encourage close cooperation between cars and kobans, patrol cars must pass each post at regular intervals and driver and partner are required to take short rest periods at kobans.

Two minor changes in the fixed-post deployment system may occur in the next few years. First, because the number of chuzaisho have been contacted, the areas to be covered are larger than before. Officers must be away for long periods which places a burden on the officers' wives to answer phone calls, take messages, and receive visitors. One suggestion that has been made to lighten the work-load on both husband and wife is to assign two officers to remote areas. This would make the posts more attractive to the families of chuzaisho officers—they would not be as isolated as before—but it would be costly since accommodations would have to be expanded. Second, in several cities a new kind of fixed post, smaller than a police station and larger than a koban, is being tried. Known as "mammoth kobans" they have been established in or near large entertainment areas where the intensity of day and night activity varies considerably. Kobans in adjacent business areas may close at night, after commuters have gone home, and their personnel redeploy to the mammoth koban. Thus, personnel can be concentrated or dispersed according to the nature of the tasks to be performed.

The most crucial function of kobans is to provide information to people about locations and addresses. Japanese neighborhoods are a maze of narrow lanes and one-way streets; houses are built on every inch of land, sometimes seeming to be inside one another, reachable only by narrow paths. To make matters worse, most streets—apart from major avenues—are unnamed, and houses are numbered in the order in which they were constructed, rather than according to location. If several houses are built simultaneously, they all have the same block number. Places are located by specifying areas within larger areas—like saying, New York, Manhattan, mid-town, east side, and then giving a number. It has been suggested that this system fits a culture in which houses have social value only within immediate families and neighborhoods. Japanese rarely entertain at home, apart from close relatives; business friends and acquaintances are entertained in public facilities.[7] There is no need, then, for an impersonal numbering system. For people who must find a Japanese home and don't already know its location, the host either arranges a rendezvous at a known place nearby or provides a small map.

Koban officers say that it takes at least two years before they know an area thoroughly. Newcomers cannot even respond to emergency calls successfully without the assistance of more experienced officers. When a patrol car receives an emergency call over its radio, a curious sequence frequently takes place: the car brakes to a stop, the dome-light is switched on, and the officers consult detailed maps. If they cannot pinpoint the location, they go to a koban in the area and look at maps there. Since koban officers are the experts on each neighborhood, patrol cars are often guided to the spot by watching for koban patrolmen on bicycles and following them. Even koban staff sometimes charge out into the night only to discover they don't know exactly where to go. They mill around, asking passersby for help, until the person who telephoned can find *them*. An illustrative case of the difficulty of finding places in Japanese cities occurred one muggy summer night when a patrol car was directed to investigate a report that a woman had been molested on her way home from work. The car roared up and down streets vainly searching for the right number. At one point the officers abandoned the patrol car and spent half an hour in a light drizzle running through meandering lanes. They finally broke off their fruitless search to spend seven minutes consulting with officers in a koban. After fifty minutes had elapsed, they succeeded in finding the unhappy woman's apartment. It turned out that the distraught woman, who claimed her breast had been touched on the stairway of a subway, had incorrectly given her block number to the dispatcher. Since she had not thought to leave her phone number, the police could not call her back to receive proper directions. Though the police were very late in this case, they performed a

7. Chie Nakane, *Japanese Society* (Berkeley: University of California Press, 1970), Chap. 4.

minor miracle in getting there at all. The officer in charge, sweat-streaked and damp, grumbled as he got back into the patrol car that it was a good thing she wasn't being murdered.

The neighborhoods surrounding kobans are generally more heterogeneous in terms of class and activity than is the case in the United States. Within two hundred yards of a koban it is not unusual to find a cluster of bars and restaurants, lower- or middle-income homes tightly packed together, a street or two of small shops, a small foundry or machine-tool factory (scarcely more than garage-enterprises), a movie theater with garish advertisements, and a clutch of expensive houses with high walls and enclosed gardens. Neighborhoods are not easy to type economically. For one thing they do not seem to have the life cycle of obsolescence so common in the United States. Though zoning is almost haphazard, economic decay is less pronounced. The explanation for this paradox may have to do with the intrinsic value of space in Japan. Space is not a throw-away item to be discarded by one class of owners when its newness wears off. Space, especially in cities, is too valuable to be left to rats, dust, and darkness. Neighborhoods renew themselves through piecemeal development.

Most people who need police help seek it in person at a koban.[8] Though there is a special emergency telephone number — 110 — that the police publicize vigorously, most people seek help directly. Kobans are near at hand and response is immediate; there is no anxious wait while an officer is dispatched by radio and the proper address located. Face-to-face encounters ensure that attention is being commanded. At the same time, the pattern of solicitation is changing as the number of telephones per capita rises in Japan.[9] In the next few years the majority of initial requests for help from the police will probably be done electronically.

To enhance the availability of koban assistance, police call-boxes have been installed in some areas of heavy nighttime activity. From the police point of view they are a mixed blessing because drunks use them to pester the police, calling for assistance unnecessarily or haranging the police for alleged misbehavior. Patrolmen encourage

8. A public opinion poll taken in 1972 found that 56 percent of people who had requested help during the previous year did so by going in person to koban or police station. Survey by Prime Minister's Office, reported in the Japanese journal, *Public Opinion* (December 1972).
9. In 1972, there were 15.2 phones per 100 persons in Japan, 60.1 in the United States, 57.9 in Sweden, and 50.9 in Switzerland. *Japan Times*, 5 June 1973, p. 3.

nearby shop owners to prevent misuse of the boxes but it is a losing battle.

Kobans are an adaptive institution, their character shaped by the setting in which they are located. They are more than sources of emergency aid; they are community service facilities. Some kobans have been equipped with area-wide loudspeaker systems for making announcements of general interest. At least one koban plays a musical chime early in the morning to serve as a time-check for a neighborhood composed largely of apartment houses. The most dramatic example of sensitive adaptation is in the Sanya section of Tokyo. This is an area inhabited by derelicts, misfits, and unskilled laborers hired each morning as casual labor. They live in flophouses and find their only pleasure in scores of small stand-bars. Because many of the people are too improvident to own watches, the koban has mounted a large illuminated clock on the front wall, which helps the men report to work on time. Many people in Sanya like to keep small fish—a Japanese passion—which they catch in small commercial pools. Because they are too poor to afford tanks and equipment, the koban has built a concrete fish pond outside its front door. Fish are deposited there and the owners come back every week or so to see their fish and leave a few hundred yen to pay for food. The police have also erected a message board where weather reports are posted daily along with notices to individuals that their families are trying to contact them. When pedestrian traffic accidents rose alarmingly, koban personnel toured the flophouses showing a film on traffic safety. Most of the accidents occurred in the evening during drinking hours. The police were instrumental in obtaining two color television sets from the municipal government which have been mounted on pedestals in the parks and are turned on for several hours every summer evening. They provide the only nonalcoholic entertainment many of these men can enjoy.

Koban officers are the first line of police response. They are the first on the scene of any emergency. They have the best chance to capture criminal suspects and the greatest responsibility for fore-stalling violence. Their decisions determine how most situations will be handled. Though they experience the excitement of jumping into the unknown, they work in anonymity and their responsibility is shortlived. The more serious a situation or the more difficult to settle, the quicker they are supplanted by specialists dispatched from the police station or prefectural headquarters. Rarely do they have the satisfaction of following a case through to a conclusion. They labor under the burden of being regarded as the foot-soldiers of police work—jacks-of-all trades but masters of none. One rainy night the phone rang clamorously in a koban; the officers on duty characteristically jumped to answer it as if letting it ring twice would be an unforgiveable sin. Informed that a traffic accident had occurred nearby, they set out pell-mell on white police bicycles. They found a sports car slewed around at the end of a long underpass, its front end shattered against the median divider. The driver had been thrown out and lay huddled on his side a few feet from the open door. Illuminated by the yellow light of sodium lamps, blood from a deep cut above the driver's ear streamed along the rain-streaked concrete mingling with the fluids from the broken car. The patrolmen diverted traffic around the scene, kept spectators back, and administered first-aid while waiting for the ambulance to arrive. It could be heard in the distance hurrying toward the accident its siren pulsating in the night "wah-oo, wah-oo, wah-oo." In a few minutes experts in traffic investigation arrived from the police station. They went to work with tape-measure, chalk, and camera, and the patrolmen returned unnoticed through the drizzle to their koban.

Investigation of all but the most trivial crimes is conducted by detectives. The koban patrolman merely preserves the scene of the crime and rounds up witnesses. Detectives also do most of the criminal surveillance, like watching for pickpockets and sex offenders. Detectives, who always work in plainclothes, use kobans as bases, coming in to use the phone, to interrogate a suspect, or to have a cigarette and a cup of tea. Outsiders are sometimes startled when a disreputable looking individual marches boldly into a koban and without a word of recognition from uniformed personnel takes over a desk and a phone. Kobans play a surprisingly small role in processing suspects. Decisions to arrest are made for the most part at the police station. Suspects are questioned briefly in kobans but if further inquiry is needed they are transported by patrol car to the station. Unless an officer is assigned to a koban where the incidence of crime is especially high, he may serve for years without filling out an arrest paper.

Generally the activities of patrolmen and specialists mesh easily. Occasionally friction develops when differences in vantage point create differing operational imperatives. For example, twice one evening patrolmen were summoned to take care of a drunken man who was pestering a bar owner. The second time they were called they took the man into custody and had him transported to the station for holding over night. The detectives in charge decided the incident was trivial and released the man. Like a bad penny, he turned up within minutes at the bar, his anger doubled because he had been reported to the police. So for a third time koban patrolmen were called out to deal with the same situation. When they returned to the koban, they spoke contemptuously about deskbound detectives who couldn't appreciate the difficulties of street work. The officer in charge of the koban—a sergeant—felt compelled to talk to the detectives by phone, explaining the koban's point of view. He then suggested firmly to his own officers that the matter had been discussed firmly enough and he didn't want to hear any more about it. Koban patrolmen also become irritated from time to time if they are asked to devote a lot of attention to matters within the purview of specialists which koban personnel do not consider very important. They often complain about the extra work involved when special campaigns are organized against illegal parking or traffic accidents. They begin to feel harried and are conscious of having to slight work which they think is more important to the safety of their immediate area.

Kobans come under the command of police stations. The station is where officers report for duty, keep equipment, train, send suspects, obtain information, and sometimes eat and sleep; it is where supervisory authority over them is concentrated. Station staffs range in size from as few as 16 to as many as 500 in Tokyo and Kita-Kyushu.[10] Stations are organized into sections according to the nature of the work performed: patrol, traffic, crime prevention, criminal investigation, security, and administration.[11] About 40 percent of total police manpower is in patrol, 15 percent in criminal investigation, 13 percent in traffic, 11 percent in security, 6 percent in crime prevention, 5 percent in riot police, and 2.4 percent in administration.[12]

Police stations in turn come under the supervision of prefectural headquarters. The prefecture is the highest level at which day-to-day command over operations is exercised. Although there are national as well as regional police commands, they provide only administrative services. Only in extreme emergencies would they direct operations. Japan has forty-seven prefectures; they are very much like states in the United States, only much smaller, on the order of a large American county. In eight prefectures where a large city dominates the prefecture—Osaka and Tokyo, for example—prefectural and city police headquarters are coincidental. In other

---

10. The smallest station is in Aomori Prefecture; it serves a remote area of fishing villages and farm communities.
11. The Security Division deals with subversive activities and counterintelligence.
12. Data provided by the National Police Agency for 1972.

prefectures, police operations in cities are managed by single police stations reporting to prefectural headquarters.

In order to function successfully as a koban patrolman, one ability above all others needs to be cultivated — the art of patient listening. Policemen spend endless hours allowing people to demonstrate that they are alive, have problems, feelings, values, and a uniqueness that is significant. Listening is often an end in itself; it makes no contribution to further action on the part of the policeman or the private individual. For example, one evening at 10:30 a working-class woman about fifty years old came into a koban. She had a nervous, tense face and was followed almost immediately by a small unshaven man of the same age. They sat side by side on a wooden bench and began to talk separately across a desk to two young officers. The woman glanced secretively at the man as she talked, her face betraying distaste and fear. Several times, when they heard their stories diverging, they broke off to shout at each other, calling one another a liar. It turned out that the woman's son and the man's niece had been caught by the police that afternoon sniffing glue. The man, believing his niece to be in bad company, came to the woman's house that evening, rudely pushed his way inside and threatened the boy if he came near his niece again. When the stories were told, the senior officer of the koban, also about fifty years old, rebuked the man sternly, his voice rising in anger, for attempting to "act like a policeman." The man had no right to enter another's house, to threaten, or to punish. Two other officers joined in the lecture and after about ten minutes the man, thoroughly chastened, went home. Clinging to what remained of his dignity, he muttered that he was satisfied that the matter was now in the right hands and he didn't intend to pursue it further. The woman, however, still agitated, settled more deeply onto the bench and had a heart-to-heart talk with the senior officer about the difficulties of bringing up an independent-minded teenage boy without a husband in the house. The officer listened sympathetically for almost an hour, gently giving advice.

On another occasion three men came into a koban — a taxi driver of middle age, informally dressed, and two rather mean-looking young men, one with a misshapen ear and a face deformed into a lopsided triangle. The taxi driver had refused to chase the car of a friend of the two young men. They had tried to goad him into it by disparaging his driving ability. He had then angrily ordered them out. But they refused to do so, arguing that it was raining hard and they were not where they wanted to go. So the driver brought them all to the koban, where they sat in a line in front of the sergeant's desk, telling the incident from their respective points of view. None of the three raised their voices or used harsh words; they sat almost companionably, exchanging cigarettes and smiling, though more out of embarrassment than warmth. Only the taxi driver occasionally showed irritation, for he still rankled from their insult to his professional ability. None of the men wanted anything from the other and the police never considered filing charges against them. The sergeant listened attentively, once in a while injecting a word or two. The rain fell, the men talked, the police listened. After half an hour they went away; they could be seen sitting together for a few mintues more in the taxi outside. The sergeant concluded simply that they had wanted to "clear up their hearts."

Kobans also attract hangers-on who ingratiate themselves with the police and with whom the officers feel involved. The police refer to them as "police maniacs." One of these has the habit of bringing gifts, such as a box of candy, to the koban when he has money in his pocket after working for several days. Another habitually tries to sleep in a koban. When the officers rush out on a call and leave the koban unattended, he sneaks in and goes to sleep on a bench. If a patrol car comes by the man explains in detail where the officers have gone, promises not to go back inside, and gives deep bows of farewell as the car pulls away. "Maniacs" are mainly a lower-class phenomena, derelicts or casual laborers, befuddled with alcohol or retarded. They are harmless and pathetic, desperately wanting a little companionship. Some retired men from higher classes are also drawn to the police, coming to kobans regularly to give advice or to assist in giving directions. Regardless of class, the motivation is the same — to provide a semblance of belonging in otherwise empty lives.

Sympathetic listening is not easy. It becomes especially difficult the more tired an officer becomes, and Japanese officers, who work incredibly long hours, have ample reason for feeling exhausted most of the time. Most patrolmen are on duty fifty-six hours an week. They work what is called a three-shift system, which involves working one day from 9 A.M. to 5:30 P.M., then the next day from 8:30 A.M. to the following morning at 10 A.M., then a day of rest, and reporting the fourth day to begin the cycle anew. Though the time served on-duty each week is fifty-six hours, official working time is forty-four hours. In each twenty-four-hour tour of duty, officers are allowed to take eight hours' rest, but they may only do so if circumstances allow. It is not unusual for officers to work the full twenty-four hours, cat-napping and grabbing bites to eat on the fly. In order to ensure that officers are on duty an average of fifty-six hours per week, a complicated scheme for distributing extra days off through the month has been devised. Tokyo prefecture is unique in the country in having recently inaugurated a four-shift system, with duty hours being fifty-five hours per week and working hours forty-four.[13] Ten percent of Japanese policemen, depending on the prefecture, still work the traditional two-shift system, where officers are on and off duty for alternating periods of twenty-four hours. They report to work at 8:30 A.M. one day and work straight through until the following morning at the same time. Then they are given twenty-four hours off.[14]

The hours that policemen work are irregular as well as long. They never work the same hours two days in a row — except on the novel four-shift system. The Japanese are familiar with the American system where officers keep to one period of duty for a substantial period of time, commonly a month. This system was tried briefly in Japan just after the war but it was not found congenial. Japanese homes are small and sleeping in the daytime is difficult. If officers are to get adequate rest, they are better off sleeping in facilities provided by the police than going home. Furthermore, because many officers do not own cars, they are dependent on public transportation. Public transportation, however, shuts down from approximately 11:00 P.M. to 5:00 or 6:00 A.M. Policemen could not get home during those hours even if they were let off work. The irregularity of working hours plays havoc with the family life of policemen. Getting home after twenty-four hours on duty, an officer is exhausted yet it is mid-morning and his family has not seen him for a whole day. He is faced with an awkward choice. He can try to stay awake and drag through the day or go to sleep immediately and find himself wide awake in the evening and faced with a new shift the following morning.[15]

13. Begun in 1972.
14. Policemen are the hardest working segment of a hard-working people. The average work week in Japanese industry in 1973 was approximately 45 hours. Japan Institute of Labor, *Japan Labor Bulletin* (May 1974), p. 10. Monthly hours worked in all industries in 1973 were 183.0. According to the *Japan Times*, 1 August 1973, p. 3, Japan is one of four countries in the world whose civil servants work 44 hours or more per week: Swiss civil servants work 44 hours; Polish, 46; and Chinese, 48. The national labor law specifically exempts police from the maximum of 48 hours per week. Policemen are given twenty paid holidays a year but few officers take all of them. It is part of the police mystique that a dedicated policeman never takes all the vacation allowed.
15. The disjointed sleeping schedule of Japanese policemen may fit deep cultural patterns with respect to sleep. Americans frequently notice that Japanese people seem to be able to take short naps any time and any place. Japanese children are

The arduousness of the Japanese system cannot be justified on the ground of putting more men on the street during peak hours of crime. The police are busiest between 8:00 P.M. and 2:00 A.M. — a pattern found in most industrial nations.[16] The two-shift system puts the same number of patrolmen on the street both day and night. The three- and four-shift systems actually increase the maldistribution: more police are at work from 9:00 A.M. to 5:30 P.M. than at any other time. Administrators recognize this. One argument in favor of Tokyo's four-shift system has been that it allows officers to begin their longest tour — twenty hours at a time — at two o'clock in the afternoon, so that they are fresher and more alert when evening comes. The four-shift system provides qualitatively, not quantitatively, better coverage.

Only patrol and traffic personnel work irregular day-night schedules. Detectives and administrators work a six-day week, composed of eight hours of duty each week day and four hours on Saturday.[17] Of course, when an investigation requires night work, detectives disregard the clock. Special precautions are taken with personnel who do exacting work where a lapse due to tiredness might have serious consequences. Patrol-car drivers, for instance, are not allowed to drive longer than three hours at a time without an hour rest and every two hours they are required to take a ten-minute break.

Tiredness, for patrolmen especially, becomes a way of life. After being on duty for a long period, fatigue becomes a throbbing physical burden, like a feverish pressure weighing down one's shoulders. Patrolmen spend much of their time on their feet, standing in front of kobans answering questions, patrolling, and responding to summonses. By night time the impulse to sit is overwhelming; an officer's feet seem to grow hot and expand in size. But it is precisely at night, when fatigue is greatest, that police

---

raised so they can sleep anywhere. A common sight in Japan is infants sleeping upright strapped to their mothers' backs. Unlike American children, Japanese children do not need to lie down to fall asleep. Sleep rituals — such as being prone, having darkness, quiet, and uninterrupted periods of time — may be less important to the Japanese. If this is true, then the irregularity of duty hours does not exact the psychic cost in Japan it would in the United States. Japanese officers are not adapting to a peculiar shift-system. Rather, the shift-system fits established sleep patterns.

16. Tokyo Metropolitan Police Department, *Keishicho, 1971* (Tokyo: Public Relations Section, MPD, 1972), p. 18.

17. Rank has its privileges. Above the rank of inspector, officers serve only during the day unless there is an emergency.

officers are busiest. They particularly dread getting a call at 2:30 A.M. just before most of them are due to get their first sleep in eighteen hours of duty.

To remain alert, let alone civil, in such circumstances is a major accomplishment. Patience is particularly needed with the happy drunks who find the police convenient objects for teasing. A party of young men, for instance, pretended to ride away on the bicycles belonging to a koban. A tall well-dressed man, sodden with drink, stood truculently in front of a koban berating the police for being lazy, unable to display authority, and wasting time. Patrolmen tried gently to move him on but he kept returning, as soon as they would turn him loose, like a yoyo on a string. Some teasers have a genuine comic gift. A short wiry man about fifty-years old, four front teeth missing and wearing a bedraggled cloth hat, spent an hour and a half one evening in front of a koban reenacting drills from his days in the Imperial Army. His stock response to suggestions from the patrolmen that he go home was to draw himself to stiff attention and give a crisp salute. The policemen always returned it, even though they knew it encouraged him. People like this mean no harm; they simply want human interaction. What few people understand is that by late evening even smiling is an effort for a policeman. And drunks are unpredictable. A policeman cannot be sure when one will begin to talk loudly, drawing a crowd, and then pugnaciously criticize the officer for the mistakes of the entire organization.

A koban is not simply a place of work; it is a home where officers eat, sleep, and relax. Housekeeping is an important part of koban life — sweeping floors, brewing tea over a gas ring, or washing cups. These chores are usually performed by the most junior officers. Every koban has an extra room, located behind or above the main office with a raised *tatami* floor where officers eat their meals and rest or sleep. Some have television sets and well-used boards and counters for playing Go. Meals are brought from home, then warmed up on the gas ring, or sent in from nearby restaurants. Green tea is always available, rarely coffee. In summer officers drink soft drinks, cold barley tea, and a sweet drink of fermented milk known as "Calpis." During the evening and night patrolmen announce their intention to go off duty and retire to the sleeping room where they unroll mattresses and bedding provided and get three or four hours sleep. Later they emerge rumpled and heavy-eyed, as their turn comes to relieve tired officers. In a few lucky kobans a woman comes regularly to prepare tea or to arrange a small vase of flowers. In one case these services were performed every evening by a cabaret hostess on her way home from work.

Services are voluntary, and they bring a welcome feminine touch to a drab male world.

Kobans are not particularly cheerful places. Like police facilities the world over, they are serviceable but dilapidated. Desks and chairs are generally bent and worn, like a collection from a used-furniture store. Floors are grimy and the walls, painted gray or dull pastels, are spotted and peeling. The only ornamentation is provided by large maps or chalk-boards. There are always a few bulky cabinets against the walls for storing confidential records, pistols, items of equipment, and the innumerable forms that plague police work.

Different generations are represented among the personnel of a koban just as they would be in a private home. The supervising officer is usually a senior patrolman, though occasionally in important locations he may be a sergeant. Senior patrolman is the first rank above the bottom and is attained on the basis of long and blameless service. To advance to sergeant, the next higher rank, a written examination must be taken. Senior patrolmen tend to be a generation older than most of the patrolmen in the koban. They have the air of wise and experienced old bears surrounded by energetic cubs. Their style is to lead their charges by example and a quiet word rather than by active command. They tend to stay close to the koban, unless a particularly difficult situation arises, letting the young officers do the running. Sharp-eyed and observant, they stand in the background allowing the patrolmen considerable freedom. When necessary they come forward unobtrusively to handle a belligerent older drunk, to calm an hysterical woman, or deliver a lecture on duty to erring teenagers.

Senior officers make sure that the routines of the koban are discharged. Patrolmen must make their personal marks—their "chops"—in the log book when going off or coming on duty. Dishes must be washed and floors swept. During the slack daytime hours, patrolmen visit the homes of the people who have recently bought cars in order to certify that private parking spaces are available. So great is the pressure on space in larger urban areas that this has become a requirement for automobile ownership. There is a lively trade in phony certificates among car salesmen. Each officer is responsible for visiting each residence and business twice a year in a designated subarea of the koban's territory.[18] This is the "residential survey" and requires considerable investment of time. From these visits the files are produced which allow koban personnel to provide

18. This will be discussed in detail in Chapter 5.

directions in an instant to almost every person or business in their area.

The procedures of kobans and the demeanor of personnel vary only slightly among different parts of the country. In Tokyo an officer is required to stand out front accessible for easy questioning twenty-four hours a day, even in the depths of winter. Other regions are more lax, partly because they are not the "front-face" of Japan and partly because patrolmen elsewhere generally serve twenty-four hour tours of duty beginning at 8:30 A.M. and are exhausted by evening. Patrolmen are not supposed to take their hats off in public and this includes the office of the koban. But they do, especially during slow hours and in less prepossessing parts of the cities.

There is more punctilio among Japanese policemen than American. Many of them put on white gloves when they leave a koban for patrol or when they drive a patrol car. When they enter or leave a koban, patrolmen salute senior officers present. They also bark a muffled, unintelligible word that sounds like "russ." It is a telescoped version of the phrase "Gokuro san desu," meaning approximately "Thank you for your trouble."[19]

The requests that flow into a koban are wonderfully varied. Most are ordinary, of course, such as directions, explanations of a law, mediation, or minor crime. But many are surprising. If people have lost their money or overspent in a night on the town, they can come to a koban and be loaned enough money to get home. Kobans in busy entertainment areas, especially those adjacent to railway or subway stations, keep a box of small change for transactions of this kind; the procedure, which involves nothing more complicated than signing a ledger, takes only a minute. Officers say the return rate is very high, as much as 80 percent. Late at night people unfamiliar with an area come to kobans to obtain recommendations about suitable hotel accommodations. Officers make suggestions and sometimes telephone to make sure a room is available. A koban is an all-purpose source of help. One day, for example, two teenage boys carrying a small plastic bag containing goldfish wondered if a koban had any distilled water so that the health of the fish would not be impaired in transit. An embarrassed middle-aged man asked if officers had a tool that might repair the zipper on his fly that

---

19. Most Japanese, I discovered, do not understand the word either. Policemen were amused that I should inquire. To a foreign observer everything is potentially significant. Separating the trivial from the important is one of the exciting features of doing research in an unfamiliar milieu, though one is frequently led up blind alleys.

would not close. A pair of needle-nosed pliers was found and function repaired.

Children emerge most poignantly out of the human parade that passes through kobans. A mother shopping on a hot, humid Saturday came to a koban to ask for water for her baby's bottle. While the officers warmed the bottle over a gas ring, she sat, tired and distracted, soothing her fretful baby. Children near public parks, especially in residential neighborhoods, drop in to say hello and in the hope that they will be given a piece of candy. The anguish of lost children is particularly moving. Some simply cry, others are frightened into vacant immobility, and some somberly talk with officers about their lives and pleasures. One six-year-old girl in a bright red dress sat bravely for fifteen minutes till her father found her. As he took her onto his lap, absentmindedly answering the policeman's questions, her face slowly crumpled and two enormous tears silently slid down her golden cheek. A young boy, not quite five, became separated from his mother during a crowded outdoor festival, and was brought to a koban. After almost half an hour the mother had sense enough to come to the koban for help. Seeing her son sitting safely on a straight chair, she flew across the room and slapped him in the face, saying "Why did you walk away?" Before the startled policemen could more than gasp in protest, she sank to her knees and put her head in the crying boy's lap, sobbing her own relief.

Children learn early lessons about citizenship in kobans. Around parks they often find coins that have dropped out of pockets of people who have sat on the benches. If the children turn them in, as well as other lost items, many kobans reward them with a small printed card filled in with the child's name, the date, and the particular deed performed. The cards ask parents to praise the child for his action.[20] Officers often make a show of receiving lost coins and putting them in a lost-and-found box. Then they give the child a reward of equal amount which in fact comes from their own pockets. The lesson is that lost money belongs to the loser but virtue has a tangible reward. Valuable losses — wallets, glasses, packages — involve more red tape. A form must be filled out giving the finder's name and address. After a specified period, the finder may claim the lost item. One child found a wallet during a summer festival. His father urged the officer not to go to the trouble of filling in the

20. I have been told that possession of such a card is a mark of status among children. So much so that occasionally a very young child will bring an object from home, saying it is lost, in order to be rewarded with a prized card.

form; he wanted to take his son back to the excitement of crowds and booths. The officer insisted, however, pointing out that this was an important occasion to teach duty to the child. The poor father, caught between responsibility and pleasure, fidgeted helplessly for twenty minutes while all the proprieties were observed for his five-year-old son.

The sheer numbers of people that pass through the kobans present peculiar problems. Throughout Japan a worn sign appears on the door of koban toilets saying "Broken. Do not use." Koban plumbing is as good as any other but assistance has practical limits.

There is a rhythm to daily life in a koban. It is marked by changes in pace of work, nature of requests, kinds of people who need help, the level of noise, and the stresses of fatigue. Each hour has a unique ambiance, so that an experienced officer knows intuitively what time it is without having to consult a clock. Take for example a warm summer night in a koban located in the middle of an entertainment section of a Japanese city. During the day there will be hardly any calls for assistance. A few people will ask directions, usually to shops and department stores. Women predominate on the streets. Officers get caught up on paper work, patrol sporadically against vehicles parked illegally, and go out on the house-to-house visitations. As the sun sets, the tempo picks up, until by eight o'clock movies, restaurants, bowling alleys, and sweet shops are pulsating with life. Streets, thronged with people of all ages and sex, are as light as day, shop windows agleam with merchandise of all sorts. A few young married couples stroll slowly in matching kimonos, often with a freshly scrubbed child in tow. Footwear is as diverse as the people — shoes, high heels, sandals, zoris, and tennis shoes with the heels folded down so they can be put on and off without undoing the laces. The clop-clop of clogs echoes in the streets, worn alike by middle-class men in kimonos and lower-class workers. About ten o'clock a change occurs. Stores begin to close, their corrugated steel shutters clanging down with a roar. Display lights are extinguished, robbing the streets of their brilliance; shadows begin to form. Two women in their early twenties come into the koban, asking for directions to a bar where a friend works. They have just arrived by train from another city and have no place to stay. Attractive, dressed in bright colors, they laugh and chatter for fifteen minutes while one officer locates the bar on a map and another makes a hotel reservation for them. As the crowds in the street begin to dwindle, the proportion of men increases. Young men with bowling bags surge suddenly out of bowling alleys as if still caught up in the excitement of sport. Small knots of men with their arm's around one another's shoulders, laughing and unsteady, stroll leisurely toward transportation terminals. Patrolmen are called to tend a drunken man who has passed out on the sidewalk near a pool of his own vomit. A friend comes with a taxi and the police return to the koban.

Just before the bars close two young men in suits and ties, slightly flushed from drinking, come to complain that they have been victimized. They had picked up two young women and gone to a cabaret. After eating and drinking for about an hour, they were presented with a bill for Y20,000 (about $75).[21] Recognizing belatedly that the girls were hustlers for the cabaret, they argued fiercely with the management and tried to bring the girls to the koban. The girls refused and several tough-looking men blocked the exit from the cabaret. The patrolmen patiently went over the bill item by item noting that the prices, though shocking, were not unusual. Unless the two young men wanted to press charges of intimidation, there was nothing the police could do. Ashamed at their naivete, the young men went sadly home, the joy of the evening turned to ashes.

At 11:30 P.M. the working day ends for legions of hostesses from bars and cabarets. They are the night's last surge of humanity in darkened and rapidly emptying streets. Carrying small bags or traveling cases like a badge of office, some are dressed in traditional kimonos, their heads piled high with shining black hair, others wear Western clothes, mostly slacks, a few shorts, and high heels. A few prance proudly like mettlesome race-horses but most shuffle tiredly. Glamor and make-believe behind them, they are like any group of working girls, glad to be done with another day.

The evening deposits people in the koban like flotsam on the shore. A tall man with glasses dressed casually in used clothes is brought to the koban after being found riding a bicycle from which all identifying marks have been removed. He will not give his name and has no written identification. His speech is halting, almost a stammer, and never consists of more than a word or two. He seems to be struggling inside himself, as if he cannot connect his mind and tongue. The officers try to coax him into a coherent response; they plead, cajole, and finally get angry. The longer they work with him the more paralyzed he becomes, collapsing into the dark world inside himself like a spent balloon. At first he was a puzzle to the police, now he is a problem. He cannot take care of himself and the

---

21. Based on an exchange rate of Y265 to the dollar, which was the rate at the time.

police do not know where he lives. After a host of phone calls have produced no clues to his identity, he is taken by patrol car to the police station for holding over night. Another man is brought in who is dressed only in undershorts and has bright orange patches of mercurochrome on his elbows and knees. He is about fifty years old, gap-toothed, with a stubbly beard and is totally bald except for a horseshoe of black hair over his ears and around the back of his head. He sits cross-legged on the concrete floor and drunkenly though coherently makes speeches to the watching officers. His wife, a drab figure in the background with an intelligent face marked by cares she cannot handle, wants him committed to a mental hospital. The man has not worked for two years due to an automobile accident that injured his shoulder. He suffers bouts of depression during which he hurts himself and frightens his wife. After a few minutes the man is carried away, shouting in protest, to a night-cell. His wife stands with simple, enduring dignity among the strange policemen and, as the night deepens and grows chill, tells them softly about her husband's tragedy. The officers listen, shuffle, and grow quiet. A little later an elderly woman, probably sixty-five, wants to spend the night in the koban. Dressed in a shapeless dress and black stocking-like hat, she moves as if benumbed, clearly unaware where she is. She is taken to the police station where she settles down for the night on a wooden bench.

So many of the people the police see regularly, and to whom only they attend, are defeated, bedraggled, and helpless. Some have been abused by their own vices, some by circumstances they could not control. All are pitiful and lost, the hope gone out of their lives.

The night runs down; midnight comes and goes. On the faces of the officers beards become noticeable. Not having shaved since early morning, they begin to look haggard and slightly disreputable, their faces etched by fatigue. Under the fluorescent lighting uniforms appear dull, colorless. Officers light cigarettes with the languid, studied deliberation of working men enjoying a symbol of respite. Policemen are not allowed to smoke in public. So they do so in the koban in interludes between activity. Patrol-car officers similary either come to the koban for a smoke or find a secluded back street or dark corner of a park. Policemen do not smoke nervously, combining a cigarette with work, but take their time, lingering over every puff, as if participating in a life-giving ritual.

The night's last task, apart from waiting for emergencies, is to discipline the cruising taxis. Because all public transportation closes down shortly after midnight, unwary revelers are at the mercy of the taxis. Exploiting their advantage, taxi drivers refuse to pick people up at the taxi-ranks where people stand in line and the driver has no choice about whom he must serve. Instead the taxis park nearby waiting for desperate people to agree to pay twice the going rate and holding out for long-distance trips. Lines at the taxi-ranks grow a block long and people complain bitterly to the police. The officers make a halfhearted attempt to stir up the parked taxis, but they snap on their lights and flee like starlings as the officers come close.

Toward two o'clock as the lines of waiting people diminish, quiet and coolness comes to streets that shortly before were fevered with activity. Shadows now are deep; a few sodden men sleep on benches. Whiffs of steam rise from wheeled stalls around which a few people sit in the light of kerosene lanterns eating noodles and boiled fish. Most of the patrolmen look forward to rolling themselves in the koban's bedding. Finally the koban is left to two bleary-eyed policemen who are charged with keeping a flickering watch over the now still night.

3. Street Behavior

Japanese policemen are addressed by the public as "Omawari-san" — Mr. Walkabout. This is an accurate reflection of what the public sees the police doing most of the time. Foot-patrolling is done out of kobans usually for periods of an hour. Patrols are more common at night, when officers work in pairs. Patrolling by foot is more tiring than it looks. Patrolmen amble at a ruminative pace that allows thorough observation. It is like browsing or windowshopping with none of the satisfactions of actually getting somewhere. Patrolling by automobile, which is much less common than foot-patrolling, can be frustrating too. Due to the narrow congested streets of Japanese cities — for example, only 13 percent of Tokyo's twelve thousand miles of streets are wide enough for two-way traffic — patrol cars are forced to move at a snail's pace.[1] There are often no sidewalks, and utility poles are built in the street several feet from the edge. Pedestrians, including small children, eddy along the streets in and out around parked cars, delivery vans, stacked crates, and utility poles. Intersections are so tight that a patrol car cannot turn from one street to another in a single motion but must jockey back and forth.

Patrolling is by no means a matter of high adventure. For the most part it consists of watching and occasionally answering questions. Patrolmen rarely discover genuine emergencies; the chances of coincidence between patrolmen and sudden need are simply too great. Patrolling does not reduce reaction time or particularly enhance availability. What patrolling does is to demonstrate the existence of authority, correct minor inconveniences — such as illegally parked cars — and generate trust through the establishment of familiar personal relations with a neighborhood's inhabitants. On patrol, policemen are alert for different kinds of problems in different places. In a residential area they watch for people who appear out of place or furtive. In public parks they give special attention to loitering males. Around major railway stations they

---

1. Information furnished by the Registration Section, Traffic Division, Tokyo Metropolitan Police Department, 1972.

look for runaway adolescents, lured by the glamor of a big city, who could be victimized by criminal elements. They also watch for "teyhaishi"—labor contractors—who pick up and sell unskilled laborers to construction companies. In a neighborhood of bars and cabarets patrolmen stare suspiciously at stylishly-dressed women standing unescorted on street corners. They determine whether wheeled carts piled with food or cheap souvenirs are blocking pedestrian thoroughfares. Throughout every city they pay particular attention to illegally parked cars and cars that have been left with their doors unlocked.

According to any objective measure, patrol work is of unquestioned importance. Officers assigned to kobans and patrol cars account for the largest proportion of contacts between police and citizens. More officers are assigned to patrol work than to any other police endeavor. Nonetheless, patrol work does not enjoy an honored place in police service. Indeed, it has the lowest prestige of any specialty. A telling indication of this is the seating arrangement of senior officers of a police station or prefecture when they meet together. Hierarchy in Japanese organizations is openly acknowledged and instantly recognized. In a police station, the chief[2] sits at the head of a rectangular seating arrangement. Immediately to his right sits the deputy chief, who is responsible for administration. Below the chief and the deputy come the heads of the criminal investigation section and the security section. Lowest of all, farthest from the chief, is the head of the patrol section. He is invariably the youngest among the section chiefs in seniority. At prefectural headquarters, division status[3] has been given to criminal investigation, security, crime prevention, traffic, and administration. Up to 1973 patrol had attained division status only in Osaka and Tokyo; elsewhere it was a section, one step below division.[4] Since then, six other prefectures have formed patrol divisions. Japan's elite police officers, who are recruited directly into the National Police Agency, view patrol work as the least-attractive steeping stone to a successful career; they much prefer to be assigned to criminal investigation or security.[5] At prefectural headquarters, the chiefs of many divisions are elite officers sent from the National Police Agency. Patrol sections, on the other hand, are directed by officers promoted from the lower ranks. The practice is rationalized by referring to the

2. *Keisatsu-sho-cho.*
3. *Bu.*
4. In Tokyo, the patrol section was promoted to division status in 1967. Before that, it had been part of the Guard Division.
5. See Chapter 4.

necessity of having patrol chiefs with extensive experience as patrolmen. There is merit in this reasoning, though it is hard to see why this should be more true of patrol work than of criminal investigation or traffic regulation or security surveillance. If the police establishment were really committed to raising the status of patrol, it would insist that elite officers be given more extensive on-street experience precisely so they could be assigned to senior patrol positions.

It is interesting to note by the way that the greatest amount of prestige after the chief in any Japanese police organization goes to the head of administration. In the United States administration is considered a necessary evil, a fit place for persons without the ability to hold active commands. The relative status of administration within the police organizations of the two countries indicates a profound difference in the evolution of each system. The Japanese police were created from the top down by explicit acts of central government initiative during the Meiji period, 1868 to 1889 especially. Function followed organization. In the United States police forces grew haphazardly out of patrol and watch activities in thousands of autonomous communities. Organization followed function. This may explain why American staff work even today is not as elaborate and well organized as Japanese.

Though American police organizations evolved out of street responsibilities, the prestige of patrol is no higher than in Japan, except in relation to administration. Most American patrolmen covet detective status. They want to get "out of the bag," as they call their uniform, and to be less bound by routine.[6] The difficulty of raising the prestige of patrol is the same in Japan and the United States: how can routine work performed by a majority of police personnel be made to seem exhalted? Because new recruits are always assigned first to patrol duties, patrol work is associated with beginners. Not only beginners but left-overs, for it is out of patrol that men are recruited to criminal investigation or any other specialty. There is a tendency for the ablest men to transfer out of patrol work as soon as possible.

The uniform of Japanese policemen is rather formal in appearance, except in the summer. It consists of a four-button double-breasted coat worn over white shirt and tie. In the winter the coat

6. In New York City, the chief of detectives is foremost among officers wearing four stars, though he commands thirty-two hundred men and the chief of patrol commands seventeen thousand. Robert Daley, *Target Blue* (New York: Delacorte Press, 1971), p. 61. Daley refers to the "mystique" of detectives among police and public alike.

and trousers are black; in spring and autumn steel blue, the material being lighter weight than in winter. A Sam Browne belt is worn over the jacket—that is, a belt with a strap diagonally over the chest to the opposite shoulder and across the back again to the belt. In summer police officers resemble American policemen, shedding coat, strap, and necktie, and wearing an open-necked steel-blue shirt with matching trousers. Short-sleeved shirts are popular, though they are not allowed in Tokyo where bare arms are considered too informal for policemen who are responsible for the safety of the Emperor. The police cap is peaked in front with a short black visor. On the front above the visor is the gold emblem of the police—a five-pointed star enclosed by pine branches. Rank insignia are worn on coat lapels or breast pocket. There are no identifying numbers or name tags. Shoes are black and vary in style. Officers assigned to motorcycles and patrol cars often affect ankle-length boots. Only socks have escaped standardization, and when policemen cross their legs a wide assortment of lengths and colors are displayed.

Over the uniform, patrol officers wear the distinctive tools of their trade. All carry a small radio receiver, located in the breast pocket, connected by a thin cord to a button-speaker worn in the ear. Patrolmen learn to live with murmuring voices in their ears and sometimes have the distracted look of people living in two worlds. The receivers allow police headquarters to send patrolmen instantaneously from one place to another, like radio-dispatched patrol cars. Two-man patrols sometimes carry two-way radios so that they can contact headquarters for information or assistance. Police batons—"nightsticks"—are straight pieces of turned wood exactly sixty centimeters long (twenty-four inches) with a leather thong that can be wrapped around the wrist. When not being carried in the hand, they are attached to the best through a metal loop. A .38 caliber revolver is carried in a holster and attached to the shoulder by a braided lanyard. Handcuffs are kept in a pouch on the belt. All equipment is standard issue and worn according to an identical format all over Japan: pistol on the right, handcuffs left-rear, nightstick down the left leg. There are no individual touches such as one sees on the uniforms of American policemen—no pearl-handled pistols or reverse-draws. Perhaps the most distinctive item of equipment is not visible—fifteen feet of light rope, strong enough to hold a man's weight, kept in a trouser pocket. Following the ancient art of rope-tying known as Hojo, officers are taught a variety of knots and ties by which they can fashion restraining lines, tourniquets, rescue hoists, and additional handcuffs.

When a Japanese policeman is out on patrol he makes a special point of talking to people about themselves, their purposes, and their behavior. These conversations may be innocent or investigatory. The law provides that policemen may stop and question people only if there is reasonable ground for suspecting they have committed or are about to commit a crime or have information about a crime.[7] Nevertheless, standard procedure on patrol is to stop and question anyone whenever the policeman thinks it may be useful. One reason for doing so is to discover wanted persons. And the tactic has proven very effective: 40 percent of criminals wanted by the police have been discovered by patrolmen on the street. Not only do officers learn to question people adroitly on the street, they become adept at getting people to agree to come to the koban so that more extended, less public inquiries can be made. People are under no obligation to do so, any more than they are to stop and answer questions.[8] The key to success with these tactics is to be compelling without being coercive. This in turn depends on two factors: the manner of the police officer and a thorough knowledge of minor laws. The first reduces hostility, the second provides pretexts for opening conversations justifiably. People who park illegally, ride bicycles without a light, or fail to wear helmets when riding a motorcycle are inviting officers to stop them and ask probing questions. The importance with which the police view on-street interrogation is indicated by the fact that prefectural and national contests are held each year to give recognition to officers who are best at it. One officer assumes the role of suspect and another is given eighteen minutes in which to discover essential facts about him. Judges evaluate the subtlety of technique. Senior officers continually impress upon new recruits the importance of learning to ask questions in inoffensive ways so that innocent people are not affronted and unpleasant scenes can be avoided.

A tall man in soiled clothes, carrying a shopping bag, was stopped along a dark street lined with warehouses. He talked amiably with one officer, readily giving his name and address. The other patrolman moved several yards up the street and quietly spoke into his two-way radio in order to determine whether the man was on the list of wanted persons. Each prefecture, or major city, maintains an "A-B-C Index" listing wanted persons, stolen objects, and criminal records. Searching these lists takes at most ten minutes, allowing

7. The Police Duties Execution Law, Article 2.
8. *Ibid.*

officers to hold people in conversation while information is un-
covered that will determine the policemen's course of action. Use of
two-way radios is often done so casually that interrogated persons
are unaware they are being investigated. When headquarters
reported that the soiled man was not wanted, the officer rejoined his
colleague and the police terminated the conversation with some
hearty advice about not drinking too much.

On another night a young man with shoulder-length hair, light-
blue jeans, white shirt, and desert boots was asked to accompany
two officers to a koban. He was questioned about his identity,
occupation, and residence and requested to show the contents of his
pockets. He wanted to refuse but his nerve failed and he meekly
complied. Finding that the young man was not on the wanted list,
the police bowed him out the koban door with profuse thanks—
"doomo arigato gozaimashita." In a small park two patrolmen
found a man in dark glasses, no tie, and with a heavily bandaged
arm; he was resting on his haunches near a low iron railing. The
man was drunk but docile and happy. One officer squatted down
with the man and talked to him while his partner determined by
radio that the man was not wanted. After providing and lighting a
cigarette for the suspect, the policemen walked on leaving the man
still hunkered down by the fence. Late at night a man in a white
shirt and good quality trousers was found in a small public garden
near the rest house of a famous temple. He was reading a newspaper
under a lamp post. Suspecting that he might be a peeping tom, the
policemen persuaded him to come to a koban. They checked
whether he was wanted, whether he had a criminal record, and even
whether the transistor radio he was carrying had been stolen.
Absolved on all counts, the man was dismissed with smiles and
thanks.

It is often helpful in an interrogation for the police to examine
personal possessions. This is a very delicate matter. Unless placed
under arrest, individuals are not obligated to reveal the contents of
their pockets, purses, or parcels.[9] For their own protection, policemen frequently pat the outside of a suspect's clothing—a frisk—to
determine whether he is carrying a weapon. And they often get
people voluntarily to show what they are carrying. For instance, a
young man was stopped a little after midnight because his motorcycle was making too much noise. His license was examined and the
identifying number on his motorcycle was checked to determine
whether it had been stolen. When the police asked pleasantly

9. *Ibid.,* Article 2(4).

whether they could see inside the satchel suspended from the handlebars, the young man readily agreed. An officer unpacked the bag item by item, asking questions about many of them. Finding only personal effects, he repacked the bag and the motorcyclist continued on his way after being warned to get his muffler fixed. A groggy bum asleep near the men's room in a park had the contents of two shopping bags searched. They contained several pounds of cigarette ends.

Cues that the police use in choosing people to interrogate are hard to pin down. Sometimes the procedure is routine, accompanying a minor infraction. Other times the police are genuinely suspicious. As in the United States, policemen are trained to recognize the incongruous: well-dressed people in low-class neighborhoods, poorly-dressed people in rich ones, heavy bulky clothing on a hot summer night, a business suit worn with crepe-soled shoes, disheveled clothing. Attention is attracted by unnaturalness of manner, such as ducking into an alley when the police are seen or, conversely, being overly casual with the police. Then again policemen may simply be curious. They select targets of opportunity as they are presented: long-haired loiterers with sandals, adolescents hanging around a railway station, unescorted young women, a group of youths walking a street at 1 A.M., a lone cyclist on a dark street, a car parked on a scenic overlook, two surly-looking men standing beside a sports car near a bar. Street "stops" and interrogations undoubtedly fall most heavily on young males. There is good reason for this: they are the most numerous part of any nighttime crowd and crime rates among them are higher than for other portions of the population. At the same time, it is an unfair imposition in that membership in a demographic category is not a crime and is certainly not evidence of individual criminal activity.

Patrolmen make other kinds of discriminating judgments as well. They decide which laws to enforce among many and whether circumstances require the application of a particular law. Patrolmen daily overlook a host of minor infractions, like spitting on the street, talking roughly in public, or carrying potential weapons such as iron bars or glass-cutters. They decide when a situation is sufficiently dangerous or disturbing to warrant action. A man urinating in the Ginza at noon will be bundled off without a moment's hesitation; late at night in a back street in Shinjuku he will be ignored.[10] In lower-class neighborhoods drunks are allowed

10. The Ginza is the downtown commercial section of Tokyo; Shinjuku is a more moderately-priced area with a more youthful clientele. It is also one of the largest urban-transportation hubs in the world and a popular shopping area.

to sprawl asleep in the entrances to movie theaters shut for the night; if they sleep on the floor of a railway station they are awakened and taken outside. A middle-aged woman, about ten o'clock at night, was displaying stuffed animals on the walkway of a shopping arcade. Two patrolmen genially said hello to her, totally ignoring a clearly lettered sign directly over her head that said sidewalk vending was prohibited by order of the police department. Several blocks further on the same officers demanded that a mobile food stall in a less crowded place be moved down the block. The difference in their responses was due to the character of the people involved: the woman was pleasant, orderly, and law-abiding and had used the spot for a long time; the man pushing the food stall was sneaky, nonchalant in a studied way, and known to be affiliated with a local gangster group. At a busy railway station on a Sunday afternoon a Communist student in a red helmet harangued the passing crowd for about forty-five minutes through an electric bullhorn. Other students passed out leaflets. Even though the activity was conducted no more than ten yards from a koban and the police knew the students did not have the required permit, nothing was done. At the entrance of a large subway station, left-wing students obtained permission from the chief of police to deliver speeches from the top of a private bus. They were allowed five minutes. After thirty minutes had elapsed two patrolmen sauntered across the street from a koban and told them their time was up. The students continued unabashedly for another hour without further notice from the police.

Traffic enforcement too raises delicate issues because most offenders do not consider themselves morally at fault. They are apt to be resentful of any regulation directed at them personally. The police are forced to calculate the value of preventing accidents against losses in public respect for law and the police. Traffic policemen openly acknowledge applying a rule of thumb to speeders —they allow between six and fifteen mile per hour over the speed limit. And they may be even more generous depending on circumstances. A man driving at 50 m.p.h. in a 30 m.p.h. zone was stopped by police officers but only given a lecture about the irresponsibility of endangering the lives of his friends. Leniency may become institutionalized. In Tokyo the traffic division publicized a policy of giving "friendly warnings" rather than citations in all but the most flagrant cases. Patrolmen learn to ignore illegally overloaded trucks, especially dump trucks hauling dirt around construction cites, because they know that to stop them would hamper completion of the work and lead to longer periods of traffic congestion. Drivers of defective vehicles are subject to fines but generally are advised instead to make repairs as soon as possible. Professional drivers tend to be treated more severely than owners of private vehicles because they are presumed to be better informed about traffic rules.

Principles governing the use of discretion are not codified or set down in writing; they have the character of custom among police officers. Several factors seem to be involved in determining when illegal behavior will be tolerated. First, enforcement is modified according to place. Officers judge what the public in a particular area has become accustomed to. Second, police foreces have their own traditions; over time notions about tolerable limits for different kinds of behavior become accepted within the police community. The policy of allowing a margin over the speed limit is an example, as is toleration of sidewalk vending in prohibited areas. Third, policemen try to judge the effect of their actions upon future behavior of the individuals involved. A warning is often as effective a deterrent as an arrest, and a good deal less costly and time-consuming. Conversely, legal penalities may be an insufficient deterrent for some offenses, so rueful toleration becomes the only practical policy. Policemen appreciate an investment of time that is commensurate with results. Drunks sleeping in public places, for instance, may be more trouble to arrest than the arrests are worth in terms of changed behavior. Fourth, policemen have their own preoccupations. They may decide, for example, that it is more important to continue to patrol against sex offenders than to check upon gambling in a Mah-Jong parlor. Fifth, policemen are some-times motivated by sympathy for offenders. On one occasion when a minor accident occurred between a taxi and a private car, officers repressed evidence that the taxi driver had been drinking. If results of the "breathometer" test had been recorded, the taxi driver would have had his license suspended. The policemen decided that the punishment would be too severe, since no one had been hurt in the accident, both drivers were adequately covered by insurance, and the taxi driver had a blameless record. The taxi driver was ordered to sleep for two hours in his taxi beside the koban before going home. Undoubtedly, he will be more cautious about drinking and driving another time, and the police will have gained a staunch friend.

Who are the people who become police officers in Japan and are required to make these discriminating judgments? Are they unusual in some respect — for example, in experience, intelligence, or pro-bity? The typical Japanese police officer is young, male, married, and high-school educated. He will come from a marginal middle-class family and have been raised outside the larger metropolitan areas.

About half of all policemen are under the age of thirty-five,[11] compared to 59 percent in the general population.[12] Relative to the general population, therefore, policemen are disproportionately in the age bracket 20-35, since the police cannot recruit juveniles. In terms of sex, policemen are not at all representative of the population. Only 1.5 percent of police officers are women.[13] Women are employed as police officers in seventeen prefectures, concentrated especially in large cities, such as Tokyo, Osaka, and Nagoya. They were recruited first in Tokyo, beginning in 1946, though only a handful were employed until 1970. Women are assigned primarily to traffic regulation, where they ticket and impound illegally parked vehicles, and to the counselling of juveniles. Other cities have female traffic wardens, who wear a distinctive uniform, but they are not sworn officers. Policewomen do some plainclothes work, mostly against pickpockets and shoplifters. A few have been assigned during daylight hours to busy kobans to assist in giving directions. No attempt has been made to integrate them into patrol work on an equal footing with men.

The educational level of policemen is higher than that of the population as a whole and strenuous efforts have been made in recent years to raise it even higher. Sixty-three percent of all policemen in 1971 had graduated from high school, as opposed to about 32 percent in the rest of the working population.[14] About 7 percent of police officers have graduated from a four-year university and 4.5 percent have had some form of advanced schooling beyond high school. In the work force generally, 8 percent have had education beyond high school.[15] Though graduation from high

11. In 1971, 0.4 percent were under twenty years old; 22.6 percent were 20-25; 18.3 percent were 25-30; and 10.6 percent were 30-35. Information furnished by the National Police Agency.
12. *Statistical Handbook of Japan*, 1971, p. 25.
13. There were about 2,850 in 1974, out of 190,350 police officers.
14. Police statistics furnished by the National Police Agency; general work-force figures from the Ministry of Education, *Educational Standards in Japan, 1970*, p. 215. The work-force figures are slightly dated, referring to 1968. In the United States, the proportion of the work force with a high school education is 30 percent. It should be noted also that the number of people finishing high school in Japan has risen rapidly in recent years. Thus, among young workers, as among young policemen, the absence of a high school diploma would be exceptional.
15. The proportion of the work force in the United States with education beyond high school is 18.6 percent. *Ibid.*

school is now a requirement for joining the police, 18 percent still have only junior-high-school diplomas and one-half of 1 percent only a grade school education.[16] Among new recruits, however, educational levels are rising sharply. Twenty percent of officers recruited in 1969 and after have been graduates of four-year colleges.

Policemen are upwardly mobile in terms of social class. The fathers of policemen are most likely to have been blue-collar workers or small enterpreneurs rather than white-collar workers in large organizations, on the one hand, or manual laborers, on the other. This is true of American policemen as well. Policemen prize advanced education highly and are determined their children will go to college. Many officers take classes part-time in order to complete a university degree. Though policemen show great pride in their vocation, few of them want their children to follow in their footsteps. Disruptive work schedules are cited as the primary detraction. A contributing factor may be uneasiness about the occupational status of policeman. Though survey data is lacking, the fact that Japanese officers consider a career in the police — apart from elite service in the N.P.A. — transitional in the history of their families indicates that they share with American policemen a sense of status inferiority.

By and large police officers grew up in the prefectures in which they serve. Interestingly, the proportion of local officers declines the more urbanized the prefecture is. In Aomori Prefecture, for example, in nothern Honshu, 99 percent of the force is local. In Osaka only half the force is local.[17] In Tokyo only 13 percent of all police officers were born in the city.[18] Twelve prefectures have chronic problems enlisting sufficient staff locally. They are all characterized by having large urban centers — for example, Tokyo, Osaka, Kanagawa, Chiba, Fukuoka, and Hyogo.

In Japan's large cities, therefore, citizens deal commonly with policemen who are migrants to those communities, officers who

16. Figures provided by the National Police Agency.
17. 51.5 percent.
18. Information supplied by each prefectural force. In the Tokyo police force, more men are recruited from the Tokyo Prefecture than any other prefecture. In order, the next major contributing prefectures are: Ibaragi, 5.3 percent; Fukushima, 5.2 percent; Kagoshima, 5.1 percent; Nagano, 4.3 percent. In terms of regions, the distribution of Tokyo officers recruited outside the prefecture is as follows: Hokkaido, 3.7 percent; Tohoku, 18.4 percent; Kanto, 18.9 percent; Chuba, 15.3 percent; Kinki, 2.0 percent; Chugoku, 4.3 percent; Shikoku, 3.0 percent; Kyushu, 18.5 percent; and from foreign countries, 2.7 percent. Information furnished by the Tokyo Metropolitan Police Department, as of 31 December 1972.

have been recruited from less urbanized prefectures. It is not clear, however, whether these officers are rural or city people. It is possible that these recruits actually came from other cities. The data available show only prefecture of origin and not the size of the community where recruits lived. It is possible that even in less urbanized prefectures most policemen grew up in the city parts of those prefectures. Observers of employment patterns generally have suggested that many employers, especially in manufacturing enterprises, prefer workers from rural area because they are believed to be more tractable, disciplined, and hardworking.[19] Though many policemen agree with this view, there is no evidence that police recruiters in the large cities deliberately discriminate against persons from the local area or in favor of noncity people from anywhere. They say that if they could fill their quotas locally, they would do so. The failure to recruit young people from the larger cities seems to be attributable to different evaluations of the attractiveness of the career between rural and urban young men. There could be various reasons for this: lack of jobs outside the large cities, appeal of a large city to people in the hinterlands, varying perceptions of the congeniality of police work. So far inquiry into factors underlying the relative failure to recruit policemen from the larger cities has not been undertaken. Results could be interesting not only to the police but to people interested in changing values in modern Japan.

When Japanese officers are out on patrol, their demeanor is self-effacing, low-key, and undramatic. Unlike American patrolmen, they do not play a visible role in public unless specifically activated to do so. In the language of the theater, they do no fill space positively unless a specific situation requires it. They do not move habitually as if laden with authority that must be defended. They do not swagger or posture. They see but they rarely take notice. Loitering teenagers or hoodlums do not draw challenging stares so typical among American policemen. In public places policemen are as inconspicuous as postmen. The public rarely gives them more than a passing glance.[20]

19. For example, James C. Abegglen, *The Japanese Factory* (Glencoe, Illinois: The Free Press, 1958), p. 137. Rural workers are supposed to have "stable natures."
20. The inconspicuousness of patrolling officers extended to me as well. Despite my height and blond hair, people took great pains to avoid noticing me. Only by turning suddenly could I surprise people glancing covertly at me. During six months of working with the police on the street, only a few drunks and two bad characters openly inquired about my presence. One evening, for example, as I was standing in front of a koban in a lower-class neighborhood, a drunk said truculently to a senior patrolman standing next to me, "I don't like to see Yanks." Gesturing down the street, the officer said calmly, "Then don't see him."

The lack of authoritative posturing by policemen is a reflection of general social mores: the Japanese seek to preserve privacy in public places. People move as inviolable units; they go to great lengths to avoid eye-contact with one another. This particular custom shows up in an extreme form among members of criminal gangs: they consider a direct stare to be a challenge and have been known to strike a person who does it.[21] So Japanese policemen are conforming to social custom when they avoid intruding visually without specific cause into other people's lives.

There is an important difference between what privacy in public means in Japan and in the United States. The privacy which the Japanese prize is a matter of sight not of sound. The reverse is the case in the United States, if police behavior is an accurate indication. Relative to one another, Japanese policemen are sound intrusive, American policemen are sight intrusive. American patrol cars carry powerful spotlights mounted on the side, sometimes more than one; Japanese patrol cars do not. Patrol cars in Japan are invariably equipped with loudspeakers; most patrol cars in the United States are not, though they are becoming more popular. Japanese policemen hardly ever shine flashlights onto people without cause. In parks they discreetly turn their lights aside from young lovers embracing on benches. American policemen make a game of seeing lovers jump when the spotlight hits them. And to catch a couple in a car *in flagrante delicto* is a great coup. American policemen shine their lights everywhere—onto the porches of private homes, at windows of stores, into yards, between buildings, and into residential areas from low-flying helicopters. On the other hand, koban and patrol-car policemen in Japan make constant use of built-in loudspeakers. The nondriving member of a patrol car team typically sits with the microphone in hand, volume on ready for instant use. They even tap the microphone in place of using their horns to move people aside. Verbal admonitions are constant. "Don't double-park along this street;" "Your door is not firmly closed," spoken to a car moving ahead in traffic; "Will the owner of car with license number such-and-such come and move it, it is illegally parked"; "You are crossing against the light, please go back"; "Stop first, then make a right turn." So natural is the commentary that whimsy as well as sarcasm creeps in. To a pedestrian hurrying across a street at mid-block, "You're looking proud"; from a koban to pedestrians, "You are now at an intersection and as the light is changing you should be thinking about

21. All Japanese I have spoken to about this accept it as being true. And with reason. I have twice heard young tough street characters excuse hitting someone because the victim had looked them in the face.

keeping your eye on the light"; as the light changes, "Time is money, better hurry across the street"; and to pedestrians defying a red light, "Red means *stop,* not *run.*" Americans would be intensely irritated by such directives. One can imagine their stony faces, mutterings of "Drop dead," and occasional rude gestures.

On patrol Japanese officers are less suspicious than their American counterparts. They seem less alert, their heads turn less frequently to see what is going on all around them. They walk through a crowd as if going for a bite to eat, not like self-conscious wardens of public order. Perhaps this is because there is objectively less to be suspicious about. But the lack of inquisitive alertness may relate as well to the norm about visual intrusions: Japanese officers may be less comfortable than American officers in prying with their eyes.

There is very little cynical posturing among Japanese patrolmen. They exchange fewer knowing smiles than American policemen when confronted with the devious, tawdry, commonplace persons of the police world. It does not seem to be essential to their image that they cannot be surprised by the foibles of mankind. They need not demonstrate publicly that they are a knowing in-group.

Japanese policemen patrol only in public places like stations, streets, and parks. They do not enter bars, restaurants, or shops unless required to do so. Even in lower-class areas where policemen are more free in their intrusiveness, they avoid public accommodations privately owned. There are a few exceptions to this. Patrolmen do enter dance halls to check for people who are under eighteen years old. They also go into movie theaters, with the permission of the owners, looking for sleeping derelicts or for underage youths if the motion picture showing has a restricted rating. Because the officers do not want to disturb or alarm the audience, they usually make their observations from the rear of the seats, which, as they admit, is not a very effective way to determine who is under age. They enter bars, cabarets, and nightclubs late at night after the customers are supposed to have gone in order to detect violations of the closing laws.

Examining Japanese and American patrol behavior together, several instructive contrasts stand out. Japanese patrolling is more pervasive, due to the proximity of kobans and the prevalence of foot-patrols, yet much less authoritative than American. They become an assertive audible part of any public scene whenever they choose. They visit private homes twice a year and conduct discreet interrogations of people who arouse their interest. But their visible presence is informal; it does not involve acting out an official role.

American police, by contrast, are more fitful in their presence, because they depend so much on the automobile, and more formal. Physical presence is more official than the Japanese; it is never self-effacing. American officers, however, are generally silent though always watchfully alert. In short, the Japanese police force is pervasive, unofficial, and low-key, while the American is occasional, official, and self-conscious. Police authority is conveyed more informally in Japanese than in American society. American police seem to make up in threatening visual presence what they lack in pervasiveness.

The language police use is a crucial variable in police behavior. As in the United States, language among Japanese policemen varies with the locality and the person contacted. To taxis and trucks clear-cut orders are given by patrol-car policemen because their drivers are frequent violators and are hardened in their relations with the police. To a double-parked taxi an officer says "Move!" rather than "Please move your car, it is double-parked," as he might to a private car in a residential neighborhood. To squabbling laborers outside a bar police say "Stop fighting!" rather than "Please stop fighting," as they would to drunken businessmen in the Ginza. In addition to varying between requests and commands, modes of address change to indicate degrees of politeness and respect. These are difficult to understand through translation but are readily recognizable to Japanese who make fine distinctions in the choice of words and grammatical forms depending on the status of the other person. Without changing tone a policeman can switch from a polite form of address in talking to his partner to a rude form in speaking to a prostitute standing on a street corner. The language policemen use with street riffraff would be deeply insulting to a respectable Japanese. They also tend to be less respectful to laborers, drunks, and young males with long hair, especially if their manner is sullen or unresponsive. Less polite language does not always indicate disrespect. Since language forms vary with class, the use of high-tone expressions with working-class people would be considered insulting because it would dramatize through its incongruity their lower status. This is true in English as well where exaggerated politeness is used occasionally to demonstrate place. For example, an American policeman may respond to the criticism of a lower-class black by saying, "Yes *Sir, Mr.* Jones."

Patrolmen are constantly reminded by senior officers to be restrained verbally. Nevertheless, anger occasionally breaks through and they become tough and threatening. When hoodlums are questioned in the back rooms of kobans, the doors are sometimes banged shut and shouting can be heard. On one occasion three middle-aged women caught for soliciting for a strip show abused the police in loud shrill voices all the way through a crowded arcade. The officers made a point of turning down a narrow well-lighted lane off the main thoroughfare, where one young officer suddenly turned on the woman and shouted "Shut up!"

Talking back to the police is not common but it does occur. The three women just mentioned—known as "catch" women—argued that they did not like being carted off "like cats" and kept saying loudly for the benefit of the crowd "Don't push me," "Don't hit me," though the police were doing neither. A drunken man who had punched a friend in a bar insisted that the police use the polite form of "You" in talking to him and refused to get into the patrol car until the officers said "please." The rudest behavior toward the police that I saw in six months of field observation was, ironically, by an American who spoke fluent Japanese. Angry because he had been given mistaken directions to a cinema by a young patrolman, the American, about thirty years old, came back to the koban and stolidly lectured the patrolman before a fascinated crowd. He badgered the officer for five minutes, deliberately calling him "Omawari" rather than "Omawari-san." Leaving off the "san" is a grave insult. The young officer took the abuse without a flicker, looking his tormentor in the eyes and standing his ground. No Japanese I have ever seen treated the police with such sustained and calculated disrespect.

Patrolmen often adopt a humorous approach to the people they deal with. Driving around a corner near a street of bars, a patrolman growled out the window like a tiger at four men urinating against a building. A patrol car came alongside a young man in sports clothes walking in a dark park. He was known to the officers as a sneak thief who robbed preoccupied lovers. "What are you doing?" said an officer. "Swimming," said the man, though the night was chilly. Rather than being affronted, the officer replied, "Pool is closed. You better go home." Three policemen were called to a home where an estranged brother had come to pester his working class family for drinking money. The policemen led the man, boisterously drunk, up the street. Patting him on the shoulder they gave him a mock lecture: "Are you a Japanese man? You don't act very manly. You should act manly or maybe we should cut off your penis. Maybe we should throw you in the river. How about that?" The man smiled groggily, wanting to play up to the humor, and finally managed to stagger to the koban.

Sometimes the humor misfires. A young hippie-type with dark glasses and red knitted cap pulled down over his head was given permission to use a koban toilet. Three of the patrolmen, the same age as the young man, kidded him about his hat. He replied that he had bad brains and the hat was to protect them. When kidded about his dark glasses, however, he produced a document showing that he was half-blind. The officers were abashed and immediately apologized. Attempting to divert conversation, they asked where he was going. Sensing his advantage, the young man wondered pointedly whether the question was official or private. If private, he said, he didn't intend to say. And with that he sauntered off, leaving the officers thoroughly discomfited.

Swearing and crude language is not common among Japanese policemen. For one thing it is difficult for a Buddhist to be blasphemous, which removes a whole genre of expressive language as Americans understand it. There are, to be sure, coarse expressions in Japan, but many of them are not understood across class lines. Earthy language is not much used among officers themselves, let alone with members of the public. Unlike the United States, it is not a badge of membership in the police community. If a Japanese policeman wants to be disrespectful, he does so by manipulating the forms of speech, especially by changing in subtle ways the indicators of status, familiarity, and respect.

The one constant element in the working life of koban patrolmen is people in endless need. In many instances there is very little the police can do to help; assistance consists largely in providing an opportunity for a grievance to be registered. For example, late one evening in July two patrolmen were called to a small bar. It was a single room scarcely twenty feet on a side, capable of serving at most twelve people sitting at several diminutive tables. Small metal Christmas trees hung from a ceiling that was barely head-high. The bar was deserted except for the three heavily made-up women who ran it. They told about a man wearing sunglasses who had drunk quickly by himself, gone to the toilet, and ducked out the back door leaving a bill of Y12,000 ($45). There was no hope the man would be found and the women seemed to know it. They talked slowly, dispiritedly, the smoke from their cigarettes drifing to the ceiling. Sometimes police assistance is rejected. Responding to a 110 call, patromen found a bedraggled young woman in a shapeless dress sobbing in a back alley, her right cheek bruised and nose bloody. A tough-looking stocky man about thirty-three years old standing nearby was questioned by the police. The injured woman, leaning against a dirty brick wall and uttering dry hysterical sobs, refused to give her name or the man's and would not even say whether he had hurt her. Two other women dabbed at the injured woman with handkerchiefs and confided to the officers that the man and woman were living together. But they too refused to give names. The police knew the woman was a prostitute, so they concluded the man was her pimp. Since the policemen had not seen the assault and the woman refused to press charges, there was nothing they could do. With disdainful nonchalance the stocky man took the sobbing woman firmly by the wrist and led her away. It was clear that the compulsions of this woman's life could not be loosed by police intervention.

Every so often the help policemen give is acknowledged, and for a moment officers feel a sense of accomplishment. A woman had an attack of severe stomach cramps. Brought to a koban, the police tried to reassure her and make her comfortable on a wooden bench while an ambulance was summoned. Three hours later her teenage son came back to report that she was fine and to offer the family's thanks to the men of the koban. Another time a blowzy woman in a yellow scoop-necked T-shirt and dowdy black skirt ran across a busy street and threw her arms around the waist of a patrolman. Her face twisted with fright, the woman used the patrolman as a shield against a crew-cut man pursuing her who had a heavily bandaged right hand. The two were living together, she said, though they were not married. He was becoming more and more violent and the woman wanted him arrested and committed to a hospital. The man was held for the night and the woman, after calming down, was sent home.

On rare occasions there may be a dramatic emergency, the kind police work is supposed to be all about but hardly ever is. Teenagers had a fight in a remote coal-mining village and a young woman was stabbed in the stomach. She was taken by ambulance to a hospital. The police wrapped up the bloody knife and brought her assailant to a koban. He stood benumbed in the center of a throng of policemen and reporters saying over and over again, "I'm sorry, I'm sorry, I'm sorry."[22] A detective became separated from his partners when he chased two gangsters, supposedly dealing in drugs, though a maze of alleys and twisting lanes. The police radio broadcast an announcement that a policeman was in danger, which brought patrol cars speeding from all over the city. On foot and in cars, a

22. *Gomen nasai, gomen nasai.*

small army of policemen ran up and down streets looking desperately for their lost colleague. Ten minutes later he turned up on his own, winded but unhurt, and the patrol cars were ordered back to routine patrol. In another incident, two patrol cars responded to a report that a fight had occurred near a Buddhist temple. They found two dirty, ragged men who had injured one another with broken beer bottles. Blood-streaked and grimy, the men sat on the steps of the temple while their heads were wrapped in incongruously clean white bandages by ambulance attendants. The policemen dispersed a small crowd of curious bystanders who were fascinated by pools of blood, almost purple in color under the light of fluorescent street lamps, that had fallen on the pitted stone steps.

The needs of most people are not dramatic and the help the police give produces indeterminate results. Many people do not even know they need help and the police grope to find an appropriate response. A typical example was a middle-aged man found about midnight sleeping on a bench in a river-front park. Near him was parked an expensive, gaudily outfitted bicycle. The man had evidently been employed at some time as a construction laborer because he wore the soft, two-toed boots that look like a dinosaur's footprint and a foot-wide woolen cumberbund. Such belly-wraps are common among manual laborers; they are supposed to prevent stomach problems by keeping the midriff warm. Sleepily rubbing his eyes in the light of police flashlights, he ruefully remarked that this was the most terrible night of his life. He had been robbed, so he could not prove his identity, and now he was picked up by the police on suspicion of stealing a bicycle. Because the handlebars of the bike had been knocked awry and the chain had come off, he could not even ride home. The police treated him with good humor and he soon began to laugh at his fate. The police took him and his outlandish bicycle to a koban where, in the course of a few hours, they would make repairs to the bicycle, find out whether it had been stolen, and try to determine whether the man's identity was genuine.

The most striking aspect of the variety of situations confronted by policemen is their compelling, unforced naturalness. The police see masses of utterly ordinary people who have become enmeshed in situations that are tediously complex and meaningful only to the persons immediately involved. The outcomes are of no interest to the community at large; the newspapers will not notice if matters are sorted out or not; superior officers have no way of recording the effort patrolmen expend in trying to be helpful; and the people themselves are incapable by and large of permanently escaping their predicaments. Policemen are responsible for tending these individuals, for showing that they appreciate — even when they are tired, hurried, bored, and preoccupied — the minute ways in which each person is unique. It is, perhaps, the greatest service they render.

4. Discipline and Responsibility

The record of the Japanese police with respect to the propriety of conduct is the envy of any country in the world. Relative to total personnel, the number of officers in Japan who are punished each year for misbehavior is many times less than in the United States. This is despite the fact that disciplinary standards are higher in the sense that Japanese are sterner with respect to infractions Americans would consider petty.[1] Informed observers, such as defense attorneys and newspaper reporters, agree that brutality is rare, restricted largely to the handling of riotous demonstrators, and corruption almost unknown.[2] Criminality by policemen is always the work of solitary individuals, never by organized groups. Complaints about police behavior are less common than in the United States and less serious, involving inadequate rather than improper conduct, even though the police have encouraged the registering of complaints by establishing special offices and telephone numbers for the purpose. A freewheeling press which is not reluctant to criticize the police has legitimatized making complaints and helped to publicize standards of propriety. There is an independent agency outside the police that reviews violations of human rights, yet complaints about the police to this agency have actually declined in recent years. numbering now scarcely more than one hundred a year.[3]

How have the Japanese been able to establish standards of personal conduct among policemen that are so high? Why are they not plagued with the kind of police misconduct that Americans have come to accept as inevitable? In discussions in the United States about ways of producing responsible police behavior, several factors are routinely cited as being especially crucial. They are recruitment, training, material rewards, supervision, and accountability. Manipulation of these factors is though to be sufficient, or at least very important, in improving police conduct. In searching for the

1. For example, some of the fewer than 600 officers punished in 1972 were disciplined because they lost the police handbook or encouraged young girls to believe they would marry them and then did not.
2. For figures on the number of officers disciplined for different infractions of departmental regulations, see Chapter 1.
3. See Chapter 1.

reasons for Japan's success, I shall begin by examining what the Japanese have done with respect to each of these. Have these factors varied sufficiently between Japan and the United States to account satisfactorily for differences in police performance?

Entrance into the police can be made at two levels — patrolman and assistant inspector.[4] Recruitment for patrolmen is conducted separately by each prefecture. Applicants must pass physical, intellectual, and vocational aptitude tests. Their personal backgrounds are extensively explored and they must do well in an oral interview. Patrolmen, who must have high school diplomas, may rise as high as their talents can take them; there is no ceiling to their advancement. Recruitment to the rank of assistant inspector is done on a national basis by the National Police Agency. Entrance has been provided at this level in order to attract personnel with the educational requirements required for staffing high administrative posts. In addition to meeting the qualifications for patrolman, applicants must have a four-year college education and have passed the advanced civil service examination.[5] Only a handful — about fifteen — are recruited at this level each year. Recruitment at two levels overcomes a criticism that is often directed at American police forces, namely that their senior officers are with few exceptions promoted patrolmen. They have not been groomed for staff positions, except for a smattering of in-service training, but have spent their formative years on the street performing routine operational tasks. Some patrolmen do rise to become senior administrators, even chiefs of prefectural forces, or assume staff responsibilities at the National Police Agency. By and large, however, these positions are monopolized by the specially recruited executive elite.

Proportionate to population Japan may have a slightly larger pool of able and interested persons from which to recruit. Manpower demands of policing are higher in the United States than in Japan. There is one policeman for ever 445 persons in the United States and

---

4. The ranks of police are, starting at the bottom: Patrolman, Senior Patrolman, Sergeant, Assistant Inspector, Inspector, Superintendent, Chief Superintendent, and Superintendent Supervisor. The chief of the Tokyo Metropolitan Police Department has the special rank of Superintendent-General. He is outranked only by the chief of the National Police Agency, known as Director-General.
5. National Police Agency, *Police in Japan, 1971*, p. 17, refers to this as the exam for "Advanced Public Service Personnel."

one for every 585 in Japan.[6] The number of applicants for positions in the Japanese police has remained steady in recent years, outnumbering vacancies six to one.[7] Comparable figures are not available for the United States. Checks of several major cities indicate that the pool of applicants is at least as large in the United States. Moreover, with the economic downturn of 1972-1973, the number of applicants has risen sharply.[8] If qualities of character and intelligence occur in similar proportions in the populations of Japan and the United States, then the Japanese have only a marginal advantage in recruitment.

In social and political outlook individuals recruited to the police tend to be conservative.[9] In the United States this is attributed to self-selection; police work attracts more conservative people. While this is probably true in Japan as well, there is a clearer element of organizational intent. Extensive background checks by the local police are carried out on all recruits to determine whether they are persons of good character. Though the constitution prohibits denying government employment on the basis of political belief or affiliation,[10] the police do reject applicants if they have "antisocial" tendencies. How often such a conclusion is based on the fact that the applicants or members of his family are associated with left-wing parties is hard to tell. That it happens sometimes is evident from the smug confidence the police have that "leftists" could not penetrate and subvert the police should they want to.

6. *Ibid.* and United States Bureau of the Census, Department of Commerce, *U.S. Statistical Abstract, 1973* (Washington, D.C.: Government Printing Office, 1973), p. 156, provides figures on the total number of police officers in both countries.
7. According to the National Police Agency, the police need about 6,000 new officers a year, a replacement rate of roughly 3.6 percent. Committee on Comprehensive Countermeasures, *Interim Report* (Tokyo: National Police Agency, 1970), Chap. 8. Close to 30,000 applicatons were received for these positions in 1971-1973. Information supplied by the Personnel Section, National Police Agency, 1973.
8. For example, in the late 1960s for about 3,000 positions with the New York City Police Department, there were 48,000 applicants. There were 9,000 approved candidates on a waiting list. Robert Daley, *Target Blue* (New York: Delacorte Press, 1971), p. 34. In Denver, Colorado, between 1960 and 1972, there were at least six applicants for every vacancy. Interview with staff member of the Civil Service Commission, Denver, Colorado, 1973. The impression of officers in the F.B.I. is that the quality of applicants as well as the number has been increasing everywhere in the United States in the last few years except in the South. Interview, 1974.
9. David H. Bayley and Harold Mendelsohn, *Minorities and the Police* (New York: The Free Press, 1969), pp. 18-30.
10. Article 14.

TRAINING

The training given recruits in Japan is much more extensive, thorough, and practical than in the United States. Formal training in a police school lasts for a year in Japan as opposed to not more than eight weeks in the United States.[11] Both the duration of training and the curriculum are standard throughout Japan. Mandatory training standards even at the state level are a fairly recent development in the U.S. Seven states still have none at all and four more introduced them only at the beginning of 1974.[12] Formal training is also a more serious hurdle to appointment in Japan. Five percent of the candidates sent to the Tokyo police school, for example, fail to complete the course.[13] Comparable data for the United States is, as usual, lacking due to extreme decentralization. However, appointment as a probationary officer has often been criticized as tantamount to final confirmation because training programs fail to weed out the incompetent.[14]

The Japanese also recognize that more learning can be accomplished in a few months on the street than in a host of school lectures and demonstrations. Accordingly they have integrated school with training on the job. After completing a year of police school, recruits are sent into the field for a year. Then they return to school for a minimum of three months to reflect on their experiences and receive additional training.[15] Furthermore, recognizing that initial experiences on the job may be unusually important to subsequent performance, the Japanese police have developed a unique tutoring arrangement whereby responsibility for teaching new recruits is given explicitly to experienced officers. "Rookies" are assigned to work with an officer who has been carefully selected and trained

11. The average length of police training in the United States is 240 hours. Interview with James Sterling, Professional Standards Division, International Association of Chiefs of Police Gaithersburg, Maryland, March 1974. At six hours per day five days a week, this amounts to an eight-week training course.
12. Information provided by the National Association of State Directors of Law Enforcement Training, 1974.
13. Personnel Section, Tokyo Metropolitan Police Department.
14. James F. Ahern, *Police in Trouble* (New York: Hawthorne Books, Inc., 1972), p.7, says that in New Haven, Connecticut, where he was chief of police, only one person in twenty-five years was washed out of the training program. He believes that failure is virtually impossible in most cities. According to informants in the Professional Standards Division of the International Association of Chiefs of Police, statistics on the rate of failure in U.S. training programs are not available.
15. The length of this period is longer in some prefectures; it is a matter of local option.

himself to provide appropriate instruction. Tutoring officers meet together in every police station to discuss the problems of teaching that arise. This arrangement raises the chances that recruits will learn what the organizations want them to rather than what a haphazard collection of "old hands" decide to pass on. Until 1972 tutoring policemen were either senior patrolmen or sergeants. They were both usually a generation older than the recruit. A new system is now being tried in which the senior partner is a young patrolman with two or three years experience. This is referred to as the "brother system."[16] It is hoped that the younger tutors will be able to empathize more successfully with the problems of new recruits. They are also likely to be more energetic than older men and can respond to the recruit's desire for activity. Some older officers have misgivings about the system, fearing that the "brother" relationship will be too businesslike, that the younger tutors cannot provide the intangible personal support that a father-figure can. They doubt that the younger tutors will give as much attention to the "spiritual" side of being a policeman, the need for pride and dedication.

There is also much more in-service training in Japan. Upon promotion to sergeant or assistant inspector, officers spend three and six months respectively at one of the eight regional training schools. When an officer is promoted to inspector he is sent for a full year to the national police college in Tokyo.[17] Every year approximately ten thousand policemen undergo training upon promotion and forty thousand do technical courses lasting from three weeks to a year.[18] Finally, serving patrolmen are often given monthly homework assignments designed to keep particular skills fresh. For example, they may be required to fill out appropriate arrest papers for a particular situation.

PAY AND BENEFITS

The material rewards for being a policeman are lower in Japan than in the United States. The total monthly salary of a Japanese

16. This is an English expression incorporated into Japanese. By avoiding Japanese words for "brother"—*niisan*, for example—the expression does not take on traditional overtones, particularly the sense of reciprocal status so common in referring to brothers.
17. This is not true in every case. Officers promoted late in their careers may not be sent at all or only for short periods.
18. National Police Agency, "Training of Police" (Unpublished paper in Japanese, p. 1).

policeman is about \$548 compared with \$700 in the United States.[19] Comparing major cities in each country, the gap between Japanese and American pay rates widens. A Tokyo patrolman earns \$390 per month while a New York patrolman earns \$1,280 per month.[20] Salary figures for Japanese policemen include base salary plus allowances. The allowances are extensive, amounting to two-thirds of base pay.[21] They include supplements for dependents, housing, commuting, assignment to supervisory positions, overtime, and working nights and holidays. The largest item is a bonus, amounting to about 40 percent of base wage and paid in three installments during the year.[22]

If base pay plus allowances were the total benefits earned by a Japanese policeman, they would be less well off economically relative to American policemen since the cost of living in Japan is comparable to that in the United States. However, Japanese policemen receive extensive fringe benefits in the form of services that American policemen supply out of their salaries. Approximately 55 percent of all policemen live in housing furnished by the police for

19. The figure for the United States is for officers in cities of over ten thousand persons as of 1 January 1972. International City Management Association, *Municipal Year Book, 1973* (Chicago: International City Management Association), p. 243. Median starting salaries were given as \$7,826 and median maximum salaries as \$9,280 per year. As one would expect, average national salary figures for the United States are much less exact than one would want. The calculation of average salary for Japanese policemen has been made from figures supplied by the National Police Agency giving the average salary for all ranks, patrolman through superintendent. Figures for the number of persons holding each rank have also been supplied by the National Police Agency. Unfortunately, they are for 1971 rather than 1972, but the difference between these two years is small. Base pay for a superintendent was Y144,894; for inspector Y126,310; for assistant inspector Y115,281, for sergeant Y105,889; and for patrolman Y74,284. For reasons given below, the average salary for each rank is figured at 66.6 percent above base pay. The exchange rate used in the calculaton of dollar equivalent of a Japanese salary is Y265 to the dollar.

20. Information provided by the Tokyo Metropolitan Police Department and the New York City Police Department.

21. Informaton provided by the National Police Agency. In effect, base pay is 60 percent of total pay; allowances are 40 percent of total pay. The ratio between base pay and allowances varies somewhat from prefecture to prefecture. Examining figures on base pay and total pay for several prefectures, I find that all allowances come to 66.6 percent of base pay.

22. Bonuses are technically allowances, known as "Term-end Allowances plus Diligent Allowance." They are set by prefectural ordinance and vary between four and five months' basic salary. Bonuses in private industry in Japan, 1970, were the equivalent of 2.9 months' salary. *Statistical Handbook of Japan*, 1972, p. 11.

which they pay little or nothing.[23] In Tokyo, for instance, where the cost of housing is astronomical, accomodations for police families are offered at less than a tenth of the market price. Free medical care and hospitalization are provided to all policemen; their families may use the same facilities at concessional rates. Restaurants, laundries, and barber shops are available to officers at a fraction of the market price. Policemen may also join two cooperative associations that provide health, disability, and retirement benefits supplementary to those awarded by the government. The associations make low-cost loans and sell consumer goods at discount prices.[24] The halls of police facilities are often crowded with racks and tables displaying clothing and household appliances. One of the associations has built hotels in famous cities and vacation resorts where policemen, their families, and even their friends (if space is available) may obtain excellent rooms and inexpensive food.[25]

In order to bring Japanese salaries up to American levels, the monetary value of fringe benefits would have to be equivalent to 46 percent of base pay.[26] This may be true but it is impossible to tell since a monetary value for fringe benefits cannot be computed.

More meaningful than comparing police salaries in the two countries is a comparison of the returns to policemen relative to other occupations. How competitive are police wages and benefits in relation to other forms of employment? The average salary of all Japanese policemen — base pay plus bonus and allowances — is 48 percent above the average for all industrial workers.[27] Policemen in the United States earn on the average 44 percent more than workers

23. In this case, of course, they would not be given a housing allowance. National Police Agency, "Pay, Benefits, and Housing" (Unpublished pamphlet in Japanese, 1972).

24. Tokyo Metropolitan Police Department, *Keishicho*, 1972, p. 32, translated these associations as the "Police Personnel's Mutual Aid Society" and the "Police Personnel's Credit Cooperative Association."

25. I have been invited to stay at several of them. The rooms are Japanese-style with tatami floors and rolled mattresses and bedding. The rooms have a wash basin and television set. Toilet and bath facilities are communal. The cost of a room and a very good dinner and breakfast is about $8.00.

26. The discrepancy between Japanese and American average pay is $152.00 per month. According to the National Police Agency, the average base pay of a Japanese policeman (as opposed to total monetary monthly salary) is $329.00 per month.

27. Y145,000 versus Y98,528. Bureau of Statistics, Office of the Prime Minister, "Monthly Statistics of Japan," January, 1974 (No. 151), p. 79. The figure is for

in private industry.[28] Only workers in the construction trades earn more than policemen. Japanese and American policemen are therefore situated similarly with respect to the overall wage structure in each country.

Japanese policemen are prohibited from supplementing their income through private employment. In American language, they may not "moonlight."[29] A Japanese policeman is doubly penalized compared with an American: he must do more work for a smaller salary and cannot earn additional income. It is like asking an American policeman to "moonlight" without pay.

To recapitulate, being a policeman is equally attractive in material terms in Japan and the United States relative to other occupations. In absolute terms, Japanese policemen are probably less well off than American, though a precise comparison of fringe benefits might change this conclusion. This is what one would expect since per capita income is lower generally in Japan than in the United States.

The amount of base salary earned by policemen in Japan depends on three factors — seniority, rank, and education. All policemen receive automatic increments in salary every year. A patrolman's salary doubles in twenty years; in thirty years in increases two and a half times. The annual rate of increase declines the longer the service. At the beginning the annual increment is 5 percent; after twenty years, it is just over 1 percent. Police service has been made more attractive for university graduates by giving them four years' seniority from the outset. This differential between college and high school graduates remains throughout their careers regardless of rank. Salary also increases with advancement in rank. Passage of a written examination is required for promotion from patrolman to sergeant, sergeant to assistant inspector, and assistant inspector to inspector. Beyond inspector promotions are made on recommendation of superior officers. From patrolman through inspector a rise in rank wins a raise in pay equivalent to between three and four years' seniority. Thus a patrolman with ten years' service earns as much as

---

average monthly cash earnings and includes overtime, bonus, and allowances. Since most policemen are male, it is instructive to compare police salaries with average cash wages for males in industry. Police salaries are 25 percent higher. *Ibid.* Cash earnings for males in industrial establishments employing more than thirty workers were Y115,592 per month.
28. $175 per week for policemen in the United States, *U.S. Statistical Abstract, 1972* p. 433. $132.82 per week for workers in private industry, *Ibid,* p. 233.
29. Some minor exceptions are allowed: with permission of a senior officer, they may help run a family store, manage an apartment, or teach English.

a sergeant with seven years' service. A patrolman with thirty years' experience could earn as much in base salary as his station chief if the chief has the rank of superintendent—which is common—and only fourteen years' seniority. Faithful service is rewarded as much as substantial promotions in rank.

In order to reward long service even more, a special rank was invented in 1967—the rank of senior patrolman, which is above patrolman but below sergeant. For appointment as senior patrolman no examination is required. Senior patrolmen are given minor supervisory tasks and a modest raise in pay. More recently a few men have also been promoted to sergeant without examination. The slight movement away from written examination at the lower ranks is in recognition of the fact that they may not adequately test skills acquired through practical experience. Many Japanese policemen agree with their American counterparts that performance on the street should play a larger role in determining promotion.

The opportunities for career advancement are greater for a policeman in Japan than in the United States. Almost one-third of all Japanese policemen hold supernumerary rank, that is, higher than patrolman. Totals for all police forces in the United States are not available, but evidence from several cities supports the conclusion. In New York City, 26 percent of the force is above the rank of patrolman; Washington, 20.3 percent; Chicago, 24 percent; and in Los Angeles, 19.5 percent.[30] In American highway patrols, 18 percent of sworn personnel are above the rank of patrolman, and among state police, 15 percent.[31] A patrolman in Japan has one chance in four of becoming a sergeant; in Chicago and New York City, one in eight, and in Los Angeles and Washington, D.C., one in six.[32] In highway patrols the chances for promotion to sergeant are one in seven and in state police one in eight.[33]

There is a constant circulation of staff in the Japanese police, both latterly and upward, which prevents units from becoming ingrown.

30. In Los Angeles there are three grades of patrolman. If an advance within the patrolman category is included, then half the police force in Los Angeles has advanced beyond the lowest rung. I am grateful to the police departments of these cities for supplying this information.
31. Calculated from ratios of supervisory officers to all personnel provided by Division of State and Provincial Police, *Comparative Data Report* (Gaithersburg, Maryland: International Association of Chiefs of Police, 1972), p. 20.
32. In these calculations, officers of detective or investigator rank are excluded. Though promotion to this position is desirable, it should not be counted as a supervisory rank.
33. Division of State and Provincial Police, p. 20.

Whenever a policeman is promoted, he is transferred to another post — either in a different specialty in the same place or the same specialty in another place. He cannot rise among the people he has worked with already. Moreover, tenure in supervisory positions — with the exception of senior patrolmen in kobans — is generally no longer than two years. The practice extends to the very top of the hierarchy.[34] Rotation prevents officers in police stations from becoming too deeply involved with local communities. Undesirable contacts or compromising decisions cannot permanently affect a station's operation. And it is almost impossible for a clique to form that can dominate the activities of a station or section.

The regular circulation of staff through posting and promotion is a function of the scale of Japanese police organization. The unit of organization is the prefecture, and prefectural forces range in size from just under one thousand officers (Tottori) to thirty-eight thousand (Tokyo). The average is four thousand officers. In organizations this size the command structure is complex, with a variety of supervisory posts, functional specialties can be developed, and lateral transfers can involve substantial geographical movement. The organization can also find places for persons who are unlikely to be promoted farther but whom it would be unjust to force into retirement and for people who need to be promoted for reasons of self-esteem but cannot be entrusted with substantial commands.

SUPERVISION

Internal supervision is considerably more strict in Japan than in the United States. American supervisors stress the development of individual initiative; Japanese supervisors, errorless performance. Koban patrolmen work under the watchful eye of a senior patrolman; sergeants tour kobans once or twice every shift. Only during

34. Retirement age in the National Police Agency is between fifty and fifty-five; in prefectural police forces, between fifty-five and fifty-eight. Though officers are not required to retire at these ages, they are encouraged to do so. For example, yearly increments in salary decline with seniority. If officers do retire at the above ages, not waiting for the statutory maximum, they receive a higher lump sum severance payment. The size of their pensions is affected only by the length of time they have served the police. In the National Police Agency, for example, an officer who retires voluntarily after twenty years gets a lump sum payment that is equivalent to 31.5 months' salary, as against 21.0 months' salary equivalent if he retires involuntarily; after thirty years, an officer gets 50.4 months' severance payment for voluntary retirement versus 41.25 months' for involuntary. Most officers choose to retire voluntarily. Information supplied by the National Police Agency.

foot patrols, which rarely last longer than an hour, are patrolmen in any sense on their own. For all but the most routine events, a sergeant or senior patrolman will come to the scene minutes after initial response. The chief of a station's patrol section monitors radio communications, especially at night, by means of a portable receiver. Even among themselves, patrolmen continually advise and caution one another. When a patrol car, for example, prepares to start across an intersection, the officer who is not driving mutters "O Rai" (all right) to the driver to indicate no car is approaching from his side. Policemen in the United States would resent this kind of routine "front-seat" driving. American patrolmen climb into their police cars at the beginning of a shift and are on their own for eight hours, unless they become involved in an unusually serious incident. American officers even eat alone, in contrast to Japanese patrolmen who are not allowed to eat in uniform in public places and so return to the koban or police station at mealtime. Senior officers in the United States continually talk about the importance of not blighting the enthusiasm of young officers.[35] The mores of the American police community militates against active on-street supervision. Challenged by public opinion to demonstrate that internal discipline is strict, American officers therefore regulate the only part of individual officer's conduct that they can get at, namely, the policeman's relations with the organization. This makes discipline a matter of nagging formalism, covering dress codes, accounting for expenditures, reporting of daily events, and indenting for equipment. Supervision in American police forces is a smokescreen for substantial freedom of action on the street. Individual performance is monitored only by peers.

The manner and perhaps the strictness of supervision in the Japanese police has changed in the past few years. Older officers say that they must command subordinates less and persuade them more. Younger policemen are not as unquestioning as their predecessors. Supervision is less intense now on matters not affecting police purposes directly. Young officers require reasonableness and intelligence to be manifest in what is demanded of them.

Variations in supervision between Japan and the United States mesh with respective deployment mechanisms. Kobans facilitate close supervision; patrol cars undermine it. In Japan most decisions about arrests are made at the police station, not on the street.

---

35. Paul Chevigny, *Police Power* (New York: Random House, 1969), p. 212, notes that if a policeman acts "in good faith," violation of a citizen's rights is rarely grounds for departmental punishment.

Except in emergencies, patrolmen ask suspects to accompany them to the police station where senior officers can dispose of the case. Patrolmen keep in close touch with senior staff and specialists by koban telephone. Because telephones are more private than two-way radios, koban patrolmen can obtain informal advice from headquarters in a way that American policemen cannot. Where American policemen have perfunctory exchanges with headquarters dispatchers, Japanese patrolmen have long conversations in which they examine the situation in great detail. Japanese officers are aware that mobility diminishes the effectiveness of supervision. They give special attention to the selection of personnel assigned to patrol cars and motorcycles, especially since increased independence is one of the recognized attractions of such work.

Supervision can be more extensive in Japan because the ratio of supervisiory officers to junior grades is higher there than in the United States. As we have already seen, patrolmen make up 68 percent of the force in Japan and approximately 75 to 80 percent in the United States. In Japan the ratio is one sergeant to every four patrolmen; in Chicago approximately one to nine, in Los Angeles one to six, in New York City one to eight, and in Washington, D.C., one to six.[36] Supervisory capacity is augmented further in Japan by the use of retired officers as overseers. They are encouraged to maintain close relations with the neighboring police station, dropping in to meet new officers and to report on the behavior of officers on the street.[37]

Strict supervision entails special obligations for senior officers. They are held accountable for the behavior of subordinates more strictly than is the case in the United States. Eight percent of officers who were disciplined departmentally in 1972 were punished for failures of supervision. The most common punishment in such cases was a written reprimand that appears on an officer's record. A few were suspended or had their pay decreased.[38] In a typical case, the chief of a detective section had his pay reduced by 10 percent for several months when a detective in his charge allowed a suspect to take poison and die. The chief of a police station was demoted in rank because an off-duty policeman had his pistol stolen in a Mah-Jong parlor. Officers are required to leave their weapons in the station, and this officer's failure to do so was attributed to inefficient

36. Daley, p. 130, says the ratio in New York was one to fourteen in 1970. However, because many sergeants were assigned to headquarters, the ratio in precinct police stations was more like one to twenty.
37. Interviews, 1972.
38. Information provided by the National Police Agency.

supervision on the part of the chief. Another station chief was demoted when a patrolman was arrested for raping several adolescent girls. Station chiefs are admonished when subordinates are arrested for drunken driving off duty. As one would expect, punishments to superiors are more severe when the subordinate's misconduct was on duty rather than off, and when there is a clear link between the activities of the superior and the mistake of the subordinate. In Japan, superior and junior officers share liability for mistakes. This creates a link between them which is symmetrical and not based exclusively on fear. A superior officer is viewed as more than a punishing judge; he is a partner in responsibility who may be punished for an error on the subordinate's part.

The responsibility of superior officers for the behavior of subordinates is not unique to the police; it is a general cultural pattern in Japan. When a military jet aircraft, for example, was involved in a mid-air collision with a commercial plane, the Director-General of the Defense Agency resigned. The Japanese government accepted responsibility for the massacre at Tel Aviv airport by Japanese terrorists in 1972 and offered to compensate the families of persons killed or injured. When the father of one of the radical youths captured at Asama-sanso in February, 1972, saw his son arrested on television, he went into the backyard and hanged himself in shame for his failure as a parent.

Because every officer is preoccupied with obtaining errorless performance, the number of policemen assigned full time to problems of internal discipline is very small. In a prefectural force of twelve thousand officers, perhaps five or six will be assigned to a small administrative unit whose function is to confirm punishments, call attention to patterns of failure, and occasionally make investigations.[39] Police station personnel do most of the work connected with investigating misconduct and deciding upon punishments. They also hold an impressive array of meetings which are devoted to the examination of conduct. The chief usually addresses the personnel of the station at an inspection twice a month. He uses the occasion invariably to discuss shortcomings in performance. Once a month a study meeting of the entire staff is held, leaving a skeleton crew on the street, which lasts a whole morning and is devoted to discussing new regulations and general problems. Some stations have regular "morale" meetings focusing on problems of misconduct which are attended by a selection of sergeants, senior patrolmen, and patrolmen from every section. There are monthly

39. This is called the Police Supervision Office.

meetings of supervisory officers above the rank of senior patrolmen, of section leaders, of shift leaders in a single section, and of the personnel of each shift. Meetings are a fixture of police life in Japan, reflecting compulsive concern with the prevention of improper as well as unsafe behavior.

The system of supervision in the police cannot be understood properly without reference to the ubiquitousness of hierarchy in Japanese social relations. Policemen are aware not only of rank gradations but seniority within ranks. They mold their speech and behavior according to whether the officer they are dealing with is above or below them in status. Even partners in a patrol car address one another differently depending on their relative roles. The senior partner will be addressed as "shacho" by the junior, while the junior partner will be called by his surname. (Americans are sometimes puzzled by the Japanese practice of exchanging name cards upon first introduction. These cards contain important clues to status, and allow each person to adopt the manner appropriate to the other's social position. Japanese travelers in the United States recount their anxiety at having to meet people socially without knowing something about their station in the world, and they find a cocktail party very unsettling.) But strenuous attempts are made to smooth the hard edges of the hierarchical system. A senior officer who could not mix on easy terms with his subordinates would not be well regarded. Supervisory personnel frequently put on fatigue clothes and perform menial work alongside their men. They also join lower ranks in playing sports or at social occasions. At a dinner or lunch for a visitor four or five ranks will be present. Conversation is general and subordinates participate without embarrassment. Though a superior can dominate if he wants to, lower ranks often inject observations and point out forgotten facts. Senior officers are pragmatic and they appreciate the value of experience. They have no trouble deferring to it over rank. In kobans, for instance, sergeants and assistant inspectors frequently step aside and allow a situation to be handled by a young patrolman who may know the area better than they.

The arrangement of furniture in police offices provides important clues to the nature of relations among ranks. In the office of a chief of a station, the chief's desk will stand on one side of the room with a chair behind it but none in front. On the other side of the room will be several sofas and armchairs grouped around a coffee table. When the chief is at his desk, he deals quickly with subordinates he summons — to give an order or elicit a point of information. The subordinate does not sit down and talk with the chief across his desk.

When the chief wants to have a discussion, he goes and sits in an armchair at the head of the coffee table. Chiefs spend much of their time sitting in overstuffed armchairs listening and talking to their staff in what an American thinks of as an informal situation. The same is true in headquarters' offices as well. The senior officer's individual work is done at his desk. When he deals with subordinates, other than in a clear command situation, he deemphasizes social distance by making himself physically accessible. In American society, on the other hand, where hierarchy is less clearly felt, a superior commonly remains seated behind his desk, inviting visitors to sit opposite him. Even staff conferences are conducted from behind the sheltering desk. Paradoxically, then, in the less rank-conscious society—where subordinates often address superiors by their first names—leaders physically demonstrate authority differentials; while in the society where hierarchy is explicit, leaders insist on collegial physical groupings. It is as if each society had developed customs for offsetting fundamental characteristics of social structure. The reason for these compromises may be pragmatic. Hierarchy and collegiality—the one to facilitate command, the other to facilitate egalitarian communication—are both necessary for the efficient operation of complex organizations. Though Japan and the United States appear at first glance to have emphasized different qualities, devices have been generated which ensure that the opposing quality is not lost.[40]

ACCOUNTABILITY

The final factor to consider in trying to explain differences in the incidence of misconduct between Japan and the United States is accountability. That is, what mechanisms have been established to enforce responsible conduct upon the police from outside? Japanese policemen are subject to the criminal law. If a policeman is accused of a crime, the public prosecutor's office—part of the Ministry of Justice—is required to conduct the investigation as well as the prosecution. The police force is not put in a position where it might be tempted to protect its own personnel. Police officers can be sued for civil damages. If damages are assessed resulting from actions occurring in the course of duty, they are paid by the government.

40. This is an excellent example of a general point that social structures arrayed at opposing ends of an abstract linear continuum tend in practice to decay toward a common center. I am indebted to Marion J. Levy for first bringing this point to my attention.

Officers are not liable personally as is often the case in the United States. Legal action against individual officers is not as easy to initiate in Japan as in the United States because policemen do not wear badges or numbers that make them identifiable individually. The introduction of such marks has been considered periodically by the police but has always been rejected. Senior officers do not consider it an important reform.

Civilian supervision of the activities of the police has been provided in several ways. First, the Human Rights Bureau of the Ministry of Justice, established in 1948, solicits complaints about infringements of civil rights by private and public agencies. In addition to an official staff in every major city, the Bureau uses ten thousand unpaid civilian counsellors scattered throughout the country to discover violations of rights. Though the Bureau does not have compulsory powers of investigation, it can ask for an accounting from the police and make recommendations concerning punishment. The police would place themselves in an awkward position if they refused to comply with a Bureau investigation. According to civil rights officials, cooperation has been excellent.[41] The number of complaints brought to the Bureau about the police has declined steadily over the past twenty years.[42] But the utility of the Bureau is seen in the seriousness of the cases they handle. Their cases tend to involve more serious infractions than those taken directly to the police. In 1972, for example, about 20 percent of the complaints received by the Bureau against the police involved physical violence,

41. For a description of the working of the Human Rights Bureau and its nationwide system of human-rights counsellors, see Ministry of Justice, *Governmental and Non-Governmental Machinery for the Protection of Human Rights and Legal Aid in Japan* (1970). An instance of Bureau intervention shows how effective it can be. In January 1966, a policeman took a youth seventeen years old to a koban. The young man, who had witnessed a traffic accident, testified cooperatively for a while but then became defiant. A policeman slapped him on the cheek, rupturing an ear drum. The Director of the District Human Rights Bureau "warned" the chief of the prefectural police to discipline the officer. He did so, ordering a reduction in pay for one month which amounted to 2 percent of base pay. Tsuneo Horiuchi, "The Civil Liberties Bureau of the Ministry of Justice and the System of Civil LIberties Commissions," in United Nations, *Effective Realization of Civil and Political Rights at the National Level—Selected Studies* (New York: UN, 1968, ST/TAO HR/33), pp. 71-72.
42. Figures are for complaints received, not for true cases. In 1972, 93 percent of all cases were found to be true, which is much higher than the percentage in most American cities. The decline in police cases conforms to a general trend with respect to the proportion of cases involving official, as opposed to private, conduct. Nineteen percent of all cases involved governmental employees in 1953; the rest were private. In 1972, only 3.4 percent involved government employees. Information provided by the Human Rights Bureau, Ministry of Justice, 1973.

10 percent illegal confession, and 15 percent unlawful arrest, investigation and seizure.

Second, prefectural chiefs of police are frequently summoned before prefectural legislatures to answer questions about performance. The prefectural legislatures, along with the national Diet, hold the purse strings.

Third, every police force is accountable to a civilian Public Safety Commission.[43] There is one in each prefecture and another at the national level which supervises the National Police Agency. Public safety commissions are similar to regulatory agencies in the United States in that their members, who serve for fixed terms, are nominated by executive authority and confirmed by appropriate legislative bodies.[44] Great pains are taken to ensure that the commissions are nonpolitical. Members cannot be appointed from legislative assemblies, hold executive office in a political party, or engage in political action. A majority of a commission cannot be from the same political party. Public Safety Commissions are charged with supervising all police operations. They appoint and dismiss prefectural chiefs of police; they must approve changes in staff positions; and they make recommendations concerning punishment for disciplinary violations.[45]

Fourth, the media in Japan is a very important though diffuse mechanism of accountability. It is free and vigorous and not reluctant to publicize police misdeeds. It is fair to say that stories about the police, especially their imperfections, are among their most popular features.

Japan, then, has the same kind of devices for making the police accountable as the United States. This is not surprising since the contemporary constitution, criminal codes, and statutes relating to police powers were laid down between 1945-1952 during the Occupation.[46] The amount of active supervision that these mechanisms exert is difficult to assess. There are certainly fewer civil suits and criminal prosecutions against police officers in Japan than in the United States. Moreover, public safety commissions do not play an active role is disciplinary investigations; they leave matters in the hands of uniformed personnel unless there is a major scandal. The

---

43. The Police Law, article 38.
44. Public safety commissions will be discussed further in Chapter 9.
45. Public safety commissions are regulated by provisions of the Police Law.
46. This is not strictly true. The Police Law was passed in 1954. However, its provisions concerning public accountability and individual duties and responsibilities changed very little from the Occupation period. What changed most was the pattern of national organization, particularly the size of police force jurisdictions and coordination between local and national levels.

press is avid but what it reports is only occasionally very serious. It would be wrong, however, to conclude that the mechanisms of accountability are not effective. The processes appear to be vital — their existence is valued, their use has been legitimated, and they are in fact used from time to time. If they are not used as often as they might be in the United States, it could be because police conduct is superior for other reasons or they are having deterrent effect.

The purpose of this discussion has been to determine whether there are sufficeint differences between Japan and the United States with respect to recruitment, training, pay, supervision, and accountability to account for markedly different records of police misconduct. The conclusion is that there are indeed important differences, and in each case the variation would have the effect of decreasing the likelihood of misconduct in Japan. Let us review these differences. First, the Japanese police have a stratified system of recruitment that permits them to recruit people directly for senior executive positions. They discriminate in recruitment with respect to the skills needed for operational and staff personnel. Second, policemen are trained for much longer periods in Japan and their vocational socialization is less haphazard; formal training is integrated with practical experience and adjustment to the job is facilitated by a carefully constructed tutoring arrangement. Third, internal supervision of individual behavior is more extensive and thorough. Avoidance of mistakes is the prime commandment, and policemen are willing to accept close supervision in order to achieve it. Fourth, supervisory personnel are rotated at regular intervals which lessens the possibility that any operation will assume an idiosyncratic character. Fifth, prospects for career development are more favorable in Japan. A larger proportion of officers are promoted and the command structure is more elaborate.

There are no features that would militate in favor of the United States having the better record of police conduct. The most that can be said is that some are similar. The pool of applicants, for example, for police service is proportionately the same. So are the rates of remuneration relative to other occupations. The same kinds of mechanisms for supervising the police from outside exist in both countries. Altogether, then, according to what Americans think are important features for producing high standards of individual police performance, Japan is doing as least as well and often better than the United States. There are objective reasons for Japan's superior record.

But analysis cannot stop here. The factors that Americans think are important for reducing police misbehavior do not exhaust the possibilities. They are a limited set — an American set. Police behavior is molded in Japan in ways that would never be thought of in the United States. What are these unique constraints? Are they applicable in the United States?

Responsible behavior is secured in Japan by developing the allegiance of the individual to the work group in such a way as to legitimate its disciplinary claims on him and to intensify his feeling of obligation not to offend against it. The work group in Japan dominates personal life. It has the emotional overtones of a family — a word policemen use frequently to describe the kind of emotional fulfillment they want to achieve in the group.[47] In such a setting discipline is generated by the chemistry of membership rather than the arrangement of formal structure. Duty is personal; it is part of belonging. Failure to act properly is an act of disloyalty against one's brothers rather than an offense against codified rules. American policemen would find supervision according to the Japanese model frustrating and repressive. Not so the Japanese. To them is is protective and liberating because it tells them how to ensure respected membership in the most important community of their adult lives. Discipline, then, is not simply a condition of service; it is a guarantor of continued emotional fulfillment.

Policemen in the United States continually ask that disciplinary rules be set forth in writing so they may know the limits of their independence. They want a clear demarcation between areas of initiative and subservience. In Japan, on the other hand, the group's oversight is constant and nearly without limit. Until 1954 policemen were not supposed to marry without the permission of their superiors. Even today they are advised to end a match when it is considered unsuitable. Senior officers frequently act as marriage brokers, arranging for young men to meet respectable young women and persuading parents that a marriage should be endorsed. Young unmarried officers are admonished to be discrete in meeting their sexual needs, to avoid unsavory female friendships, and to visit professional women outside the jurisdiction in which they serve. In police school they are counselled about personal finances, especially the importance of saving. Personal appearance must be sober at all times, hair is not to be worn long and civilian clothes must be subdued in color and conservative in style. Vacations can be taken

---

47. For example, see Christie W. Kiefer, "The Psychological Interdependence of Family, School, and Bureaucracy in Japan," *American Anthropologist* (February 1970), p. 71.

only with the permission of superior officers; word must be left where the officer may be reached.

Even in informal groups of officers there is an acknowledged leader who, by virtue of rank or seniority, is responsible for the behavior of the others. If an accident occurred or an individual behaved badly, the leader would be ashamed for failing to discharge his responsibilities. To give an illustration, four police superintendents on a study-tour of the United States were teasing one of their number about wanting to run away with an actress. One officer commented ruefully that if that did in fact occur, he would be disgraced because he was senior among the group.

Japanese policemen constantly exhort one another to live up to the ideals of the organization. Signs are hung in every station, often framed in glass, bearing mottoes about conduct. The year's slogan in one prefecture was "Create a grass-roots police." The motto was not hung and forgotten, an empty ritual, but was continually referred to by all ranks of officers. Supervisors seize every opportunity—inspections, shift-meetings, athletic tournaments—to deliver short lectures about duty and responsibility. There is a great deal of talk about the "police spirit"—attributes all policemen should display. Policemen pridefully say they are not "sarariman" (salaryman), working only for a wage. They are the new samurai, infused with "Nihon damashii"—Japanese spirit.[48] The constant inveighing about duty and spirit sounds forced and artificial to an American, more appropriate to a Boy Scout meeting or a Sunday School class than to seasoned police officers. To the Japanese it is part of the style of the organization, as unremarkable as the air they breathe.

The work group can legitimately and effectively play a larger role in maintaining responsibility in Japan because the organization is more than an instrument for accomplishing tasks; it is a community. Being a policeman is not just a job; it is a way of life. Long hours on duty in an unrhythmic shift-system separates policemen from the rest of the world. Opportunities for socializing outside the fraternity are limited, even with one's family. The work itself is conducted in groups. The koban assures this, though it is also true for administrative offices and detective sections. The introduction of patrol cars, it should be noted, in place of kobans threatens not only customary relations with citizens but the group-basis of life in the police as well. This undoubtedly accounts as much for the reluctance to rely

48. Officers had a long discussion on one occasion about whether the most appropriate phrase for what they had in mind was "Yamato damashii" or "Nihon damashii." "Yamato damashii" means ancient Japanese spirit, and was considered to have too many feudal overtones.

on patrol cars as concern about close public relations. Policemen work together, eat and sleep together, and share mundane house-keeping chores. They relate to one another along many dimensions of activity, not simply the few associated with police tasks. Police-men describe the relations they want with one another as "wet" rather than "dry," indicating an empathic involvement.[49] Life in the police has the ambiance of an American army company, a touring theatrical troupe, or a college fraternity—people with a job of work to do requiring total involvement, multiple role-playing, and intimate conduct.

Because group relations in the Japanese police are so distinctive, the number of hours spent on duty each week should be looked at differently than they would be in the United States. Indeed, it is misleading, psychologically, to have compared them at all. Hours served in the United States are spent at work; hours served in Japan are spent living communally, producing a crucial nonwork conse-quence. Duty hours in Japan help to form and develop a community of a particular sort. Though the work-week is long, it would feel much longer if served in the American way.

Japanese policemen often live together off duty. This is more than the coincidence of private residence that occurs in the United States. All Japanese policemen are required to live in a dormitory during the year in police school, even if they are married. Furthermore, dormitories are provided for bachelor officers after police school. They must live in them during the first six months on the job, though many stay for longer periods because of the high cost of providing food and housing privately. In the dormitories curfews are maintained; officers must get permission if they want to stay out past 11 P.M. Since most patrolmen are young and therefore unmarried, it is common for as many as half the personnel of a shift to live together in a dormitory. Housing is provided for about half of all married policemen, mostly in large apartment houses. Occupan-cy is sometimes limited to a fixed term, during which officers are urged to save enough money to cover the cost of a down-payment on a house.

Athletics play an important part in knitting the police community together. Despite the fact that space is scarce, every police station sets aside a large room for practicing judo and kendo.[50] Time is set

49. Americans would say warm, but more than warmth is involved. "Wet" connotes moistness, stickiness. Americans consider these unpleasant in human relations; Japanese do not.
50. Kendo is derived from traditional sword fighting. Combatants dress in helmets, body-armor, and ankle-length blue skirts. They fight barefoot, dealing hard blows to the head and body with bamboo staves about four feet long.

aside during duty-hours for practice of one or the other. Stations reverberate all day with the thump of bare feet, shouting, and the hollow sound of the judo drum. Officers fight, sweat, and bathe together before going back on duty. This is one way of promoting what are graphically referred to as close "skin relations." In midsummer and again in midwinter two weeks of competition are held within each police station and prefectural headquarters, culminating in an intramural tournament. At these times all officers, often including chiefs of sections and stations, practice daily with their men. Some stations also have baseball teams that play in a police league. It is common to see policemen together with civilian staff playing volleyball or badminton outside on warm days. In large office buildings deskbound workers are invited by loud-speaker to rise and participate in calisthenics as a midafternoon break.

The intensity of community spirit is dramatically expressed during the annual prefectural judo-kendo tournaments. These are really three tournaments in one: station against station, section against section from headquarters, and company against company from the riot police. Teams practice daily for months under the eyes of police coaches. During the tournaments, which are held in large municipal arenas, the galleries are packed with spectators, mostly nonparticipants from the work group and some families. Top officers from the prefecture are on hand accompanied by distin-guished guests. Long signs and banners are hung over the balcony railings. Men and women, the latter usually traffic aides, stand in the crowded aisles and lead cheers by means of complicated arm and body movements. The noise is deafening and keeps up all day long. Partisanship among participants is intense: they lose their tempers, refuse to quit when injured, and hang their heads in shame when they lose. Winning teams celebrate by throwing their coaches and chiefs into the air. One hardbitten coach, fifty years old, admitted to me that when his team lost he felt like crying. To an American the atmosphere is identical to a traditional college rivalry — the same emotion, identification, and singlemindedness.

Symbols augment group solidarity. Stations create their own mottoes and hang them on the walls. Every prefecture has its own police song. So too have various training schools, units of the riot police, some of the larger police stations, and occasionally a bachelor dormitory.

A variety of publications circulate within the police force devoted to matters of community interest. Each prefecture publishes a

monthly journal and most stations print a pamphlet about important occurrences.[51] The Tokyo metropolitan police force has a
printing run of fifty thousand for its monthly magazine. And for
over twenty years the Patrol Division in Tokyo has printed its own
magazine, circulation about ten thousand. The "Daily Police
News," published privately, is available throughout Japan on a
subscription basis.

The immediate work group also does a great deal of socializing
together outside of duty. Though for the most part informal, a spur-
of-the-moment drink or meal after work, senior officers deliberately
contrive occasions for fostering "wetter" relations among members
of the group. Overnight trips are arranged for hiking, fishing, or to
seaside resorts and famous gardens. Groups stay at inexpensive
police hotels at which they eat and drink together wearing traditional kimonos ("yukata") after bathing communally in large tubs.
They sleep three and four to a room on movable mattresses
("futon") on the floor. Boisterious, lighthearted, noisy, and ribald,
such groups develop the kind of comraderie that is found on a
hunting trip among close friends in the United States or at a
professional convention.

Supervisors make a point of taking bachelor officers home for a
meal and sometimes a bath. To be entertained in a Japanese home
is very unusual, and the bath is a symbol of total hospitality. Or they
organize a party at a restaurant or a bowling alley. Social occasions
are organized quite calculatingly, senior officers saying to one
another that "It is time for a party" or "We haven't had a section
party in two months." More is at stake than simply avoiding friction
among workmates; the purpose is to develop a special intimacy, a
climate of emotional trust. Money is provided by the organization to
defray expenses, otherwise the burden on supervisory staff would be
unacceptable.

Group parties, especially if they involve drinking, serve to foster
closer communication among ranks. This is important because
where hierarchy is pervasive, candor may be inhibited. The Japanese compensate in an interesting way. What an individual says when
he has been drinking is by accepted custom forgiven; it is not to be
remembered. Japanese get "high"—loud, happy, bawdy—more
quickly than Americans who, by comparison, seem controlled and

51. These pamphlets go back many years and could be an important source of
historical information. They are not public documents. Each station maintains a
file of them.

inhibited in their drinking. The apparent susceptibility of Japanese to alcohol is psychological rather than physiological. The whole point of drinking is to obliterate the constraints of hierarchy. There is no virtue in "holding one's liquor" when the purpose of drinking is to create unstructured interaction. Policemen recollect many instances when hidden feelings were revealed during a drinking party, an unburdening that benefited group relations later on. Two young officers spoke fondly about carrying their gruff sergeant home one night after a drinking bout. Now they felt they knew him as a person; he had entrusted himself to their care. Where an American sergeant would be embarrassed, the Japanese sergeant undoubtedly felt that the evening had served its purpose.

Japanese policemen view Americans as being too homebound, too private, and neglecting to develop "wet" relations with workmates. A person who does not socialize with his colleagues is guilty of "my home shugi" (*mai homu shugi*) — antisocial privacy. Note that the phrase has incorporated English words into Japanese: this kind of isolation is associated with the United States. Japanese do not entertain colleagues at home, at least not commonly. They do not invite acquaintances to meet their wives, see their children, "make themselves at home." Consequently, the Japanese do not understand that when an American goes home, socializing with colleagues is not precluded. The Japanese are right, however, in appreciating that the demands of home and work may conflict, but while a Japanese policeman is concerned about home threatening the work community, the American policeman is concerned about work threatening home life.

It should be noted in passing that the police community is an intensely male world. Integration of women on an equal basis is impossible without sacrificing its distinctive closeness. A woman cannot participate in the fraternal life of eating, sleeping, bathing, and drinking without offending against morality. Women as police officers pose a more perplexing problem for the Japanese than for Americans, for they threaten the sense of community itself.

The intensity of involvement with the work group is not unique to the police, nor its centrality of moral tone.[52] Most large scale organizations — banks, ministries, laboratories, factories, insurance companies — have work communities much like the police. As one American observer has said:

The corporate group, characterized by exclusiveness and loyalty, is a common structural element of Japanese institutions — a mode of

52. I am indebted for this phrase to Professor Lawrence W. Beer.

integration for the individual that contributes both to developing his identity and his socialization.[53]

Industrial firms have company songs, flags, and lapel pins. They arrange marriages, provide free bathing facilities, and organize classes in birth control, dressmaking, calligraphy, and budget management. They provide an assortment of fringe benefits including housing, vacation accommodations, and health care. Work affiliation in Japan is the basis of life's most crucial rewards — affective as well as material.

American policemen too are conscious of belonging to a distinct group. But there is a crucial difference. The Japanese police community has been deliberately created; identity, entailing distance from others, has been fashioned in order to augment pride. Community spirit is fostered to facilitate the carrying out of organization tasks. In the United States, identity is a consequence of perceived resentment and antagonism. It is founded on rejection. American policemen have been driven inward against their will; their communitarian spirit is defensive, like that of a persecuted minority group. The basis of community among the police in Japan is pride; the basis of community among the police in the United States is shame.

In generating responsible police behavior, Japan and the United States have emphasized different strategies. In Japan reliance is placed primarily on the police community itself. The police are self-disciplined. In the United States the burden of achieving responsible behavior is placed upon mechanisms of constraint external to the police organization. When scandals occur Americans reflexively think of providing better external supervision — by elected representatives, civilian review boards, or courts. This is not to say that external mechanisms do not exist in Japan nor that internal disciplinary procedures are nonexistent in the United States. But faith in each strategy differs substantially between the two countries.

The readiness with which Americans resort to external constraints in order to achieve responsible police behavior can be counterproductive. External intervention in police affairs is viewed by policemen, justifiably, as a threat to the autonomy of the organization. Defenses are erected against these intrusions, which have the effect of making the organization more resistant in the future. As in

53. Robert E. Cole, *Japanese Blue Collar* (Berkeley: University of California Press, 1971), p. 14.

the case of innoculating a living organism, infection generates an immune reaction. One indication that this has occurred in the United States is the "blue power" movement in which police officers, feeling embattled against the outside world, have organized for political action. They have campaigned for the election of officials sympathetic to them, lobbied for stricter criminal legislation, mounted campaigns for the abolition of civilian review boards, publicly criticized other agencies in the criminal justice system, and condemned special investigations of police misbehavior.[54] This is unheard of in Japan. There is no "blue power" movement because there is no object to organize against. Discipline comes from within; it is not the result of probings from outside. Japanese policemen see their environment as benign.

American policemen often reject outside criticism as being ill-informed because it lowers their self-esteem. They feel belittled by it. They continually argue that no one can appreciate police work except another policeman. Japanese officers too become irritated occasionally when they are criticized publicly, but it is irritation tinged with pride. They realize that high public expectations are a mark of respect. American officers do not salvage pride from criticism. It wounds; it does not ennoble. So while Japanese officers angrily accept the public's standards, American officers angrily reject them.

Comparing Japan and the United States, certain characteristics pertaining to conduct and discipline in the police form strikingly contrasting patterns. In the United States where police scandals are recurrent, public respect for the police is low, policemen feel invidiously exposed to public gaze, their self-esteem is precarious, they are defensively assertive in politics, and their sense of group solidarity is based on feelings of rejection. In Japan where scandals are infrequent, public regard for the police is high, policemen pridefully accept the applicability of high standards to their conduct, their self-esteem is solid, they have not organized in defense of their autonomy, and solidarity is founded on pride. Is it a coincidence that these patterns respectively are associated with very different practices for achieving responsible police behavior? It is at

54. Their sensitivity to outside criticism, even when well supported, can be seen in the intemperate remarks of Robert M. McKiernan, head of the Patrolman's Benevolent Association of New York Cty, to the report of the Knapp Commission on corruption in the police department. McKiernan called the report the "wild ravings of a sick man with a sick man. . . . The Knapp Report is a fairy tale, concocted in a whore-house, told by thieves and fools." *New York Times,* 29 December 1972, p. 1.

least worth asking whether so great a reliance on external checks in the United States is not in some measure responsible for the disciplinary problems so often deplored.[55]

The key to police morality is public respect. If policemen believe they are damned stereotypically, they have little incentive to behave properly — one may as well be hung for a sheep as a goat. Public expectations of police impropriety act not as an impediment to such behavior but as an excuse for it. Furthermore, police officers are more likely to internalize moral principles out of pride than out of fear — though there are undoubtedly punishments so fearful as to produce assured compliance. An individual's self regard is a function of the way he is perceived by others. The effect of relying on external constraints is to augment the policeman's sense that he is unfavorably regarded. Punishments from outside lower the policeman's sense of worth as a policeman; his occupation appears to be under attack. Discipline generated internally, however, cannot be confused with an attack either on the group or on the role; it is directed unambiguously at the individual. Therefore, reliance primarily on external checks can be counterproductive because by demeaning the group, it undermines the individual's will to reform.

The United States has harassed its police without producing responsible behavior. Each turn of the disciplinary screw from outside the police organization results in demoralized policemen. Contrarily, the organization becomes reform-resistant as acceptance of outside criticism is equated with disloyalty to the organization. This is not to suggest that external mechanisms are the only cause of police misconduct. There are undoubtedly others. But continued reliance on external checks impedes the development of community pride that could provide a basis for responsible self-discipline and identification with the larger community's standards of appropriate behavior.

The implications of this discussion for the United States are tragic in the classical sense that the future is inevitably contained in an

55. There is an interesting parallel between the thinking of Americans about curbing deviance generally in society and curbing improper behavior in the police. Reliance upon external checks is similar to depending on punishments from the criminal justice system to prevent crime. Formal punishment and external checks both fail to reshape the social circumstances from which criminals or police officers come. In order to reduce criminality in society, it is important to change the social conditions in which people live; in order to reduce the incidence of improper behavior in the police, it is important to change the organizational context within which police work. The Japanese have given greater attention to life-circumstances within the police organization and relatively less to punishments from outside.

unchangeable past. The way each country addresses the problem of ensuring responsible police conduct reflects deeply rooted beliefs, practices, and values. Americans could not give up their faith in the efficacy of external checks any more than they could manufacture the tightly disciplined work communities of Japan. Indeed, as long as distrust in police performance is so pronounced among Americans, an act of perverse courage would be required to entrust them more fully with their own discipline. Current circumstances and American culture inhibit a shift in emphasis between internal and external mechanisms. Therefore, if the American strategy of accountability is counterproductive, the United States will continue to sow the seeds of the behavior it wants so much to eradicate.

The Japanese model for achieving responsible police behavior has much to commend it. But approval should not be unqualified. An organization that so effectively shapes and manages individuals could be massively irresponsible without fear of dissent within or exposure without. This potentiality must be examined.

Because the work community is so dominating economically and emotionally, officers must consider carefully any action that could jeopardize their standing in it. Occupational mobility is much lower in Japan than in the United States which makes the consequences of losing one's job even more catastrophic. Choosing an occupation in Japan is like choosing a wife in a society which regards divorce as a sin. Moreover, where mild rejection, let alone ostracism, can be emotionally shattering, the primary ethical injunction easily becomes "Don't rock the boat."[56] But the inhibitions against dissent are even more subtle. Decisions are made collectively in the police, as in other Japanese organizations.[57] Before a decision is made extensive consultations take place between a superior and his immediate subordinates. Every senior officer feels obliged to discuss alternatives and solicit opinions extensively. Every person has his say. After consensus has been reached, any act of dissent seems ungracious and lacking in magnanimity. If, therefore, misbehavior is the result of policy or is tacitly condoned by the group, the chances seem slight that an officer would step outside the group to condemn what is taking place.

56. Referring to Albert O. Hirschman's provocative analysis in *Exit Voice, and Loyalty* (Cambridge: Harvard University Press, 1970), Japanese officers cannot exit. Though they can voice dissent, they do so at the risk of seeming disloyal.
57. James C. Abegglen, *The Japanese Factory* (Glencoe, Ill.: The Free Press, 1958), pp. 85-86.

In small ways too criticism of the organization is discouraged among policemen. For instance, there are no formal grievance procedures. One would have thought that since a police union was prohibited by law, the organization would have mechanisms for ventilating internal discontent. Senior police officers believe that formal procedures are unnecessary because they are so close to their subordinates. They cannot conceive that they are not fully aware of the difficulties in the personal situation of their subordinates. Perhaps indeed they are. Communal closeness and the emphasis on empathic understanding may successfully bridge rank gradations. This is very difficult for a foreigner to judge. Several times, however, junior officers have confessed that they found the organization's view of itself intimidating. Having been told almost daily that an individual with "police spirit" does not count his days of holiday or pay much attention to the precise amount of his pay check, policemen are reluctant to express dissatisfaction about these matters to superiors. In this way behavior at junior levels becomes what superiors say it is rather than what policemen actually perceive it to be.

Loyalties within the police are personalistic. They are particularly intense between an officer and his immediate superior, and they may undercut attachment to universalistic norms. Senior officers speak eloquently of the need to take the blame for honest mistakes of subordinates. They refer graphically to the need for "maintaining a strong stomach" — Americans would say "guts" — in such a situation, having the courage to take responsibility themselves. By showing they understand the predicament of the subordinate and protecting him from the consequences of his mistake, the superior forges a bond of obligation between the subordinate and himself. One effect of such bonds is that junior officers think twice about exposing superiors to censure for their own mistakes; they become cautious. Another is to thicken the silence around mistakes. Personal obligations overwhelm the requirements of accountability.

Some thoughtful Japanese officers have questioned whether the community of the police is not too self-contained. Policemen are recruited young, trained intensively for a year, monitored closely during probationary periods, and imbued with the peculiar customs of the organization. Though officers so trained have an almost intuitive grasp of the needs of their work mates, they have not had much opportunity to develop an empathic sense for others. It would be easy for them to become righteous about the values extant within the police, dismissing without reflection the perspectives of others.

There are persuasive reasons, then, for believing that the dynamics of Japanese social organization can discourage candid testimony about what goes on within the police. But this is true for other societies as well, through for different reasons. In the United States the defensiveness of the police certainly discourages individual officers from assisting outside critics. They run the risk of being regarded as traitors by their colleagues every bit as much as Japanese officers do. Moreover, the police in the United States, like those in Japan, are organized along authoritarian lines. A career can easily be wrecked if a policeman becomes known as a troublemaker. It is not clear on a priori grounds that internal dissent is more inhibited in Japan than in the United States. Damaging revelations about police behavior by policemen are more common in the United States but this may simply reflect a different incidence of misconduct. Without participating for a long time in the life of each organization, judgments by an observer about duplicity are bound to be vague and unsatisfactory.

The conclusion to be drawn form this comparison of Japanese and American practices for ensuring responsible police behavior is that too exclusive reliance upon the Japanese model would be as mistaken as too exclusive reliance upon the American. The approaches are complementary. External checks are needed in both countries to ensure that police standards of propriety are coincidental with those of the society at large. External checks reduce the danger that either police force becomes hermetically sealed—the one out of pride, the other out of alienation. The point that Americans must reflect on is whether the Japanese have been more successful in providing external accountability than Americans have in creating internal responsibility.

There is a vicious cycle in attempts to improve police conduct in the United States: public criticism lowers the self-regard of the police, undermining their enthusiasm for setting their own house in order; failure to be responsible for the conduct of one another within the police leads to further deterioration in conduct, producing another round of public criticism. The nub of the problem for the United States is to restore pride while maintaining active external mechanisms of accountability. This is more difficult than adding external checks to a pridefully cohesive police force, as happened in Japan twenty-five years ago. In the United States mutual distrust between public and police plus cultural values less hospitable to the formation of tightly knit professional communities undercut the possibility of generating police forces more actively responsible for the conduct of their members. Public regard, police pride, and responsibility are tied together. In the United States the linkage has operated to the detriment of responsiblity; in Japan the linkage has operated in favor of responsibility. Is the United States locked into this cycle? Is the pattern of recurrent scandals, lack of pride, slack discipline, and ineffective intrusion into police affairs doomed to be repeated indefinitely?

5. Community Relations

Twice a year uniformed patrolmen knock on the door of every residence in Japan and ask questions about the people living there. How many people live there? Are they related to one another? What are their ages and sex? Are they employed? If so, what kind of work do they do? Do they own a car? What are its make, model, and license number? The answers to these questions, usually supplied by women since calls are made during the day, are written down on printed forms. The police invite residents to list especially valuable items of property with the police, so that they may be identified in case they are stolen. The police elicit information about happenings in the neighborhood generally. Have new people come to the block? Has the resident noticed any people acting suspiciously? What crimes have occurred recently? They encourage people to discuss problems of living in the neighborhood, such as the quality of municipal services or troublesome neighbors. Policemen visit small businesses as well, obtaining a roster of employees with information about their background. A special point is made of discovering the hours of work of the business and whether someone stays overnight on the premises.

These visits by policemen are referred to as the residential survey and are a fundamental part of Japanese police work. Japanese officers are surprised that American policemen do not do the same. They cannot understand why Americans would find such visits distasteful and would object vehemently. To the Japanese the residential survey is as natural as rain. It is a dramatic indication that the role of the police in Japanese society is not the same as in the United States. Though both police forces have the same general responsibilities, they relate to the people in intriguingly different ways. Two features are especially striking. First, Japanese policemen penetrate the community more extensively than American policemen but they do so in a more routine, less formal fashion. Second, police and public in Japan share tasks more fully than in the United States; the boundary line between the police and the citizen is more permeable in Japan. I shall examine each of these features in turn.

The Japanese force is neighborhood-centered. Its personnel are deployed in fixed posts—kobans—scattered throughout every community. The residential survey is a device for extending the koban's knowledge of its community, for demonstrating the availability of police service, and for developing personal relations between police officer and citizen. The information collected through the residential survey is used almost exclusively by local officers alone. It is not filed or collated at some central headquarters, not even at the level of police stations. The bound notebooks that officers carry, which seem so ominous to Americans, are kept in a locked case in the koban. They are used primarily for locating people and premises. Indexing of the files is primitive, usually only by name and address. In order to be used in criminal investigations or intelligence operations, koban staff must be told what to look for in their files. The residential survey provides a dencentralized memory that has to be jogged by directive in order to be exploited. The information is not shared with other government agencies, a point which officers stress with residents. Unlike the prewar period, residents are not required to answer questions of policemen calling at their homes. Frequently officers simply leave the form and ask that it be filled out and returned to the koban. Most people cooperate readily; outright refusals are uncommon though not unknown. Refusals in principle come, according to policemen, primarily from left-wing people—a point that may be inferred from a refusal and duly noted on the information card. In some university areas the survey has been eliminated altogether because of the angry reactions of students. Resistance is undoubtedly greater than it was two decades ago, though it still cannot be called strong. By and large it can be overcome by persistence and affability on the part of individual officers. A more serious impediment than ideology is the attenuation of community that has occurred in some neighborhoods. Officers complain particularly about the difficulty of carrying out the survey in the large apartment complexes of the burgeoning "bedtowns." Working wives are common and no one is left at home for the policeman to contact. They have to come back in the evening or leave the form in the mailbox. Apartment residents take less interest in one another than people do in older neighborhoods composed of detached homes and they are not well informed about community happenings.

The salience of ideology as an attribute of identification in Japan is a point worth underscoring. When policemen are asked to specify the characteristics of people that determine responses to the police, they repeatedly cite ideological predispositions. These are as important in explaining public cooperativeness, rudeness, or disregard as race is among policemen in the United States. Japanese policemen hardly ever mention ascriptive characteristics, such as race or national origin. In part this is due to the remarkable homogeneity of the Japanese population: the largest minority groups are the Koreans and the Chinese, constituting respectively about a half of 1 percent and less than one-tenth of 1 percent of the population.[1] The *burakumin*, tradition outcasts who are ethnically Japanese, number about two million, roughly 2 percent of the population.[2] Discussion of these minorities is referred to by officers privately as a "taboo" subject.[3] It is clear, however, that it is not just official policy that accounts for lack of reference to minorities. Relative to ideology, the attributes of birth are considered by policemen much less important in explaining differences in public behavior.

The residential survey is usually carried out in the morning or afternoon when emergency demands on the police are slight. It is not a chore policemen enjoy. The work is slow, dull, and sometimes awkward. Rarely do residents notice anything either intrinsically interesting or relevant to the serious side of police work. They complain about a neighbor's loud radio, inefficient public services, or door-to-door salesmen. They imagine suspicious behavior without being able to provide any specific details. Conversations once begun are often difficult to shut off, especially if the people contacted are old, retired, or simply lonely. Officers occasionally accept a cup of tea or a cold drink. Though this deepens contact, it prolongs the round and establishes future obligations. Visiting officers volunteer to inspect the locks on doors and windows in order to give advice about crime prevention. Younger officers complain that door-to-door visitations make them feel like salesmen, and they are showing increasing distaste for the enterprise. There is no sorrow in a koban if the pressure of work is so great that officers are unable to make the rounds twice each year, as is recommended by national headquarters. Senior officers are aware of this reluctance and have sought to rekindle enthusiasm by stressing the survey's importance for criminal investigation and surveillance of radical people. This is not make-believe: many student radicals were located during 1970 and 1971 by timely tips from anonymous citizens to koban personnel. Patrolmen who carry out the survey with particular skill are honored with special awards. Since the problem of morale has been recognized and is being met, it is most likely that the residential survey will continue to be a fixture of Japanese police work.

American policemen frequently complain that most of the people

1. Information furnished by the Japanese Consulate, San Francisco, 1974.
2. George A. De Vos, *Japan's Outcastes* (London: The Minority Rights Group, 1971), p. 3.
3. The expression is "Japanese-English." Policemen are taught in police school not to refer to people by their "historical classifications." This applies to Chinese and Koreans as well as *Burakumin*, sometimes called *Eta*.

their work brings them in contact with are unpleasant and unsavory individuals that the rest of society wants to ignore—crooks, perverts, alcoholics, bums, prostitutes, and thugs. The residential survey is an antidote to this. It forces officers to meet normal people in home surroundings on occasions not marred by stress or demands. Officers meet the respectable people they are protecting rather than the sordid people they are protecting society from. The survey helps the Japanese policeman as well as the Japanese citizen to recognize the humanity of the other.

The Japanese police have long recognized that they are in a unique position to provide advice and assistance to people about a host of nonpolice matters. Accordingly, all prefectures have set up general counselling offices. They go under various names—"Komarigoto Sodan" (Trouble Counselling), "Keisatsu Sodan" (Police Counselling), "Kaji Sodan" (Domestic Affairs Counselling), and "Seikatsu Sodan" (Life Counselling).[4] All police stations assign an experienced older officer—usually a sergeant—to general counselling. In order to coordinate the variety of requests for counsel that come into most police headquarters, an experiment in the consolidation of counselling facilities was begun in Aichi Prefecture in 1972. At prefectural headquarters "Jumin Corner" (Citizen's Corner) was established to coordinate handling of any request for counsel, whether it involved personal problems, complaints against the police, advice about crime prevention, or resolution of a police case.[5] The office also supervises counselling officers in all the police stations. People are no longer shunted from office to office until they find the appropriate place; specialists are summoned by the personnel of Jumin Corner according to the nature of the inquiry. Consolidation has also transformed counselling into a coherent specialization, making it more attractive to the career-minded officer.

Few citizens know quite where to turn to obtain help in solving their problems. Since the police are the most pervasive government agency in society, advice from them can save people agonizing steps. In most cases police counsellors simply refer people to appropriate nonpolice offices. In Aichi Prefecture, for example, only 40 percent of approximately twelve thousand cases brought to the police for counselling each year involve the police directly. They involve complaints about police behavior, advice for protecting the home, traffic accidents, questions about the criminal law, or complaints

4. I am indebted to Inspector Noboru Watanabe, Aichi Prefecture Police, for providing information about police counselling.
5. A Jumin Corner has also been established in Aomori Prefecture.

about pollution.[6] Indicative of the acceptance of the police counselling role is the fact that a large number of people bring personal
troubles to them — marriages, debts, disputes with landlords, and
nonfulfillment of contracts. In Aichi Prefecture again, 41 percent of
all cases brought to the police were of this kind. The Family Affairs
Counselling Officer in Tokyo handled almost twelve thousand such
cases in 1972.[7] Police counsellors must be careful not to infringe on
the prerogatives of either lawyers or civil courts. Their function is to
listen and provide informal conciliation. Representatives of the
lawyers' association periodically inspect the counselling work of the
police to ensure that they are not exceeding their authority.[8]

The ingenious potentialities of police counselling can be seen in
another example from Aichi Prefecture. The policewoman of Jumin
Corner prepared a selected list of people who were known to live
alone. Then they telephoned almost a thousand of them to demonstrate that they had not been forgotten, that someone still cared. In
some cases follow-up visits were made in person. The campaign was
enormously popular and attracted considerable attention from the
press. An ironic tribute to the impact of the effort came from a few
"left-wing" politicians who complained that this kind of work should
be left to political parties.

Counselling of a general sort is something that American police
officers do too. Studies have repeatedly shown that most calls made
to the police in the United States do not involve law enforcement.
The proportion may be as high as four out of five.[9] Police officers
spend most of their time advising, mediating, referring, listening.
What is different is that American police organizations have not
adapted willingly to performing this function. The nonenforcement
part of police work is considered a recent discovery in American

6. One-third of the counselling cases in Aichi Prefecture were brought directly to
the Jumin Corner; the rest to individual police stations. Questions about pollution
arise because the police have recently been empowered to enforce antipollution
ordinances.
7. Information supplied by the Family Affairs Counselling Office.
8. Information on counselling activities in Japan is wonderfully complete, including analyses of the backgrounds of clients, disposition of cases, and mode of
conduct.
9. Arthur Niederhoffer, *Behind the Shield* (Garden City, New York: Doubleday
and Co., 1967), p. 26; The President's Commission on Law Enforcement and the
Administration of Justice, *Task Force Report: The Police* (Washington, D.C.: U.S.
Government Printing Office, 1967), p. 13; David H. Bayley and Harold Mendelsohn, *Minorities and the Police* (New York: The Free Press, 1969), Chap. 3; and
National Advisory Commission on Criminal Justice Standards and Goals, *Police*
(Washington: Government Printing Office, 1973), pp. 12-17.

police circles, giving rise to cliches about policemen being "peace officers" rather than "law officers." In Japan the first family counselling office was set up in 1919 in Tokyo. Though Japanese officers do not consider counselling a glamorous part of police work, they have not resisted shaping the organization to accommodate it. They do not grumble, as American officers do, that policemen are not social workers. Moreover, counselling in Japan is not a response to a deterioration in public image; it is not a public relations gimmick, though it undoubtedly pays public relations dividends. Counselling has been accepted as an inseparable part of the police function. As a clue to American priorities, it is worth noting that though many American policemen have visited Japan to study police practices, none of them, according to Japanese informants, have visited the Family Affairs Counselling Office in Tokyo or Jumin Corner in Aichi Prefecture.

Another dimension of routine nonemergency contact between police and public involves crime prevention. The Japanese police devote more attention to this than is the case in the United States, though this judgment is necessarily impressionistic. Crime prevention is a major field of specialization within the Japanese police. This is reflected by the fact that organizationally it has the same status as criminal investigation, security, patrol, and traffic. In Tokyo about 6 percent of the uniformed personnel serve in the crime prevention division. This figure is somewhat misleading in that crime prevention in Japan also covers what Americans know as vice control, drug abuse, juvenile counselling, and regulation of firearms. Nonetheless, officers assigned to this unit are specifically charged with developing and supervising programs designed to produce that ounce of prevention that will make an emergency response unnecessary.

Police officers consult frequently with homeowners and businesses about security. Technicians are provided by the police to install pick-proof locks for doors. Koban officers couple crime prevention checks with the residential survey, making on-site inspections and leaving printed pamphlets. If a resident is not at home when an officer calls, he often leaves a printed card on which he has noted defects in security—doors unlocked, inadequate safety-catches on windows, valuable property left unattended in the yard. Women and children come to police stations for films on molestation, street safety, and household security. With appropriate fanfare the police award medals and plaques to citizens for outstanding assistance or timely 110 telephone calls. Signs about crime prevention are seen everywhere in Japan, which seems incongrous considering the low crime rates. Notices reminding people to use the police emergency number are tacked in public places, stuck on the front of private homes, and on banners across major streets. On the top of one of the largest police stations in Japan, the admonition "Keep all doors locked" is displayed in letters two feet high. When a law was passed making glue-sniffing a crime,[10] hand-painted signs appeared at subway entrances in Shinjuku in Tokyo setting forth the new penalties.[11] Notices are erected on beaches warning couples about sexual attacks by hoodlums. In a well-to-do suburb placards six feet tall and one foot wide were put up printed with the legend "Watch out for lechers."[12] Kobans have created a curious kind of folk literature in connection with crime prevention. Each month they circulate single mimeographed sheets filled with admonitions, information, and hand-drawn cartoons designed to teach lessons about crime prevention. Each koban adapts to local circumstances the directives sent down from prefectural headquarters. The circulars may note that summer is coming and more children will be playing in the street; that alcoholism rises at New Year's; that purse-snatching has become common at a particular shopping center. Kobans take great pride in their creations, and national and prefectural awards are given for the most original bulletins.

The Airin area of Nishinari ward in Osaka, like the Sanya section of Tokyo, has been troubled since the early 1960s by summer-night riots among its floating population of derelicts and day-laborers.[13] As a result, crime prevention activities have become unusually elaborate. Twenty officers out of the area's complement of four hundred are permanently assigned to a counselling office located just inside the main door of the police station. Their function is to alleviate frustration and anger by providing timely advice and mediating disputes. Twice a month the station distributes copies of a popular commercial magazine to the area's three hundred flophouses. A simple message is stuck inside the front cover, usually stressing the availability of the police and the importance of remaining law-abiding. A single-sheet newsletter is printed twice a month giving advice appropriate to the moment—tips on how to

10. Effective 1 August 1972.

11. Sinjuku had been notorious for glue-sniffing in public places.

12. These signs were put up by the local community, not the police. The Japanese word I have translated as "lecher" is *chican*. It is sometimes used teasingly by girls to their boyfriends, as an American girl might refer archly to her boy friend as a "sex fiend."

13. Airin is the new name for Kamagasaki, a famous slum. Airin literally means "Love your neighbor." This is a case of social reform through verbal benediction.

stay healthy in the winter or warnings about disregarding the lies spread by agitators. A small library has been provided for public use in the police station. Police personnel monitor living conditions and advise government agencies about particular needs, such as neglected refuse pick-up, improper sanitation, or needed medicines. The police talk to the owners of flophouses and bars about the need to keep their facilities cheerful and healthy. They prevailed on the city to replace sidewalks with asphalt so that broken concrete could not be ripped up and thrown during riots.

In sum, then, police penetration of the community in Japan is more routine and personal than in the United States and it is more active in ways unrelated to law enforcement. Deployment in kobans forces police officers in Japan to play a role in the community as known persons, not like American policemen who are seen as anonymous faces flickering by behind a facade of steel. A koban is an active force in community life; it is not simply a passive source of police assistance. In the United States the justification for contact between police and citizen, apart from criminal activity, is overwhelming need, and initiative belongs to the citizen. An American policeman is like a fireman, he responds when he must. A Japanese policeman is more like a postman, he has a daily round of low-key activities that relate him to the lives of the people among whom he works.

The second point of contrast in the ways in which Japanese and American police relate to their respective communities has to do with the permeability of the boundary between police and citizen roles. In Japan private persons are mobilized in explicit ways to assist policemen in the performance of their duties, creating a cooperative relationship between police and public that is unknown, if not unthinkable, in the United States.

Every neighborhood in Japan has a Crime Prevention Association composed of resident volunteers who work closely with the local police station. Activities of the associations vary considerably from place to place, depending on the imagination and enthusiasm of members. They erect signs in public places—such as "Beware of pickpockets" and "Beware of Lechers"—and distribute leaflets about home protection. They bombard the community with reminders about the importance of calling 110, the police emergency number. Small square 110 notices are one of the most common items of graffiti in Japan. No pretext is too trivial for a call to the police; seeing a "suspicious person," as Association literature puts it, is sufficient justification. Associations publicize and sell improved locks and window catches. They contribute money to police stations to defray the cost of crime prevention booklets. In some places they have underwritten the construction of outdoor phone-boxes connected directly to nearby kobans. Association members are on the alert for situations that can cause accidents—open trenches, unguarded canals, or defective playground equipment. They maintain informal surveillance over trouble-making people, such as gangsters and student radicals, Intimidating door-to-door salesmen are frequently warned away by association members. Lists and pictures of wanted persons are circulated through neighborhoods.

Crime prevention associations organize their own street patrols, each member wearing an armband, that sometimes accompany the police but most often go on their own. Patrols are especially common at New Year's time when businessmen transport substantial amounts of cash and public drunkenness is a major problem. Many patrols specialize in juvenile problems and concentrate upon downtown areas where they watch for runaways and caution against unseemly behavior. Women participate in these patrols as well as men. They take the names of juveniles and notify school authorities and parents about their behavior. Civilian patrols augment police coverage during emergencies. In one city when a rash of fires were suspected to be the work of an arsonist, members of the local association walked the streets during the night carrying lanterns, like a medieval watch. Civilians took up the slack in night patrolling when the police were occupied with large-scale student demonstrations. In one city in Aomori Prefecture association members patrol regularly out of kobans, dressed in a distinctive uniform, and hold annual training exercises under police direction which stress preservation of the scenes of crimes, accurate notification of emergencies, crowd control, and cordoning of areas. The activities of this association are more elaborate than most, but they indicate the kind of momentum that can be generated.

Another unusually vigorous local endeavor is the "Setagaya Woman's Apartment House Lock Troop" in Tokyo. When a burglary occurs, the police drive a mini-van through the streets carrying the flag of the lock troop—the figure of a key on a bright green background trimmed in gold. This is a signal for members of the troop, wearing green neck-scarves or billed caps, to collect at the scene of the crime. Using a hand-press in the mini-van, policewomen mimeograph circulars giving information about the crime and precautions that might have been taken to prevent it. Members of the troop distribute the sheets through the immediate area, enlisting other women in the cause of burglary prevention. Residents are urged to purchase pick-proof locks which the local association makes available for about Y450 ($2.00) and police technicians install free of charge. Residents are also urged to paste small green signs at eye-level beside the doors of their homes which stress the importance of calling 110. The theory is that thieves may be deterred by this display of crime awareness.

Crime prevention associations are intertwined with a system of informal local government that reaches into every household. The smallest unit of formal government is the *ku*—township—in cities and the *buraku*—hamlet—in rural areas. Under these, like spreading vines on a forest floor, are centuries-old institutions of unofficial neighborhood governance called the *han* and the *cho-kai*.[14] A han consists of twenty to thirty adjacent households.[15] Several hans form a cho-kai.[16] Membership in the han and the cho-kai is automatic. Their vitality varies from place to place. In most places notices from government are circulated to heads of the cho-kai and then through the community. Message-boards are passed from house to house containing information of all kinds—the fire season has arrived, water will be stopped on the day after tomorrow, the crime prevention association will hold a meeting, and so forth. Households are obligated to participate in projects undertaken by the cho-kai. For example, each household may be asked to send one person on a designated day to help clean out the drains of the neighborhood. The cho-kai leaders make sure that the neighborhood garbage box is cleaned twice weekly by members of each household in rotation. A household that fails in its duties to the community atones by sending a small gift to the other houses. The cho-kai collects money for services not provided by formal government, such as maintaining a pump which supplies the neighborhood's water. The head of the cho-kai, like the head of the han, is called on to mediate disputes, as when two neighbors quarrel over the placement of a wall or a branch that overhangs a property boundary.

All of Japan is covered by crime prevention institutions linking the citizen and the police. At the bottom are 560,000 "contact

14. David W. Plath, *The After Hours* (Berkeley: University of California Press, 1964), p. 142, says that neighborhood government associations are six hundred years old. Because the system was exploited by Japan's military government during the war for purposes of regimentation, the Occupation tried to discourage its continuation.

15. Names differ from place to place: *kumi* in some rural areas; *tonari-gumi* in Osaka; *han* in Tokyo and Aomori.

16. R.P. Dore, *City Life in Japan* (Berkeley: University of California Press, 1958), p. 269, calls them wards, characterizing them as more than postal districts, less than communities. Plath, p. 142, compares them with Air Raid Block Warden organizations in the United States during World War II.

points."[17] Originally created by action of the prefectural police, they have been taken over by the crime prevention associations. A contact point is a residence or business, designated by small yellow and green signs fixed near the door, where people solicit police help or obtain information. Making rough calculations, there is about one contact point for every fifty households in Japan, assuming of course that contact points are distributed proportionately to population density. Crime prevention associations are usually organized on the basis of police station jurisdictions. There are approximately 1,200 constituent associations in Japan, the same number as police stations. Each association supervises the work of the contact points. Twenty-eight prefectures report that their associations sometimes have "branches," an organizational layer between the station-level headquarters and the contact points. In some places these coincide with elementary school districts; in others they are ad hoc divisions created for administrative convenience, as when a village is annexed to a city. When a cho-kai becomes a member of a crime prevention association, as some do, they are referred to as branches. There are also 8,000 specialized crime prevention associations based upon occupations and work places. They are members of station-level associations. For example, there are crime prevention associations of pawnshops, restaurants, factories, bars, banks, and department stores.

The 1,200 geographical and 8,000 functional crime prevention associations are federated into prefectural crime prevention associations. In some places there are intermediate city associations — Tokyo, Nagoya, Nagasaki. But some quite large cities have no separate association, such as Osaka, Kyoto, and Hiroshima. The 47 prefectural associations[18] are members of a National Federation of Crime Prevention Associations. Thus Japan is linked from top to bottom, central government to neighborhoods, by a network of crime prevention institutions that can be used to inform citizens about crime and its prevention at great speed and very little cost.

Total membership in crime prevention associations is impossible to determine because membership criteria vary. In some places every resident who accepts the authority of the cho-kai, which means almost everyone, is automatically a member; in other places membership is by application. Financing is equally unstandardized.

17. I am profoundly indebted to Mr. Koji Kasahara, National Federation of Crime Prevention Associations, for providing me with information about these associations.
18. Forty-six prefectures on the main islands plus Okinawa since 1972.

In most places the cho-kai contributes some of its resources to the local crime prevention association. Thus all residents, whether they know it or not, make some financial contribution to crime prevention. Special levies earmarked for the association are sometimes made through the cho-kai. Amounts vary considerably, from Y30 to Y400 per year ($.10 to $2.00).[19] Dues from voluntary members are not standard either. Some associations allow businesses to join like individuals; others create special functional associations, as I have shown. A large part of association income comes from business enterprises either as voluntary donations or membership fees. General tax revenues also find their way into crime prevention work. Just as cho-kai often contribute to local associations, so other units of government, such as cities and prefectures, make grants to the federations. The largest source of income for the national federation, for example, is the national government. There is a delicious element of poetic justice in this gift. A foundation has been established into which a fixed percentage of the profits from legalized gambling are paid. Operating under a mandate to promote the public welfare, the foundation's governing board has repeatedly selected the National Federation of Crime Prevention Associations as one of its beneficiaries. Proponents of legalized gambling in the United States should take note.

Because the system of crime prevention associations is so decentralized, a national figure on crime prevention expenditures is not available. Examination of some local records shows that the amount of money involved is not particularly large. The budget for Tokyo's ninety-three associations in 1972 was Y161 million ($609,000). This included money from dues, donations, and cho-kai contributions. The Tokyo city federation office had a budget of Y58 million in 1972 — 4 percent coming from member associations, 33 percent from the Metropolitan Government, 62 percent from its own enterprises (magazine subscriptions, sales of locks, posters, and protection paraphenalia), and 1 percent from private donations.[20] Labor costs, however, are very small, since only a handful of staff at headquarters of the national and prefectural associations are salaried. If the value of donated labor were added to the budget totals,

19. Receipts for the payment by households to the crime prevention association are pasted to the door-posts, along with metal disks showing payment of fees for radio license, water, Red Cross, and Community Chest.
20. The monthly magazine sells for Y60 per copy; it is sold through local associations, not through commercial bookstores. Seventeen thousand copies are printed each month.

the scale of crime prevention activity would be more adequately reflected.[21]

Leaders of crime prevention associations tend to be elderly, male, and conservative. Women and youth are seriously underrepresented although there are usually women's units within the associations that are active in youth counselling. Retired people are the backbone of the associations. Leadership appears to be self-perpetuating though the mechanisms are unclear and undoubtedly vary from place to place. In order to be an effective leader, say association officials, one must have sympathy for the police. They indicate firmly that people with leftist political leanings are not encouraged to assume leadership positions. Contradictorily, association officials and police advisors strenuously insist that the vitality of local associations is not affected by the ideological complexion of neighborhoods. Everyone, they say, is concerned about crime and even communist working-class neighborhoods have active associations. It is hard to know whether such claims can be taken at face-value. It seems doubtful that people affiliated with Socialist or Communist parties would be attracted to participation in associations whose upper eschelons are so conservatively oriented. These doubts are strengthened by the admission of association officials that only "leftists" object to compulsory cho-kai levies for crime prevention activities and are reluctant participants in campaigns of the associations.

Selectivity in the choice of association leaders is undoubtedly essential, especially in light of events after World War II. Whether selection is wisely done depends on the criteria chosen. During the late 1940s, when the police were operating on an austerity budget, the public became agitated about rising crime rates and by what appeared to be a dissolution of national spirit. There were also some ethnic overtones in this, directed at Koreans and Chinese particularly. Crime prevention associations tried to step into the breach, collecting considerable sums of money for law enforcement purposes. Unfortunately some of the money was given directly to local police officials. Since some association leaders had commercial interests on the margin of the law, money was used to obtain favors

---

21. The practice of contributing labor voluntarily to assist government agencies is not confined to the police. Volunteers also serve as civil rights commissioners, probation officers, welfare administrators, court arbitrators, and administrative consultants. Tsuneo Horiuchi, "The Civil Liberties Bureau of the Ministry of Justice and the System of Civil Liberties Commissions," in United Nations, *Effective Realization of Civil and Political Rights at the National Level—Selected Studies* (New York: UN, 1968, ST/TAO HR/33), p. 61.

and several scandals arose. The police recognized that they were being compromised and deliberately pulled away from the associations in the early 1950s. They established strict policies about the acceptance of cash donations.[22] With these experiences still relatively fresh in people's minds, police and association leaders are very sensitive to conflicts of interest. Although money is still contributed to the police for certain purposes, it cannot go to individual officers. Local associations subsidize crime prevention publicity gotten up by police stations; occasionally they purchase a substantial piece of equipment, such as a metal shed for parking police cars. Benevolence to individual policemen is limited to cards and flowers for injured officers and sometimes a contribution to the family of an officer killed in the line of duty.

The police are undoubtedly the dominant partner in the relationship with the crime prevention associatons. Associations are viewed, by their own leaders as well as the police, as auxiliaries. Associations submit plans for crime prevention campaigns to the police, taking their cues from police perceptions of public need. In every police station, as well as higher levels, officers are assigned to work with the associations, providing information, coordinating activities, and informally monitoring performance. The police quietly inform associations when a member serving on a council or as a contact point has a criminal record or undesirable business connections. In many places office space for associations is provided in police buildings. Headquarters for the National Federation, for instance, is in the office building of the National Police Agency in Tokyo. Secretarial assistance for local associations is provided by police station staff. Retired police officers monopolize salaried positions in prefectural and national federations; they are also prominent, though not paid, in local associations. But the associations are not completely passive. They are conduits for community input into police policy, especially when matters of local implementation are involved. The process of consultation seem to be informal, founded on personal relations rather than institutional procedures. Since association leaders are prominent people locally, their opinions are important to the police. On occasion personal as opposed to community interest may not be easily distinguishable. Police officers testify that association leaders sometimes protest to the police about the enforcement of parking regulations, usually asking that the

22. Harry Emerson Wildes, "The Postwar Japanese Police," *Journal of Criminal Law, Criminology, and Police Science* (January-February 1953), p. 663; Dore, p. 275ff; and interviews with newspaper reporters, 1973.

police be more lenient. There is general agreement that certain areas of police activity are out of bounds for association commentary—for example, criminal investigation. It appears that associations are reluctant as well to criticize the behavior of individual officers. Being protective of the image of the police, they do not want to be the agency for publicizing police misbehavior.

The police value the work of the crime prevention associations and encourage their growth. They view the associations as valuable instruments for developing a sense of neighborhood identity, a need the police view as acute in the suburbs of modern Japanese cities. Individual officers display genuine appreciation for the work of the associations. Like professionals in any line of work, they occasionally find the volunteers underfoot. Nonetheless, they do not deprecate association activity nor patronize their members. The public as a whole is probably not as favorably disposed toward the associations as the police.[23] Left-wing political parties have often criticized the assertiveness of crime prevention associations in particular places. Some university students condemned the Setagaya Woman's Apartment House Lock Troop as a police conspiracy to repress people. Even people who are conservative politically sometimes criticize the associations for being cliquish and ingrown. Sometimes individual members anger people by throwing their weight around too much. The police occasionally have to restrain volunteers who think they have the authority of full-fledged police officers.

Extensive though cooperation is between police and public through the crime prevention associations, they represent only the tip of the iceberg. Most neighborhoods also have Traffic Safety Associations. Like the crime prevention associations, they are embedded in institutions of local government and integrated upward into federations. They do various good works, such as organizing traffic safety campaigns, putting up signs about avoiding accidents, and serving as traffic wardens to assist in re-routing traffic around dangerous situations. In addition, Japanese society is honeycombed with committees made up of private citizens and officials that consult on matters of public safety. In most prefectures, for example, there are committees on juvenile delinquency, child welfare, violence, outdoor advertising, construction hazards, and gas-main explosions. There are hundreds of private organizations representing almost any role a person can play in society that

23. There have been no public opinion surveys on this that I know of. Items about crime prevention associations have not been included in the periodic surveys on crime and police conducted by the Prime Minister's Office.

petition the police about matters affecting their members. There
are organizations of mothers, taxi drivers, high school teachers,
attorneys, automobile driving instructors, owners of bars, theaters,
and so forth. All in all, the police operate within an intricate
network of civic associations, all of which insist on being consulted
on matters of mutual concern.

In 1960 a special organization was formed, national in scope, to
foster high morale among the police by demonstrating public
support. Known as the "Friends of the Police," it was a response to
attacks on the police made in conjunction with the riots over the
U.S.-Japan Security Treaty. Membership, which numbers about ten
thousand, is by invitation only. The organization solicits prominent
people who are willing to lend their names to support of the police.
Activities of the organization are financed by dues and donations
from large corporations. The association holds two banquets a year
in Tokyo honoring policemen who have been selected from all over
Japan. They and their families are brought to Tokyo for several
days. Delegations of association members visit sick and wounded
policemen in hospitals. Association leaders speak at police schools,
telling the recruits how valuable the police are in society. Celebrities
entertain at police installations and free tickets are distributed for
baseball games, wrestling matches, and theaters. Families of policemen killed on duty are given the officer's portrait in oil painted by a
famous artist.

In the United States private groups rarely give the kind of
assistance to the police that is routine in Japan. As concern about
crime has grown in the past few years, a few neighborhoods, mainly
in urban ghettoes, have organized crime prevention associations.
Some of them have experimented with street patrolling. Cash
awards are being given in some communities by private organizations to persons who furnish information leading to the arrest and
conviction of a criminal.[24] Telephone numbers and post-boxes are
being publicized where tips about criminal activity may be com-
municated anonymously.[25] Parents have volunteered for training to
deal with drug problems and a few neighborhoods have held
meetings about crime prevention. Activities of this sort are still rare,
so much so that the National Commission on Criminal Justice

24. Denver, Colorado, and Battle Creek, Michigan. For a review of efforts to
encourage citizen participation in crime prevention, see U.S. Department of
Justice, Bureau of Narcotics and Dangerous Drugs, *Citizen Support for Law
Enforcement Efforts* (Washington, D.C., no date).
25. *Ibid.*

Standards and Goals reporting in 1973 made a point of recommending that attention be given to organizing civilian groups to do crime prevention work.[26]

The American tradition of law enforcement is not at all hospitable to the development of private groups to assist the police. Law enforcement is a task which is to be carried out by formal agencies of government. The private citizen, though enjoined to obey the law, is not encouraged to play an active role in catching lawbreakers. Invidious words have been invented to describe such people — snitch, tattletale, fink. People should cooperate with the police when asked but they are not expected to take initiative themselves, unless of course they are victims. Encouragement of private people to share responsibilities with the police is considered dangerous to liberty, an invitation for people to intrude into other people's lives. The only time Americans consider banding together for law enforcement purposes is when official agencies have lost control. Citizen assistance does not supplement police efforts; it replaces them. This is the vigilante tradition, which is regarded very suspiciously by Americans for good reason: vigilantes are creations of desperate circumstances, unrestrained by ordinary processes of law.

Though in relation to Americans, Japanese display a remarkable appreciation of their own responsibility for law enforcement, they frequently criticize themselves for not having a well developed sense of civic consciousness. They refer especially to reluctance of individuals to come to the assistance of strangers. Japanese visitors to the United States often come away praising its tradition of mutual assistance and kindness shown foreigners by anonymous people in public places. And the Japanese observation is acute: being a Good Samaritan *is* esteemed in the United States. This is indicated, backhandedly, by the concern Americans have expressed in recent years about a decline in willingness to come to the assistance of criminal victims. Stories of people failing to respond to screams for help in the night invariably draw considerable press attention; people are shocked by such clear evidence of indifference. But the conclusion that Japanese in comparison lack a high standard of civic responsibility misses the point. One of the most remarkable sights I ever saw in Japan occurred at 12:30 A.M. one warm summer night near a municipally owned working-class apartment building. A

26. National Advisory Commission on Criminal Justice Standards and Goals, *Police*, p. 66.

young man had crashed his sports car into the median divider of a four-lane thoroughfare. Glass, bits of metal, and personal belongings were scattered along the highway for seventy-five yards. Miraculously the car was still upright on its wheels and the driver escaped with minor bruises. As the police made inquiries, twenty people of varied ages — men clothed in pajamas and knee-length underwear and women in bathrobes and hair curlers — came out of the apartment house carrying brooms and sacks and began sweeping up the debris. They swept the litter into piles, carefully separated the driver's personal belongings, and stowed the rest in bags. In ten minutes the street was spic and span, not a scrap of debris to be seen anywhere.

The Japanese do not lack civic responsibility as compared with Americans; they simply articulate it in a different way. They participate in the community in groups rather than as individuals; they respond to individual needs collaboratively. In order to enhance public safety the Japanese establish volunteer organizations in each neighborhood. Americans, by contrast, react as private individuals, purchasing guns, raising dogs, and buying security devices. Apart from paying taxes Americans cannot conceive of contributing to public security other than through acts of individual self-defense. This is one reason why private gun ownership is so important in the United States. Americans, for all their reputation as joiners, have virtually no organizations that provide assistance to the police on a day-to-day basis.

The contrasting reactions of Japanese and Americans to problems of public security reflect different historical traditions with respect to the relation of society and government. Since colonial times Americans have been preoccupied with limiting governmental authority. Governmental power is created reluctantly to accomplish particular purposes. People invested with these extraordinary powers must be carefully specified; private citizens cannot be entrusted with public authority.[27] Similarly, the powers themselves must be carefully delineated so that officials can be held accountable in law. In Japan, on the other hand, government is not an explicit creation of society. In philosophical terms, there is no social contract. Government is an expression of community just as parenthood is an expression of family. Government is not a separable function

27. Since there are private security forces in Japan as in the United States, it is necessary to make some distinctions. Acting in a police-like way may be done by three kinds of agents: public police, state-regulated private police, and private citizens. The Japanese have all three; the U.S. lacks the last.

grafted on to preexisting communities.[28] Therefore the dividing line between policemen and citizen is more vague than in the United States. The responsibilities of the citizen are not eclipsed by creation of policemen. Though the policeman is designated in law to preserve public safety, the citizen bears a moral obligation to do as much. In the same way, the policeman's duties are not exhausted by what is specified in law. Policemen are moral not just legal actors. They are expected to play an informal role in creating a consensus within the community about right behavior. That the Japanese people actively assist the police in law enforcement is the obverse of the active unstructured role the police play in community. Because the line between government and society is unclear, both policeman and citizen are responsible for law enforcement and both policeman and citizen are moral actors.[29]

The sharpness of the separation between the roles of policeman and citizen affects the demeanor of policemen in an unexpected way. Pervasiveness in the Japanese case is not associated with an ostensibly authoritarian police presence. Though the Japanese police penetrate social life more extensively than policeman do in the United States, their manner is much less formal, less self-consciously authority-bearing. Japanese police penetration is pervasive but low key. They do not need to display authority precisely because justification for intervention is not exclusively legal; it is founded on a sense of fitness shared with citizens informally. American police, on the other hand, though they intervene less often, always do so as agents of law. They are cast in a formal role. Because, figuratively, the sirens are always wailing when the police act in the United States, a uniform is more essential to police function there than it is in Japan.

28. In the early Meiji period as Japan came in contact with the West, the Japanese had to coin a special word to mean "society" in the Western sense. It is still a difficult concept for them to articulate.
29. See also comments by Albert Craig in Asahi Shimbun, *The Pacific Rivals* (New York: Weatherhill-Asahi, 1972), p. 303; Richard Halloran, *Japan: Images and Realities* (New York: Alfred Knopf. 1969), pp. 100-101; and Masao Maruyama, *Thought and Behavior in Modern Japanese Politics* (London: Oxford University Press, 1963), Chap. 1.

6.The Pursuit of Pleasure

In both Japan and the United States police must deal with a special category of offenses commonly referred to as victimless crimes or vice—gambling, prostitution, drinking of alcohol, pornography, homosexuality, and drug addiction. Victimless crimes have peculiar features compared with other criminal offenses. First, there is generally no complaint. Because no one feels victimized, police intervention is not impelled by a specific request. Cooperation in prosecution is invariably low, since neither buyer or seller has an incentive to do so. Because the police must obtain information from uncooperative participants about what is essentially a private transaction, questions of infringement of individual rights continually arise. Search and seizure issues are common in narcotics cases; enticement in prostitution; wiretapping in gambling; invasion of privacy in homosexuality; and freedom of expression in pornography. Second, most people involved in victimless crime, whether seekers or purveyors, think of themselves only technically as criminals. They may be ashamed but they think of their acts as no one's business other than their own. When legal prohibition is coupled with substantial demand as well as a fitful sense of moral guilt, corruption becomes inevitable. Police scandals in the United States have chronically involved the regulation of vice.[1] Third, the number of people involved in victimless crime is enormous. In the United States half of all arrests made by the police are for victimless crime.[2] Isn't it odd that at a time when crimes against persons are rising disturbingly, a very substantial portion of police resources is being devoted to offenses in which there is no aggrieved party? Fourth, demand for illegal pleasures creates a clandestine world where the ordinary protection of the law ceases to exist and huge amounts of money are generated for invisible purposes. In the United States organized crime has fed on prohibited pleasures.

1. Roger Lane, *Policing the City: Boston 1823-1885* (Cambridge: Harvard University Press, 1967); James F. Richardson, *The New York Police* (New York: Oxford University Press), Chaps. 7 and 9.
2. Norval Morris, "Crimes Without Victims," *New York Times Magazine*, 1 April 1973, p. 11ff.

How have the Japanese handled this vexing set of enforcement problems? Have they devised distinctive measures for regulating the pursuit of pleasure? Have they been able to insulate their police from the corroding effects of having to regulate what many want but the law prohibits? In order to answer these questions, I shall examine police enforcement of laws pertaining to drinking, gambling, prostitution, pornography, and drug addiction.

DRINKING

Proportionate to population six times as many Americans as Japanese per thousand are held by the police for drunkenness.[3] At the same time, drunkenness accounts for a smaller proportion of the people detained by the police in the United States than in Japan. In the United States, drunkenness accounted for 20 percent of all people arrested by the police in 1972; in Japan, 32 percent.[4] In other words, the Japanese police are more preoccupied with regulating drunkenness relative to other crimes than the American police are, even though a smaller proportion of the population is involved in Japan. The most likely explanation for this is that because total crime is substantially lower in Japan than in the United States, the police devote more time to the minor offense of drunkenness.

Drinking alcohol is not a criminal offense in Japan, nor has it ever been. Japan has no "dry" areas. People cannot be arrested for being drunk, only for giving offense to public order while being drunk.[5] At the same time, people who are drunk may be taken into protective custody if they are unable to take care of themselves. Relatives and an appropriate court must be notified.[6] Protective custody fulfills the same function as a misdemeanor arrest in the United States, only no charges are filed.[7]

Japanese policemen show an almost exaggerated solicitude for drunken people. They stand by impassively when teased by them,

3. The rate is 1.4 per thousand in Japan, 8.0 in the United States. In Japan, 1972, the police detained 150,490 persons for drunkenness. Ministry of Justice, *White Paper on Crime*, 1972, p. 10. In the same year, the F.B.I. estimated that 1,676,800 persons were arrested for drunkenness in the U.S. U.S. Department of Justice, Federal Bureau of Investigation, *Crime in the United States: Uniform Crime Reports—1972* (Washington: Government Printing Office, 1972), p. 119.
4. *Ibid.*
5. "Law to Prevent Drunkards from Giving Nuisance to Other People," Article 4.
6. *Ibid.*, Article 3.
7. In 1972 out of 150,490 drunken persons detained, charges were filed against only 1,415. *White Paper on Crime*, p. 10.

sometimes enduring a bleary baiting that would anger most American officers. Unless an individual is sodden or wild, they will allow him to go his befuddled way. Japanese drunks tend to be "happy drunks"; they are neither mean nor surly. On the street they are usually found in small groups, arms around one another's shoulders, reeling, staggering, singing, and joking. Policemen treat drunken people according to the general view that they are children and not responsible for what they do and say. The duty of a policeman is to protect them from their own excesses. Censorious law enforcement would be very unjust since, as noted in chapter 4, a major purpose of drinking is to relax tensions among a people always conscious of interpersonal status and obligation.[8] The object of drinking is to create ties of personal warmth and sympathy; to "hold one's liquor," to fail to show its effects, amounts to the wasting of a precious opportunity.[9] So the police show endless patience in dealing with drunks, maintaining a light touch so as to sustain happiness. It is no wonder that Japanese policemen often lament that Japan is a "paradise for drunkards."

While Japanese society excuses drunkenness, it does not excuse all behavior that results from drinking. Drinking to excess is tolerable as long as it does not encroach on duty. A man would be strongly condemned if drinking forced his family into bankruptcy or caused him to miss work. Similarly, verbal indiscretions are forgiven in one's cups but not negligence that endangers others. The Japanese are exceedingly strict, for example, on drunken driving. The police regularly set up check-points on major roads late at night as the bars are closing. All cars are stopped and each driver is made to say a few words so that officers, leaning in the driver's window, can smell whether he has been drinking.[10] Policemen also watch for the driver who keeps his face averted, trying to hide his "sake flush."[11] If they have been drinking, drivers are given the choice of pleading guilty to a charge of drunken driving or submitting to a breath-analyzer to

---

8. Chie Nakane, *Japanese Society* (Berkeley: University of California Press, 1970), pp. 124-126.
9. David W. Plath, *The After Hours* (Berkeley: University of California Press, 1964), pp. 87-88.
10. Because this duty is unpleasant, an electronic gadget has been invented that makes a beeping sound in the presence of alcohol. It is about as big as a three-cell flashlight.
11. Many Japanese react in a unique physiological way to the consumption of alcohol. Their faces become flushed, turning quite distinctly red. Some find this so embarrassing they refrain from drinking.

determine the quantity of alcohol in the blood.[12] Conviction for drunken driving carries a penalty of immediate license revocation and up to two years imprisonment at hard labor or a fine of not more than Y50,000.[13] Japanese standards for the proportion of alcohol in the blood sufficient to render a person drunk are the most stringent in the world.[14] An ounce of whiskey, if the balloon test is administered immediately, will produce a reading of drunk.[15] Many Americans and Europeans have bitter memories of being caught driving in Japan with an amount of drink in their systems that would not have caused a flicker of concern at home. There are three outcomes for the driver who has submitted to the breath-analyzer at a drunk-trap: if drinking has been in small amounts, the driver will be given a warning; if moderate, the driver will be given a citation and told to rest in his car beside the road for an hour or so; if heavy, he will immediately be arrested and taken to jail.

Most social drinking in Japan is done in public accommodations concentrated in almost unbelievable numbers in well-known entertainment areas. In the Minami area of Osaka, which is hardly more than a quarter-mile square, there are 4,900 establishments serving liquor.[16] It is like a rabbit warren. Bars, nightclubs, and cabarets are tucked into corners, upstairs, downstairs, and behind one another. Narrow alleys branching off small streets are completely lined with miniscule bars, sometime arranged in tiers two stories tall. Entire floors of large buildings are given over to separate bars. Yet if all one wants is a quick drink of beer, it is not even necessary to go inside: in many places beer is dispensed on the street from sidewalk vending machines, like soft drinks in the United States.

The entertainment districts of Japanese cities are like adult versions of Pleasure Island from Walt Disney's version of Pinochio. Built close to mass transportation terminals, they are brightly lit areas covering several square blocks interlaced with pedestrian malls and covered arcades. Every kind of entertainment imaginable is

12. A balloon test is used. A suspect blows up a balloon and the contents are analyzed by passing them through a heated pipette containing a substance reactive to alcohol. The material changes color depending on the concentration of alcohol.
13. Just under $200.
14. 0.25 milligrams per liter of exhalation versus 0.8 in Canada and 0.5 in Europe. The Road Traffic Law, Article 65, stipulates that these standards are to be set by Cabinet order. Information provided by the Traffic Enforcement Section, Tokyo Metropolitan Police Department.
15. This was demonstrated to me by the police.
16. Seventeen hundred bars, 3,200 restaurants and snack shops that serve food and also liquor. Information provided by the local police. Distinctions among liquor-serving businesses will be explained below.

provided — movie theaters, bowling alleys, restaurants, bars, Mah-Jong parlors, department stores, strip shows, nightclubs, pinball galleries, snack bars, and dusky hotels. Like the midway at Coney Island, the sights are dizzying in profusion and glitter: glass elevators that rise gracefully on the outside of buildings, vast underground shopping arcades linked to the surface by moving stairs and decorated with tinkling water fountains, cabarets three stories tall built to resemble turreted castles complete with inset stained-glass windows, sleazy nightclubs bedecked with enormous cut-out figures of half-clad women, ice cream parlors large enough to have a mezzanine and an arched ceiling sixty feet high, restaurants displaying in glass cases plastic imitations of their food so real as to make the mouth water, and stunning women in beautiful kimonos and high black wigs standing discreetly inside the glass doors of posh cabarets. The air throbs and shimmers with tantalizing pleasures.[17]

Every city has these pleasure islands; the larger the city, the greater the number, Location and clientele give each one a distinctive character. The Ginza in downtown Tokyo is for the well-to-do. Chauffered limousines jockey for position along tree-lined streets, waiting for their owners to be deposited unsteadily in the backseats by nightclub hostesses. Kabukicho, near Shinjuki station in Tokyo, is for the middle class and for young adults. The crowds are more diverse than in the Ginza. T-shirts and blue-jeans mingle with business suits and ties. Dating couples are common, walking hand in hand amid the swirling throng. Many young men carry bowling bags and families with small children spill out of movie theaters to enjoy an ice cream before going home. The automobiles nosing slowly along the crowded streets are sporty and bright, crammed with grinning young men. Garish floodlit sign-boards tower over the street advertising risque movies. The crowd's pleasure seems to come as much from inspecting itself as from actually buying. Life is outdoors, on the street, rather than shut discreetly behind closed doors. There are lower-class entertainment areas too, such as Nishinari in Osaka and Asakusa in Tokyo. Men in open-necked shirts and workers' knickers squat in groups along the sidewalks. Many have battered puffy faces, bruised from work or recent fights. Stand-bars are crowded with people and cases of beer bottles are piled to the ceiling. Refuse is heaped in piles and

17. The attraction of these areas is shown by an interesting fact discovered by Professor George De Vos. He found that juvenile delinquency is more common in the pleasure islands than in any other area. The incidence of juvenile delinquency cannot be mapped by residential neighborhoods, as it can in the United States. Conversation, summer 1973.

pedestrian underpasses smell of urine. Shops draw down their shutters early in the evening; streets are more shadowed. Grimy merchandise is sold from the sidewalk by peddlers, forcing pedestrians to push together to get by. Late at night, wheeled food stalls provide cheap bowls of noodles and fish to weary revelers.

For the police, fights are the major problem arising out of drinking. On Friday and Saturday nights especially they are called out repeatedly to remove quarreling drinkers from bars and cabarets. When drinkers become violent or helplessly sodden, the police take them to special cells, aptly called "Tiger Boxes," where they are held overnight.

Regulation of drinking involves more than holding people responsible for the consequences of their actions. The places and hours of drinking are strictly controlled. Establishments that serve alchohol, along with dance halls, Mah-Jong parlors, and pachinko houses, must close at eleven o'clock at night. In summer these hours are often extended until 11:30 P.M. Drinking places require some prodding, so patrolmen make spot checks after closing hours. They are not unreasonable, usually allowing leeway of about half an hour, long enough for patrons to finish their drinks. The police have a unique and powerful ally in the enforcement of closing hours. Public transportation throughout Japan shuts down during the middle hours of the night. Buses stop as early as 10:30 P.M. and most trains and subways close by shortly after midnight. Since the proportion of car owners is much lower in Japan than in the United States, closing public transportation at night leaves most people stranded. They are forced to stay overnight in a hotel or take a taxi home at extortionate rates. Between ten and twelve o'clock at night streams of people hurry toward homeward-bound buses, trains, and subways; public transportation drains people out of the entertainment districts like water from a leaky barrel. The police do not enforce closing hours so much as they preside over them.[18]

Commercial establishments that are allowed to sell alcoholic drinks come in a variety of types, and the distinctions among them are subtle.[19] First, traditional Japanese restaurants are usually walled houses with a garden, diminutive fountain, and raised floors

18. Closing public transportation at night causes particular problems for employees of night-entertainment establishments. Cabarets and nightclubs sometimes band together to provide private bus transportation for their employees, especially their hostesses. A common sight in entertainment districts around midnight is tired women boarding buses while a few male patrons cluster around the doors and windows for a last few words before the evening ends.
19. Interviews with crime prevention officers. Also Crime Prevention Division, Tokyo Metropolitan Police Department, *Crime Prevention Police* (no date, *circa* 1971), p. 11.

of tatami mats. Food is served by kimono-clad women, usually middle-aged, who participate in the conversation. Second, cabarets, which provide hostesses, are Western in decor, and allow dancing. Some of them are large enough to hold several hundred people. Third, nightclubs, which are smaller version of cabarets but without hostesses. Floor shows are not standard at either night clubs or cabarets. Most make do with a small band or a piano player. Foreigners are frequently disappointed because Japanese nightclubs seem more like glorified cocktail lounges. Fourth, bars which come in Western and traditional sytles. Oddly, it is the Western ones that have hostesses; in Japanese-style bars hostesses are optional. Neither kind allows dancing.

Drinking places, especially bars, are small by Western standards. Many have room for scarcely a dozen people. Prices are high, probably a function of high overhead costs and low turnover. In the posh entertainment areas, the cost of a night's drinking can be astronomical. An hour in a Ginza cabaret for three men drinking only beer and nibbling hors d'oeuvres can easily come to eighty dollars.[20] Hostesses are a substantial part of the cost. At some cabarets they are provided in relays every twenty minutes, always one hostess to each man. They sing, joke, make light conversation, and invite patrons to dance. At a high-priced cabaret a hostess costs Y1,500 an hour (about $6.00), more if the customer designates a particular girl. Entertainment at these prices cannot be afforded by many people out of private income. Expense accounts are the foundation of the night-life economy. All large firms, including government ministries, provide money for lavish entertainment. Wining and dining at the expense of one's employer is a prized perquisite of promotion. A government report estimated that Japanese businesses spent yearly about two billion dollars on entertainment.[21] Expense-account entertaining is so common that cabarets and their hostesses present monthly bills to regular customers rather than itemizing each evening's cost.

The enforcement of drinking hours calls for considerable judgment on the part of the police because different kinds of establishments are subject to different rules. The great division is between places which serve alcohol and also food — like bars, cabarets, and

20. Two young men complained to the police about a bill for Y22,500 — about $85 — from a cabaret. The bill was for two beers, two plates of hors d'oeuvres, four Japanese brandies, one double brandy, and four dishes of snacks. The police told the men the prices were not out of line. Summer 1973.

21. Harumi Befu, "Bribery in Japan: When Law Tangles with Culture" (Paper presented to a colloquium at the Center for Japanese and Korean Studies, Berkeley, California, 21 April 1971). The government report was issued in 1968. Total expenditures would be much higher today.

nightclubs — and those that serve food and also alcohol — like restaurants and "snacks."[22] The first group must observe the 11 P.M. curfew; the second group can stay open later, precise hours determined by each prefecture. Even in restaurants and "snacks," alcohol cannot be served all the time, but the hours at which they must stop are always later than bars — usually between midnight and 2 A.M. The problem for the police is that many "snacks" are indistinguishable from bars and small nightclubs. How is a patrolman to determine accurately whether food complements drink or drink complements food? Duplicity can be quite blatant. Some "snacks" advertise "Snack and coffee" on illuminated signs picturing a bottle of White Horse scotch and do not close until 5 A.M. Furthermore, early closing hours must be observed by all places that serve alcohol and have hostesses. But many "snacks" employ waitresses. An amusing waitress plays very much the same role as a fetching-and-carrying hostess. Policemen shrug their shoulders about these matters, and follow a policy of being stern with only the most indescreet offenders.

Though the police officially deny it, closing hours for drinking establishments are enforced with varying degrees of strictness in different places. In skid rows, which are not numerous in Japan, closing the bars can lead to a riot. The police are more concerned with bars that open too early in the morning as the day-laborers are collecting for work rather than too late at night. Parts of some cities gain a reputation for having lenient closing hours or where the distinction between bar and "snack" has been fudged sufficiently that the dedicated night-owl can continue to drink into the small hours of the morning. There are well-known migration patterns among night-people as one area closes and another stays open. Closing policies are set by prefectures but implementation rests with the chiefs of police stations. If nonenforcement becomes too notorious, prefectural headquarters may suggest to a station chief that standards should be tightened. The Crime Prevention Division has plainclothes squads, operating out of prefectural headquarters, that monitors such matters. Enforcement that is too strict can lead to the transformation of bars into snacks. This weakens the control of the police over them since they are then licensed by the Board of Health as opposed to the Public Safety Commission. Public Safety Commissions, as I shall show in chapter 9, control and supervise the police. If an establishment is licensed by a Public Safety Commission, a threat of license-suspension by the police is more credible

22. "Snacks" is the word the Japanese use.

than if it is licensed by the Board of Health.[23] Though closing hours are observed more often than not, they are stretched in some places depending on three factors: the historic traditions of the area, demands of a peculiar clientele, and competition felt by businessmen from other parts of town or other businesses providing similar services.

The police also try to discourage various rackets associated with drinking. Though customers cannot be solicited on the street, in most entertainment districts "catch girls"[24] are often seen enticing men to come drink at a particular place. Price gouging is notorious, and almost impossible to stop. Some bars change prices at different hours of the evening, raising them according to demand. Others charge separately for entry, service, food, drink, hostesses, and the table. Policemen repeatedly advise the inexperienced to be wary, but sympathy is about all they can give to the disgruntled customers who flock forlornly to kobans late in the evenings.

GAMBLING

In the United States the major form of victimless crime, at least in terms of money spent, is gambling. In Japan as well gambling and running a lottery are offenses under the Penal Code.[25] Yet gambling is a minor problem compared with the United States, the incidence of gambling offenses running less than one-fourth the American rate.[26] In Tokyo, which has a population slightly larger than New York, there are about 700 gambling offenses each year.[27] The explanation for the low incidence of offenses in Japan is simple: gambling is allowed under state auspices; only private gambling is prohibited. The government provides enough outlets through authorized channels to assuage the public's gambling itch. This is no small accomplishment in a country that has been characterized as a

23. Public Safety Commissions license other places where men and women mix under commercial auspices, notably dance halls and dance schools. Mixing of men and women is considered "morals" business, hence the preserve of the Public Safety Commissions. *Crime Prevention Police*, p. 11.
24. Americans would call them "B-girls."
25. Penal Code of Japan, Chapter XXIII, Articles 185-187.
26. This generalization is based on data which are not strictly comparable. In 1971, 12,508 suspects were investigated by the police in Japan for gambling. *Summary of the White Paper on Crime*, p. 9. In the U.S., 93,300 arrests were made for gambling during the same year. *Crime in the U.S.—1971*, p. 115. The respective rates are 0.12 and 0.44 per thousand. Since more people are investigated in any country than are arrested, these figures exaggerate the incidence of gambling offenses known to the police in Japan relative to American ones.
27. *Crime Prevention Police*, p. 3.

nation of plungers.[28] The government runs horse, bicycle, car, and boat races, including the gambling on them. Legalized betting is very lucrative for the state: in 1970 government earned almost $294 million[29] from gambling on all forms of racing.[30] The state also sponsors over 500 lotteries a year, some of them enormously rich.

The major participant-betting sports are Mah Jong and Go.[31] Though prohibited, a lot of quiet betting undoubtedly goes on, generally for small stakes. The police occasionally make raids, but, as the statistics show, the police are not very attentive.

Probably the most popular game of chance is Pachinko. Very much like pinball, the game involves injecting a small steel ball into a maze, as the ball falls through bells ring and lights record a score. The ringing, clattering noise of pachinko machines is a fixture of most entertainment districts. Pachinko machines are crammed by the score in narrow rows into sleazy, smoke-filled halls. No skill is required to play and patrons thumb the handle as fast as they can, sending a cascade of balls through the machine. Pachinko narrowly avoids being gambling because prizes and not cash are awarded. But there are ways around these rules that put pachinko on the border of legality. Though pachinko parlors cannot buy their own prizes back, private persons can. In some cities there are even licensed stores for buying pachinko winnings. The National Police Agency condemns this practice. Dealing in pachinko winnings is compli-cated by the fact that cigarettes are the most common prize but dealing in cigarettes is illegal without a tobacco license and authorized tobacco dealers are prohibited from buying pachinko cigarettes. Nonetheless, late at night in back streets near pachinko parlors people can be seen darting into ill-lit doorways to trade winnings, including cigarettes, for cash. Once in a while the police crack down but by and large they consider it too insignificant to bother about.[32]

PROSTITUTION

For the first time in Japanese history prostitution fell under legal censure in 1958 when, amid considerable public controversy, the

28. Kazuo Akasaka, "Wanna Bet? A Nation of Gamblers," *East* (April 1971), pp. 32-35.
29. Y78,000 million.
30. Akasaka.
31. Mah-Jong parlors are licensed by Public Safety Commissions. They cannot admit people under eighteen years of age and must be located more than a certain minimum distance from schools or temples. No license is needed for Go.
32. There are some esoteric gambling games run sub-rosa like the numbers racket in the U.S. They are unimportant in financial terms. One of them, known as "Hanafuda," involves putting together pieces of a picture.

"Anti-Prostitution Law" was enacted.[33] To many observers, especially foreign ones, it appeared as if Japan had overthrown an historic tradition of legalized prostitution. Famous red-light districts three hundred years old, such as Yoshiwara in Tokyo, Shinmachi in Osaka, and Shimabara in Kyoto, were closed. The reality is significantly different from the impression.

The famous law of 1958 does not prohibit prostitution in terms that American expect. The law prohibits three acts: public solicitation, provision of facilities, and management of prostitutes.[34] The law does not prohibit private sex acts for money.[35] A man and a woman may legally negotiate a price for sexual services and go to a hotel to consumate the arrangement. As long as everything is discreetly done, neither party is punishable. It is not commercial sex that the law enjoins but public display and knowing facilitation by third parties. A prostitute and her clients cannot be punished but a landlord who knew her trade could be. The prosicute herself is liable to legal sanctions only if she solicits publicly.[36] In the United States, where prostitution is illegal everywhere except a few counties in Nevada, participation in sex for money is the key prohibition. In many states fornication outside of wedlock, with or without payment, is still a criminal offense. In Japan neither the act of sex nor the commercial nexus is punishable.

This explains why, compared with the United States, antiprostitution enforcement is much less a burden on the police and the rate of arrests per unit of population is one-fifth as much. In 1971, 5,073 persons were prosecuted in Japan for offenses under the law, compared with 55,100 who were arrested in the United States.[37]

33. 1958 is the year commonly associated with passage of the law, but this is wrong. The law is No. 118 of 1956, May 24. It was enforced for the first time 1 April 1957, but had no punishments for offenses. The law was then revised, Chapter Two being added. These portions came into effect 1 April 1958. Though the law was passed in 1956, it is fair to say that it did not become effective until 1958.

34. Specific provisions of the law punish streetwalking, acting as a go-between, furnishing accommodations for purposes of prostitution, inducing a person to become a prostitute, and participating in the earnings of a prostitute.

35. The law does condemn prostitution as being "against the dignity of human beings, sex morals, and good manners of the society." Article 1. The law articulates a high moral standard, then, but does not enforce it.

36. The law refers to "persons," not just "women," as I have implied. Male prostitutes are subject to the same restrictions as women.

37. *Crime in the U.S.—1971*, p. 115. Japan, Criminal Affairs Bureau, Ministry of Justice, "The Operation of the Anti-Prostitution Law in Japan" (Mimeographed statement, 1972, in English). The offenses covered in the American statistics are: prostitution, managing a brothel, pandering, procuring, transporting, or detaining women for immoral purposes, and attempts to commit these offenses. Private correspondence with the F.B.I., 1974.

Most offenders in Japan are apprehended for streetwalking, followed by persons who have acted as go-betweens.[38] Since 1959 the number of persons prosecuted has declined steadily each year. There were about one-third as many arrests in 1971 as in 1959. Decline in apprehensions does not mean that prostitution is withering away. Rather, as an official report states, methods of operations "have become more cunning and clandestine."[39] It is also apparent that the police are not as attentive in enforcing the law as they once were. The *White Paper on Crime*, 1972, refers to the "decrease in the number of investigations by the police" in connection with prostitution.[40] This may reflect a growing realization within criminal justice circles that the rehabilitation of prostitutes is not realistic. Convicted prostitutes can be sent to Women's Guidance Homes for up to six months. In 1965, 253 were so committed; in 1971, only 46 were. Most prostitutes are now fined or dismissed without charge. Only 3 percent are sent to jail.[42]

Because commercial sex acts are not punishable per se, police tactics against prostitution differ considerably from American. Plainclothes policemen are not sent out to pose as customers, making an arrest either after solicitation or occurrence of an overt act indicating willingness to participate in sex. Thus the legal problems of entrapment are avoided altogether. Japanese antiprostitution squads operate against women behaving indiscreetly in public, accosting men on the street or bargaining openly. They round up the "catch girls"—most of them are middle-aged women —who solicit for prostitutes. Many stations have photograph albums with pictures of the most notorious "catch girls." Policemen question prostitutes and their clients about third parties who abet their arrangement—landlords, pimps, procurers.

The police in Japan, as in the United States, know quite well where prostitution is going on. The great difference is that there is legal justification in Japan for ignoring it. Keeping prostitution out of public sight in the United States, which is all that police forces really do, is the same as winking at prostitution; officers are conscious that they are acting contrary to law. Keeping prostitution discreet is precisely what the Japanese law enjoins. Therefore, Japanese policemen are not conscious of doing wrong when they

38. Between 1959 and 1971 streetwalkers accounted for between 52-72 percent of persons apprehended each year; go-betweens from 13-24 percent. *Ibid.*, p. 1.
39. *Ibid.*
40. *Summary of the White Paper on Crime, 1972*, p. 20.
41. "Operation of the Anti-Prostitution Law in Japan," p. 5.
42. *Ibid.*, p. 2. In 1970 out of 3,215 prostitutes charged with soliciting, 1,297 were fined, 90 were sent to jail, and 43 were put under guidance measures.

point out to an observer where prostitution is being practiced—
though they may be willfully ignoring the extent of complicitous
involvement by third parties.

Patrolmen will point out that a particular area is an "ex-red light
district," adding with a smile that perhaps it is not so "ex-." Though
Yoshiwara has had its name changed, the area still has more arrests
for prositution than any other place in Japan.[43] Officers know in
most cases when a traditional restaurant advertised as a geisha
house is really a house of prostitution. The most flagrant disguise
for prostitution is the ubiquitous turkish bath. They cluster in
certain areas, just as drinking establishments do, and not by
coincidence are commonly found in red-light areas. There is
nothing illegal in a masseuse offering very personal services. The
culpable individuals are the knowing proprietors. By custom many
hotels make available massage services. By paying the girl more
than the regular price, clients obtain extraordinary services. There
is hardly anything the police can do to prevent prostitution under
this guise.[44] At least one prefecture—Aomori—has abolished turkish baths.[45] In Chiba Prefecture, northeast of Tokyo, just before the
opening of an all-Japan high school athletic meet, the police
arrested the manager of one turkish bath charging him with
providing quarters for prostitution. This was a warning and immediately understood. The association of turkish-bath owners—forty-
two baths were located in one place—decided to close on the
opening and closing days of the meet and to limit business by one
hour per day.[46] Hiroshima Prefecture recently adopted rules, com-
mended by the National Police Agency, requiring that no doorways
be closed or screened within turkish baths so that the interiors of all
rooms remain clearly visible.[47]

The strictness of antiprostitution enforcement varies from place
to place. Tokyo is known as a particularly clean city, probably
because it is the "front-face" of Japan where almost all foreign
tourists come. Just across Tokyo's borders, however, are several
notorious red-light districts. Around the harbors of major ports
regulation is often lax, the police recognizing that sailors have fierce
expectations on this score. In lower-class entertainment areas

---

43. 169 in 1971. Statistics furnished by the local police.
44. Massage parlors are a disguise for prostitution all over the world. They have
become common recently in London and New York, and cries have been raised
about the need to close them down. *Japan Times*, 27 June 1973, p. 4, and 29
August 1972, p. 4.
45. The law was passed in 1967, according to informants.
46. *Asahi Shimbun*, 6 June 1973. Japanese language edition.
47. *Ibid.*, 14 June 1973.

streetwalking can be found fairly openly. The phone numbers of prostitutes are pasted by pimps in public telephone booths; more brazenly they pass out printed cards to automobile drivers stopped in traffic. Certain areas are known historically as being centers of prostitution. The police may reason, though this is conjecture, that since commercial sex is not illegal per se, it is better to contain it within designated locations than to drive it underground and perhaps disperse it over a wider area. From time to time the police undertake campaigns to curb flagrant practice. The impetus usually comes from prefectural headquarters which, in turn, has been prompted by reports from its own plainclothes patrols, local police stations, or citizens group complaining about unseemly behavior.[48] But because police manpower is not unlimited, antiprostitution work must be balanced against other demands. Since discreet behavior of a freelance sort is what the law allows, regulation within the bounds of decorum—a standard which varies from place to place—is what the police in fact provide.

Around major entertainment areas patrolmen quickly learn to recognize habitual prostitutes and their protectors. They may even be able to address them by name. Police and prostitutes are both street people and they exchange banter like opponents in a well-understood athletic contest. Verbal exchanges are often quite matter of fact: "Why are you sitting down?" spoken to a group of women at an intersection; to a single girl on a corner, "Are there any new ones in your group?" As a patrol approaches, loitering men can be seen giving hand-signals, warning prositutes down the street to walk purposefully and not stand around. One summer night patrolmen saw two suspected prostitutes standing at the far end of a dark city block; tucking their caps under their arms and hiding their batons behind them, they sauntered slowly down the street. Too late the girls realized the ruse and tried to run away. They were caught and given a lecture. Officers from a patrol car saw a saucy young woman with red hair talking to two men on a street corner. As she walked away, one officer stopped her and asked questions while his colleague talked to the two men. The men refused to implicate her and she volubly protested her innocense: "If people ask me directions, I can answer them if I want to!" "I wasn't *standing*, I was *walking*." There are moments of humor in these relations. A patrol

48. According to the Japanese-language edition of *Asahi Shimbun*, 6 June 1973, there are twenty-two women's organization active against prostitution. Pressure from women's groups was important in enactment of the 1958 regulations against prostitution.

car in which I was riding drove up quietly behind a tall short-skirted young woman in the middle of a bar-lined street. Though we could not hear her, she was saying something to two men walking away. Turning around and seeing the patrol car stopped immediately behind her, she gasped in surprised and her hand flew ingenuously to her mouth. Appalled at the narrowness of her escape, she did a slight knee-bend like a curtsy and gave a smile of mingled relief and embarrassment.

Prostitution's customers are easy marks for fraud. If they have drunk too much, prostitutes take them to apartments where they are robbed. If they are unwary enough to pay in advance, prostitutes find some excuse to leave the room and then run away. In Tokyo a gang of seventy-one persons used this method to bilk over two thousand men of almost ninety-three million yen until the ring was broken by the police.[49]

Cultural mores shaping the law and police practices pertaining to prostitution are very different between Japan and the United States. In Japan a sexual double standard is socially sanctioned. Infidelity is not a source of guilt to men; they do not suffer a bad conscience from being sexually incontinent. Nor do wives feel that infidelity necessarily threatens their marriage. Going with a prostitute is spoken of as being therapeutic, a way of releasing tensions, much like drinking is. A man's duty to his wife and family are not conceived in sexual terms, apart from siring offspring. Standards of acceptable conduct are breached only when extramarital sexual activity is allowed to impinge on the husband's performance of nonsexual duties to his family.[50] As long as infidelity does not lead to public indiscretions and profligacy, morality is not considered to have been violated.

Perhaps the clearest illustration of the difference in national values with respect to extramarital sex is provided by respective public reactions to alleged sexual infidelity by Prime Minister Tanaka and Senator Edward Kennedy. During the 1972 general election the Communist Party revealed that the Prime Minister had maintained a mistress for years, producing two children by her that he supported. The tactic backfired. Tanaka earned considerable sympathy for admitting the truth of the charges publicly, while the Communists were criticized for boorish bad manners.[51] Prime

49. Interviews with local police station personnel, summer 1972.
50. Ruth Benedict, *The Chrysanthemum and the Sword* (Boston: Houghton Mifflin, 1946), Chap. 9.
51. *The Denver Post,* 10 December 1972, Section B, p. 25.

Minister Tanaka and his party won the election handily. The Chappaquiddick incident raises several questions about Senator Kennedy's behavior, but one of them clearly is that he may have been cheating on his wife.[52] In the eyes of many Americans, the situation raised suspicions of immorality regardless of the death of the girl and the post-accident behavior of Kennedy. The political effects of the senator's career are considered by political experts to be very damaging.

Marriages have customarily been arranged because marriage was viewed as an institutional relationship between families, not simply an emotional attachment between individuals.[53] Although virginity is assumed in a bride, it has never been a part of Japanese custom among good families to demand proofs, nor have illegitimate children been stigmatized in law.[54] There was often a trial period in marriage to determine whether the woman fitted into the new household. Even today, there is sometimes a delay between the ceremony of marriage and notification of the government, without which the marriage is not legal. Divorce by mutual consent has always been possible in Japan and never for infidelity on the part of the man.[55] When the penal code was redrafted after World War II, Occupation authorities recommended that adultery be included as grounds for divorce for the woman as well as for the man. The Japanese legislature objected, with the ironic result that adultery by either party was eliminated as an offense under the code.[56]

The climate within which prostitution is tolerated may be becoming less hospitable. The agent of change is the growing presence of love in marriage. Though families still pay an important role in bringing prospective partners together and in investigating the other party, young people by-and-large insist on the right of

52. This is a revealing American idiom.
53. Tadashi Fukutake, *Japanese Rural Society* (London: Oxford University Press, 1967), pp. 44-45.
54. R.P. Dore, *City Life in Japan* (Berkeley: University of California Press, 1958), pp. 107-108. Until 1948, the Civil Code referred to two categories of illegitimate births—"recognized illegitimate" and "strictly illegitimate." A child was "recognized illegitimate" when the father assumed responsibility for it even though he could or would not marry the mother. The status of "recognized illegitimate" was eliminated because it was considered demeaning to women, implying the status of a concubine. Shirley Hartley, "The Decline of Illegitimacy in Japan," *Social Problems* (Summer 1970), p. 81.
55. Yozo Watanabe, "The Family and the Law," in *Law in Japan*, ed. Arthur T. Von Mehren (Cambridge: Harvard University Press, 1963).
56. Chalmers Johnson, *Conspiracy at Matsukawa* (Berkeley: University of California Press, 1972), p. 37.

veto.[57] While they may not insist on prior emotional attachment—
though that is not uncommon—they do want a partner with whom
the formation of an emotional bond is possible. The tendency of
young people to reject the traditional saying that "Those who come
together in passion stay together in tears"[58] may have important
effects on the way in which infidelity is regarded. Marriage based on
passion, or the possibility of passion, leaves less room for extramarital dalliance. Sex assumes a more central place in the definition of
the marriage relationship with the result that sexual continency
becomes a duty of the husband. Since love is a reciprocal relationship, marriages based on it weaken the acceptability of a double
standard.[59]

The increasing popularity of dating also affects conceptions of
marriage and hence sexual customs. Until a few years ago young
male-female couples were rarely seen in public. Now the "abeks"[60]
are seen everywhere. For young Japanese men there is beginning to
be an alternative to commercial liasons or early marriage. Park
benches and scenic overlooks are crowded with couples on warm
evenings. This has created a disturbing problem for the police.
Young hoodlums victimize these couples, stealing purses, intimidating the man, and molesting the woman. Policemen patrol parks
intensively at night, watching for unattached men. Some observers
believe that sexual frustration lies behind these attacks. They note
that dating, though growing in popularity, is still exceptional; the
rules of the game have not been thoroughly worked out. At the same
time, men under twenty are not allowed in bars or turkish baths
where arrangements with prostitutes might be made. Undoubtedly
they sometimes are, but the proprietor runs a risk. There is a
Catch-22 quality to their predicament: dating is tantalizingly
acceptable but not fully available; prostitution is not available
because of their age.[61]

57. Dore, Chap. 11; Ezra F. Vogel, *Japan's New Middle Class* (Berkeley: University of California Press, 1963), Chap. 8.
58. Fukutake, pp. 44-45.
59. Note that this formulation suggests that women's militancy against prostitution
can come from an intensification of the emotional basis of marriage rather than
from insistence on marriages as arrangements of convenience. It also follows that
the subservience of women in marriage may decline with intensification of the
romance of marriage.
60. From the French "avec."
61. It should be noted that Japan in the years since 1958 does not provide an
acceptable test of the relationship between criminalizing prostitution and the
incidence of sex crimes. It is frequently suggested that prostitution provides an out-
let for people who would otherwise engage in criminal sex acts. Japan has not
abolished prostitution; it has only abolished the brothel, and that only in law.

The fact that sex outside marriage is widely excused is part of a larger pattern. Entertainment for men is centered primarily outside the home and it does not involve wives. Social activity is based on workplace friendships supplemented by lingering ties to school and university friends. Men do not generally entertain one another at home; they go to public facilities. Such places then provide female companionship. In effect, the feminine element is provided impersonally by the marketplace. The ambiance of this form of socializing is unfamiliar to Americans, indeed almost unimaginable.

There are different styles to the way in which female companionship is provided. In high-class traditional restaurants the women are often well over fifty; in cabarets and nightclubs they are young, the emphasis being on physical attractiveness. In both settings parties can become quite bawdy. With older women it takes the form of verbal suggestion, innuendo, and double-entendre. There is elaborate playing on words, rather like Elizabethan humor. With the young women, bawdiness is physical as well as verbal. Distributed among a table of men, the girls deliberately intrude into the physical space of men. They hold hands, press knees together, rest a hand on the knee or thigh of the man. The men put their arms around the girls, allow their hands to drag across breasts, or rest their hands on thighs. Conversation is suggestive and not too subtle. Men pretend to unzip their flies in response to imagined invitations; the physical endowments of the girls are openly complimented.

For the young hostesses the work is tiring and degrading. Their faces, caught unawares, frequently register disgust or boredom. At the same time, there is no question about who is in control: it is the women. They ply the men with food and drink, ordering without being asked; they make sure that the men do not spill on themselves, spreading napkins and cutting food into bitesized bits; they restrain the men's hands, keep tempers calm, and guide unsteady patrons to the men's room and to the street at evening's end. Responsibility belongs to the hostesses, which is why the men can relax. Sexually there is no ambiguity in the situation at all. The night spots are for the most part well lit, unlike American cocktail lounges. Flirtation is vigorous but thoroughly ritualized. A man can try to arrange a rendezvous and the hostess is free to accept or reject. The men are not engaged in seductions; at most they enter into a business transaction under cover of stylized risqueness. The hostesses are being used but they are not helpless.[62]

---

62. I was taken to a nightclub one night in the company of several off-duty policemen. One unusually candid hostess told a story to the group about the first time she agreed to meet a man at a hotel. She was blissfully unaware that she was

The contrast between behavior in an American cocktail lounge and a Japanese cabaret is striking and revealing. In the Japanese case flirting is open, not arch or furtive, and there is no ambiguity about outcome. Both parties are free to offer and refuse. The presence of a man's wife or date is unthinkable. In an American cocktail lounge, on the other hand, flirtation is less open, more furtive, and outcomes are uncertain. Wives and dates are encouraged.

Japan has another unique institution that throws light on sexual customs — the "Lovers' Hotel." Clustered on the fringes of entertainment areas, they look like small modern hotels, neon lit, multistoried, shadowy in appearance. Illuminated signs advertise rooms for rent by the hour or the night. No questions are asked, no registers are signed. Many have covered parking places which make coming and going more private. At some hotels parking attendants place placards against the front and rear of the cars so that license plates are obscured. There is no fuss about marriage licenses, no fear of a nocturnal visit by a hotel detective. Parents know that these are not hotels for families; should they be unobservant enough to enter, they would be turned away. Japan has solved at a stroke a problem that plagued generations of American lovers. Until the recent revolution in sexual mores, Americans either had to be rich or use disreputable motels in order to arrange assignations. The Japanese approach was more straightforward, recognizing a difficult problem made more acute by small houses and fewer motorcars. "Lovers' Hotels" undoubtedly facilitate prostitution but the police say that problems of disorderly conduct are few; all parties are anxious to avoid publicity.

Private prostitution is tolerated in Japan because it is not considered an insidious social force. Male sexual activity before as well as outside marriage has been legitimized, subject to the one qualification that the family must be protected. There is a parallel between the Japanese handling of sex and alcohol. Both indulgences are allowed under regulation so long as the duties of one's station do not suffer. Contrary to what Americans believe, stable family life and prostitution are not incompatible. Divorce rates have fallen in the past several decades in Japan, despite the fact that divorce is obtainable by mutual consent or by suit of either party.[63] In

---

talking to police officers — not that it would have mattered a great deal. Sex was clearly for sale.

63. The divorce rate is between 3 and 5 percent of all marriages. Between 1950 and 1970 the number of marriages per 1000 people occurring each year has risen, while the number of divorces has declined. Bureau of Statistics, Officer of the Prime Minister, *Japan Statistical Yearbook, 1972*, p. 31.

comparison to the Japanese, Americans appear to have overemphasized the influence of sex outside marriage on social life; they see in it an insidious social force. In the name of the family they have sought to prevent infidelity under commercial auspices. Because sexual practices and beliefs about the social impact of sexual practices are tightly interlocked, the role of the police with respect to sex in any society cannot be easily changed. The Japanese see no social need for the police to act as sexual censors; Americans do. Japanese results would seem to belie American belief, but then Americans are not Japanese. Perhaps Americans would be unable to buffer the social effects of legalizing prostitution. It is important to bear in mind when dealing with culture that what is real is what people believe — things are indeed what they seem.

Lack of censoriousness about the practice of prostitution applies to homosexuality as well. Homosexuality is not a crime in Japan, unlike the United States where in many states it is a felony.[64] Homosexuality is subject to precisely the same rules that apply to heterosexuality — prohibition of solicitation and performance of indecent acts in public places. A movie theater, for example, that becomes the haunt of homosexuals will be patrolled by police in plainclothes to prevent indecent behavior. There are "gay bars"[65] in most cities, some of which have hostesses who are "blue boys," meaning female impersonators. Some of these bars have become famous and are visited by the general public; "blue boys" have appeared on national television and some have become celebrities. Police encounters with homosexuals, both male and female, are unstrained; they are not marked by the contempt and covert baiting found in the United States. Even in tough neighborhoods among derelicts and hardened day-laborers, "blue boys" can be seen mixing, talking, and drinking without attracting hostility.

PORNOGRAPHY

Pornography is a matter of growing concern to the police. The press refers to a "poruno bumu" — porno boom — during the last five years. There are nude floor shows; bookstores have "erotic corners"; women's magazines serialize sexual adventures; and there are a growing number of specialized stores, usually found in back streets, displaying and selling erotic objects and devices. Fairly explicit

64. Morris, p. 61. Consensual homosexual acts are legal in Illinois and Connecticut; they are misdemeanors in New York.
65. A Japanese-English expression.

advertising for films can be seen in most major cities.[66] Though police believe that unremitting effort on their part is required to prevent a flood, the number of cases arising each year is still small by American standards.[67] In 1973, there were 369 cases of indecent acts, such as strip shows, and 247 of exhibition of obscene materials, such as films, books, and pictures.[68]

The selling, distribution, and public exhibition of obscene materials are a crime in Japan. No qualifications are made in law for consenting adults and discreetness of activity.[69] Japanese courts have been required to make judgments about the lewdness of materials, balancing them against artistic merit. As in the United States, private possession of obscene material is not a crime, nor is the private, nonprofit showing of pornographic films. Enforcement policy in practice, as with prostitution and homosexuality, appears to turn more on the discreetness of the activity than the nature of the act. Limited access to commercialized pornography is tolerated, as long as the scale of activity is small, the public not exposed against its will, and minors are excluded.

Obscenity standards are fairly uniform, more so than in the United States. Each prefecture makes its own judgments in particular cases, with the National Police Agency advising about principles. Evaluations made by the Tokyo Metropolitan Police Department are exceptionally influential because Tokyo is the center of the publishing industry and public sales occur there first. The Tokyo police have set up an eleven-member committee of private persons, including several women, to advise on cases where lewdness and artistic merit are in fine balance. The police are sensitive about reviving memories of prewar police enforcement of censorship, so they take action against books and magazines only in the most extreme cases. Obscenity as far as media presentations are concerned consists of display of the genitals, pubic hair, or intercourse. For example, the centerfolds of *Playboy* and *Penthouse* are inked

66. The pornography "boom" is described by Sidney Schanberg in the *New York Times*, 14 April 1974, p. 14.
67. A committee of the National Police Agency has recommended tightening the pornography laws in several ways. Committee on Comprehensive Countermeasures, *Interim Report* (Tokyo: National Police Agency, 1970), Chap. 5.
68. Information provided by the Tokyo Metropolitan Police Department.
69. Penal Code, Article 175: "A person who distributes or sells an obscene writing, picture, or other thing or publicly displays the same, shall be punished with penal servitude for not more than two years or a fine of not more than five thousand yen. The same shall apply to a person who possesses the same for the purpose of selling it."

over before sale.[70] Privately exhibited erotic films are referred to as "blue" films; commercial films shown in public theaters with erotic scenes that may be obscene are called "pink" films. The police show no compunction in making arrests connected with "blue" films. "Pink" films are another story. The motion picture industry has established a Motion Picture Ethics Committee to approve commercial films. Police standards are stricter than those of the industry body, so that police enforcement produces awkward and well-publicized confrontations.[71]

DRUG ADDICTION

The pattern that emerges from this examination of Japanese policy toward victimless crimes is that acts themselves are not prohibited. Outlets have been allowed for adults, especially men, for drinking, gambling, and sex as long as indulgence is discreet, does not harm others, and compulsion is avoided. Japanese and American policies toward the pursuit of pleasure are, therefore, substantially different. The keynote in Japan is regulation; in the United States, prohibition.

This conclusion is compelling only so far, for there is one form of victimless crime where prohibition is strict and the police unrelenting in their enforcement. This is the area of narcotics addiction and drug abuse. Using and dealing in narcotics, hallucinogens, and stimulants are subject to stern criminal penalties. There is no movement toward legalization of any forms, including marijuana, excepting of course for licensed medical purposes.[72] Nor are there any programs for maintenance of addicts on drugs under medical auspices, as in Great Britain. The only acceptable goal of treatment is permanent abstention. Hallucinogens are classified as narcotics and penalties for marijuana use are almost as severe as those for use of opium derivatives.[73] Punishments allowed under Japanese law

70. This service is performed by the Customs Bureau under a law dating from 1911. Schanberg, p. 14.
71. Such a clash occurred in late January 1972 and was widely reported in the press.
72. Decriminalization of marijuana use was recommended in the United States by the National Commission on Marijuana and Drug Abuse, *Drug Use in America: Problem in Perspective* (Washington: Government Printing Office, 1973), pp. 458-459. The Comprehensive Drug Prevention and Control Act, 1970, reduced the penalty under federal law for marijuana use privately from a felony to a misdemeanor. *Ibid.*, p. 245.
73. The penalty for possession of marijuana for use is imprisonment up to five years; for opium, up to seven years. Ministry of Health and Welfare, *A Brief*

tend to be as stiff, and often stiffer, than those in the United States. Because the United States does not have a uniform penal code while Japan does, comparison of statutory penalties between the two countries is difficult. On the assumption that federal laws are a bellwether of American policy generally, I shall cite federal laws in comparison with Japanese.[74] In Japan possession and use of narcotics are punishable with jail sentences up to seven years—five years in the case of marijuana.[75] Under federal law possession of any narcotic, including marijuana, for personal use is subject to sentence of imprisonment not exceeding one year.[76] Possession of stimulants in Japan can earn an offender five years in jail; under federal law in the United States, one year.[77] In both countries selling, distributing, and possessing drugs for gain is regarded more seriously than possession for personal use. The punishment for dealing in opium and cocaine derivatives in Japan is a jail sentence of from one to ten years. In the United States the maximum penalty is fifteen years and there are no mandatory minimum sentences.[78] Japanese law requires minimum sentences for persons who are convicted of dealing in narcotics for gain, including import and export, while mandatory minimum sentences were eliminated from federal narcotics laws in the United States in 1970.[79] Japanese law provides for compulsory hospitalization of addicts, including marijuana users, for periods up to six months.[80] Though procedures vary a great deal in the United States, the federal government and all but four states have some measures for compelling persons dependent on drugs to undergo treatment.[81]

The Japanese have had remarkable success in dealing with drug problems. The number of persons arrested for hard drug use has

---

Account of Drug Abuse and Countermeasures in Japan (Tokyo: 1972), Table II. This document is in English and provides a very complete and useful summary of drug enforcement in Japan.

74. The Comprehensive Drug Abuse Prevention and Control Act of 1970. This act has served as a model for the revision of state statutes dealing with drugs. See Andrea M. Corcoran and John Helm, "Compilation and Analysis of Criminal Drug Laws in the 50 States and Five Territories," in National Commission on Marijuana and Drug Abuse, *Drug Use in America,* Appendix, Vol. III, pp. 240-334.

75. Narcotics Control Law, 1953, Article 64; Opium Law, 1954, Article 51; Cannabis Control Law, 1948, Article 24(2).

76. U.S. Code, Title 21, section 844.

77. It is only a misdemeanor in twenty-three states in the U.S. *Ibid.*

78. U.S. Code, Title 21, section 841.

79. In 1973 New York State went against the trend of reducing penal punishments by enacting a law providing mandatory life sentences for drug dealers.

80. Narcotics Control Law, Article 58, paragraphs 6-10.

81. National Commission on Marijuana and Drug Abuse, p. 327.

declined steadily over the past decade, after rising during the 1950s and early 1960s.[82] This is not because the police adopted a more tolerant policy or because arrests became more difficult to make. The peak year was in 1963 when 2,988 persons were arrested and tried.[83] In 1973 only 591 narcotics arrests were made. Violations involving opium continued to rise a bit longer, peaking in 1968. By 1971 they too had fallen, being one-half the incidence in 1963. The number of addicts reported to authorities shows a similar steep decline since the early 1960s. In 1961, 2,194 were reported, in 1971 only 63.[84] The Japanese experience shows that hard-drug use can, through official action, be dramatically reduced.

In terms of numbers of persons involved the major postwar drug problem has involved amphetamines.[85] By 1954 amphetamine use had risen to what the Japanese thought was epidemic proportions. In that year, 55,664 persons were arrested for stimulant violations. Three years later only 271 arrests were made. Through the 1960s the number of arrests remained stable, about 800 a year. In 1970 the number began to rise and has been increasing each year. Almost 3,000 persons were arrested in 1971 and 8,000 in 1973.[86] The Japanese have become alarmed and are now speaking of a new "stimulant boom."[87]

Marijuana arrests too have risen since the mid-1960s, from 158 persons arrested in 1966 to 617 persons in 1973.[88] Still by American standards marijuana use is a negligible problem.

And this of course is the point. Drug problems in Japan and the United States are incommensurable. In 1973 Japan arrested 9,509 persons for drug offenses, 6.2 percent in connection with hard drugs. In the United States, with a populations twice as large as Japan, 628,900 persons were arrested in 1973, twenty percent in connection with hard drugs.[89] In Tokyo there were only 449 drug arrests in 1971, 4.9 percent for hard drugs, 32 percent for marijuana, and 62 percent for amphetamines.[90] In New York City, with

82. Arrested under the Narcotics Control Law and the Opium Law.
83. *A Brief Account of Drug Abuse and Countermeasures in Japan*, p. 16.
84. *Ibid.*, p. 20.
85. "Hiropon" in Japan, which means "fatigue killer"; "speed" in the U.S. Chemically, phenil-amino-propane or phenil-methyl-amino-propane.
86. *Mainichi*, 28 December 1973.
87. *Ibid.*
88. *A Brief Account of Drug Abuse and Counter-Measures in Japan*, Table 1, and information provided by the National Police Agency.
89. *Ibid.; Crime in the United States—1973*, p. 121.
90. Information provided by the Tokyo Metropolitan Police Department.

a smaller population, there were 41,266 narcotics arrests in 1971, 68 percent for heroin, 12.7 percent for marijuana, and 2.7 percent for cocaine.[91] The total number of drug-dependent persons in either country is not easy to estimate. Though the Ministry of Health and Welfare in Japan reports only about 60 new addicts reported each year,[92] Tokyo Metropolitan Police Department sources say there are 6,000 addicts in all of Japan, most of them undergoing therapy. For the United States the Drug Enforcement Administration has estimated conservatively that there were over 600,000 drug-dependent persons in 1973.[93] New York alone may have 300,000.[94] Because drug involvement is not a serious criminal problem in Japan, it does not play a significant role in other forms of crime. By contrast, in New York City 24 percent of robbery suspects and 33 percent of burglary suspects admitted being drug users, chiefly heroin.[95]

What is the secret of the Japanese success? How have they been able to reduce the incidence of drug use so dramatically during the past twenty years? A definitive analysis of the causes of drug addiction and its responsiveness to official policy is beyond the scope of this study. It is instructive, however, to examine what the Japanese themselves say are the reasons for their success, comparing that with American experience. Japanese experts attribute their enviable record to two factors: strict law enforcement and a climate of public opinion implacably hostile to drug use.

The Japanese claim that narcotic enforcement is particularly strict in relation to the United States is exaggerated. It is true that statutory penalties for narcotics use and dealing appear more severe than in the United States, but in evaluating the strictness of law enforcement, one must look at the implementation of statutes, and particularly, at the kinds of sentences handed out. Summary data on sentencing is available for Japan but not for the United States — once again due to decentralization of criminal justice

91. Robert Daley, *Target Blue* (New York: Delacorte Press, 1971), pp. 446-447. Also, private correspondence with New York City Police Department, 1974.
92. *A Brief Account of Drug Abuse and Countermeasures in Japan*, Table 9.
93. *Drug Enforcement Statistical Report* (no date). The estimate is based on states with a valid data base, so the estimate is conservative. Donald E. Miller, chief counsel for the Drug Enforcement Administration, estimated that there are 3 million addicts in the U.S., 300,000 of them addicted to heroin. "The Drug Abuse Dilemma" (Mimeograph copy of a speech delivered in 1973), p. 5.
94. *Drug Enforcement Statistical Report.*
95. Yorihiko kumasaka, Robert J. Smith, and Hitoshi Aiba, "Crimes in New York and Tokyo: Sociological Perspectives" (Unpublished paper, 1972), p. 5.

among state jurisdictions. Sentencing practices of U.S. District Courts for offenders against federal narcotics laws, however, are much stiffer than the Japanese. The average sentence under federal law in 1971, excluding marijuana violations, was five years and five months.[96] In Japan, the average prison sentence for violations of hard-drug laws was about two years.[97] In the United States, 67 percent of all persons sent to prison under federal laws were sentenced for periods of five years or over; in Japan, only 1.4 percent were sentenced for terms that long. It can be argued that using federal sentencing data overstates the strictness of criminal penalties in the United States. Federal agencies tend to concentrate on dealing and overlook simple use and possession; the latter are left to local authorities.[98] At the same time, many states have much stricter laws than the federal government, so it is not possible to assume that federal sentences are more severe, on the average, than state sentences. In lieu of adequate sentencing studies for most states, the question of the representativeness of federal sentences remains moot.

With respect to sentences for marijuana offenses, American federal courts are again more severe than Japanese courts: the average prison sentence is three years and four months in the United States, as opposed to less than one-and-one-half years in Japan.[99]

Japan's policy of compulsory hospitalization probably exposes narcotics offenders more certainly to treatment than the patchwork of laws under which states commit persons in the United States. Considering that provisions for hospitalization were enacted in 1963, the year that the number of arrests for hard-drug use peaked, and the crest of the amphetamine wave passed several years before, it is not entirely clear that hospitalization made a major contribution to breaking the back of drug addiction, though it may be helping in keeping addiction down.

96. U.S., Administrative Office of the U.S. Courts, *Federal Offenders in the United States District Courts, 1971* (Washington, D.C., 1973), p. 134.
97. Calculated from data on sentences provided by the Ministry of Justice for all courts of first instance.
98. Interview, Drug Enforcement Administration, 1974.
99. *Ibid.* In state courts, according to the National Commission on Marijuana and Drug Abuse, 24 percent of all persons convicted for marijuana possession are sent to jail, usually for a year or less. The remainder are put on probation. Of persons convicted for the sale of marijuana, 65 percent are sent to jail, usually for more than a year. *Marijuana: A Signal of Misunderstnding* (Washington: Government Printing Office, 1972), p. 112. The report of sentencing practices in this account is not sufficiently precise to determine whether state courts are more or less lenient than federal courts.

Law enforcement is certainly stricter in Japan than in the United States in the sense that a much larger proportion of users and dealers feel the bite of the law. The scale of narcotics use is so much smaller than in the United States that enforcement is more manageable. Mild punishment awarded to almost all offenders in a category may be more effective as a deterrent than stern punishment awarded to a small proportion. This is an interesting application of the old adage that nothing succeeds like success—the smaller the number of offenders, the more certain the punishment, and the greater the deterrence from criminal sanctions.

Japanese experts also argue that enforcement efforts are facilitated by Japan's being an island, therefore making access easier to control, and by the fact that its organized criminal gangs are more easily identifiable than American. Japanese gangster groups appear in public for ceremonies, leaders are well known, and gangster offices are set up overtly. Membership in a gang is a matter of pride for individuals. Therefore, gang activities can be monitored more thoroughly and accurately than in the United States.

The second major reason cited for Japan's success in meeting the drug problem has to do with the climate of public opinion. Drug use in Japan is not considered a private matter, like drinking or going with a prostitute. It is an offense against the community, an antisocial act which weakens the nation. A drug addict is not a private sinner; he is a subversive.[100]

The effectiveness of social pressure at work in the Japanese community can be seen dramatically in the case of smoking. Though the Japanese are heavy smokers, they have effectively enforced a prohibition against smoking in public by persons under twenty years of age.[101] Smoking is considered a presumptive sign of juvenile delinquency. Teenagers discovered smoking will be admonished by the police, their names taken and parents and school authorities notified. Police officers as well as civilian juvenile counsellors demand that adolescents destroy their packs of cigarettes on the spot. I have seen teenagers taken out of dance halls by

100. The link between patriotism and condemnation of drug use may be based on memories of the Opium Wars in China. China's penetration by European powers and her ultimate prostration are attributed in part to the wholesale importation of opium. The Japanese themselves took a leaf out of the European book in the 1930s and exported huge quantities of opium from Manchuria into China as a means of expanding Japan's empire.
101. This policy goes back to the Meiji period. Baron Kanetake Oura, "The Police in Japan," in *Fifty Years of New Japan*, ed. Count Shigenobu Okuma (London: Smith, Elder, and Col, 1909), Vol. 1, p. 291.

the police and made to shred their cigarettes one by one on the street. In Tokyo in 1971 7,000 juveniles were admonished by the police for smoking in public.[102] A patrol car cruising one evening in a residential neighborhood suddenly made a U-turn and dashed back half a block where two teenage boys were lounging on a low wall. The driver had noticed one of the boys throwing a cigarette-end away. The officers found the stub and confiscated a pack of cigarettes. The boys were taken to the home of the younger, where the mother apologized for their behavior and thanked the officers for being so attentive. A report was made to the juvenile delinquency office. It is intriguing to speculate on the reactions of American parents in the same situation. Would they respond as gratefully as the Japanese mother did or would they be inclined to mutter about policemen with nothing better to do? The smoking prohibition is enforced only against teenagers still in high school. Once they have gone to work, they are considered of age and the police wink at their smoking as they do at their drinking. College students are also exempt.[103] American teenagers in Japan are unaware of the impact they have on Japanese who see them smoking on the street. To the Japanese it appears brazen, and though police and private citizens are generally too polite to say anything, they resent this disregard of Japanese custom. If Japanese public opinion supports—not just tolerates—this kind of enforcement in the case of smoking, is it any wonder that drug problems among youth are minimal?

Public opinion about drugs is not only adamant, it is united. Japan is probably the largest homogeneous nation in the world. There are no large racial, national, or linguistic subgroups that can form pockets of deviance due to the mechanics of cultural domination. Class barriers too are relatively permeable, lessening even further the possibility that alienated groups will seek to develop identity or assuage frustration by consuming drugs.

In conclusion, Japan's success with stemming drug use is not due to more severe prison sentences, though it may be tied to stricter enforcement in the sense that a larger proportion of offenders are caught and subjected to offical sanctions. The primary reason for success undoubtedly is near-unanimous public hostility to drug use, an antagonism that is acted out in informal ways and clothed in the sentiments of national pride and identity.

102. Information provided by the Tokyo Metropolitan Police Department.
103. Haruhiko Ando and Etsuko Hasegawa, "Drinking Patterns and Attitudes of Alcoholics and Non-Alcoholics in Japan," *Quarterly Journal of Studies in Alcohol* (March 1970), p. 159.

Stepping back and looking at victimless crime as a whole, it is apparent that the Japanese have avoided many of the problems that strain law enforcement in the United States. The police have not been corrupted or demoralized by having to enforce laws against victimless crime. The number of offenses committed each year is not large. Since this is not due to indifference on the part of the police, the law and public opinion would seem to be in substantial harmony. Few people are brought into conflict with the law in their pursuit of pleasure. What are the lessons that can be drawn from Japanese experience that might help Americans as they wrestle with this unique catagory of offenses?

Success in managing the pursuit of pleasure does not depend on the harshness of criminal penalties. Without the reinforcement of an active public opinion, police enforcement cannot be effective, unless the populace will tolerate Draconian enforcement measures.[104] Conversely, the more adamant the public is against a particular form of victimless crime, the less reliance need be placed on official instruments of regulation. Therefore, the development of enforcement policies must involve an assessment of public opinion toward particular indulgences. The key feature about public opinion to assess is whether the act involved is perceived as a private vice or a public menace. That is, is its indulgence viewed as compatible with the performance of necessary social obligations? If it is viewed as not inevitably harming others, then its unpleasant effects should be contained through regulatory supervision and not through prohibition. Japan has criminalized an act of vice only in the one instance where there is an overwhelming consensus that the act is antisocial—namely, drug addiction. The United States prohibits many kinds of vice—prostitution, gambling, narcotics, and sometimes alcohol—regardless of whether the public considers them inherently antisocial.

The harmful social effects of the pursuit of pleasure may be eliminated in various ways. The choice is not, as many Americans think, between prohibition or license. There are in fact four alternatives. First, prohibition—that is, penalizing the indulgence itself. Second, regulating the circumstances under which indulgence is permitted. This was the tack taken in the United States with respect to alcohol after the repeal of the Volstead Act. It is the policy the Japanese apply to alcohol, prostitution, and gambling. Indulgence is allowed so long as it does not transgress the rights of

104. As Paul Freund has said, "Not every standard of conduct that is fit to be observed is also fit to be enforced." Quoted in Morris, *op. cit.*, p. 11.

others. Third, not acts themselves, but consequences arising from indulgence may be penalized by criminal sanction. Such a policy recognizes that indulgence does not always compromise responsibilities but only sometimes does so. The Japanese tolerate drinking but are implacable toward drunken driving. Americans, on the other hand, though they once tried to prohibit alcoholic consumption, are comparatively lenient toward the drunken driver. Similarly, the Japanese, who tolerate prosititution, look with enormous misgiving at the emotional promiscuity involved in the so-called sexual revolution and have preserved very stable families; Americans, who prohibit prostitution, accept the sexual revolution almost with enthusiasm and tolerate high divorce rates. The Japanese are more responsible in their indulgence; they do not act as if they believed indulgence and duty are incompatible. Fourth, informal sanctions can be developed that help to reduce unpleasant consequences from private indulgence. These informal sanctions may supplement as well as exist in lieu of legal prescriptions. One problem with any criminal regulation or prohibition is that it thrusts responsibility onto offical agencies. It tends to blunt public discussion of what is right and proper. In a new version of Gresham's Law, legality drives out reasonableness. Consider the case of marijuana. People in the United States who oppose criminal penalties for private use spend so much time speaking for decriminalization that they give little attention to the question of whether to smoke it or not. Few people are able to maintain that penalties for marijuana smoking are too severe and at the same time that smoking is harmful in general and that marijuana smoking is intoxicating and should be avoided as much as possible. Similarly, the American approach to containing sexual immorality is to prohibit prostitution. Few people discuss circumstances in which infidelity may be inevitable, possibly justified, and ways to cushion those effects. Informal social sanctions constraining the manner in which infidelity is indulged may be more salutory in terms of human effects than banning prostitution entirely. In the United States, unfortunately, being a libertarian often does sound very much like being a libertine.

The difficulty with the precept that enforcement policies must fit concepts of social effect lies in knowing when to shift from one mode to another. Just as public opinion legitimizes enforcement, allowing it to work, so legal prescriptions help set community norms about what is proper. Laws have a pedagogical function; they are a useful standard of appeal. Attempts to prohibit drinking in the United States through the criminal law were founded on a widespread view that society was in grave and immediate danger. It is clear that spokesmen for prohibition misassessed the opinion of their fellow men. Most people did not believe that drinking was incompatible with the performance of social duties. The alcohol-prohibition experience shows that there is no quicker way to determine the moral context of an offense than to criminalize it. If alternatives to prohibition are recognized, then criminalization of indulgence can be looked upon as a controlled experiment, the implication being that if it fails repeal should be immediate and other policies substituted. This should not be a cause for anguish. Shifting from prohibitory to regulatory modes and informal sanctioning is not capitulation. Indeed, such a shift may be the only successful way to contain the harmful effects of the pursuit of some pleasures. Minimization of harmful effects is much more important than moralizing through prohibition.

The Japanese experience suggests a last sobering thought. The relation between what a society believes about a particular form of pleasure and how it chooses to supervise it may be self-fulfilling. A society that believes a vice is containable through regulation without dissolution of the community may be more effective in containing that vice than a society that believes the vice is only containable through prohibition but is ineffective in doing so. Even narcotics addiction can be stemmed and its social effects limited by means of regulation if the community as a whole reinforces the norm that containment is necessary. Conversely, a society may be effective in prohibiting indulgence in a vice if people believe that this is necessary to save society even though in fact they are mistaken. The point is that effectiveness in regulating the pursuit of pleasure depends on a community's conception of the social effects of indulgence. The community's conception varies from pleasure to pleasure, so policy must be discriminating. Unfortunately, attitudes such as these are rooted deep in popular culture; they change very slowly. It follows that enforcement difficulties may be as peculiar to different countries as views of morality.

7.The Individual and Authority

One Sunday afternoon a man about forty years old dressed in a neat suit and tie was brought to a koban by two patrolmen. He had parked illegally on a narrow residential street. He was thoroughly chastened and the officers, after talking to him for several minutes, decided that instead of issuing a parking ticket, which would require payment of a fine, they would have him send a formal letter of apology to the chief of the local police station. So the man sat down at a koban desk and wrote out a letter in longhand. After giving his name, address, age, occupation, and nature and date of the offense, he wrote as follows: "I am very sorry for the trouble caused by illegal parking. I will be very careful in the future that I will never repeat the same violation. For this time only please I beseech your generosity." After signing his name and adding his seal,[1] he was allowed to go on his way, justice having been done in the minds of all concerned.

Variations of this quaint little drama occur frequently in relations between the Japanese police and public. Policemen freely adapt their responses to misconduct according to the personal background and demeanor of offenders. The most important basis for doing so is a display of contrition by the offender. Apology is one form repentance takes. Written apologies, as in this case, are widely used by policemen in connection with relatively minor offenses where an automatic fine is levied.[2] The letter written by this man was copied from a form kept in the koban under a clear plastic cover. Some offenders, knowing about the procedure, ask to be allowed to give an apology in lieu of fine. The decision depends totally on the judgment of the officers involved. Unless they believe an offender is truly contrite and will not offend again, they insist on due punishment. To Americans, giving an apology would seem a minor price to pay. One can imagine them being irate at not being allowed to apologize, and wondering about what kind of favoritism was

1. A seal (hanko) is a small wooden stylus imprinted with a Japanese character. It is legal authentication of a signature.
2. Automatic fines are not paid to the police; they are collected for government by banks and post offices.

involved. To the Japanese, however, apologizing can be acutely embarrassing. So much so in fact that often the police simply warn the offender rather than demanding a formal apology.

Late one night koban officers were summoned by a young woman to save her from a man who, she said, had tried to force her to come to a hotel. It turned out that they had had an affair some time before and he, meeting her by accident, wanted to resume it on the spur of the moment. The woman was both furious and scared. The man, flashily dressed in a pink shirt and white slacks, was very embarrassed and steadfastly maintained that he had only asked her to come for a cup of tea. Discounting his denials, they lectured him sternly about using threats. Then the officers arranged that if he apologized to the woman and wrote a letter saying he would not do this again, the woman would sign an undertaking that she would not press charges. Taken into the room where the woman was, he shuffled his feet reluctantly and with a bad grace mumbled "Sumimasen ne" — "I'm really sorry."[3] Drunken men who relieve themselves outdoors are often let go if they are cooperative and apologetic; if they try to run away, they are fined. Youths under twenty found smoking in public can be taken to juvenile guidance centers, but they often are not if they voluntarily destroy their cigarettes on the spot and apologize. Late one evening two patrolmen on bicycles stopped a man for drunken driving; he tried to escape by reversing his car, which narrowly missed one patrolman and punched a hole in the side of a small wooden house. A breath-test showed he was drunk and he was marched on foot to a koban. The policemen wrote up the incident in detail and asked the man extensive questions about himself. As the interrogation dragged on, the driver became progressively more clear-eyed, subdued, and finally penitent. One of the young bike officers and the senior patrolmen of the koban disagreed sharply about the appropriate penalty to assess. The patrolman wanted as severe a punishment as the law allowed — after all, it was he who had almost been run over — and the senior patrolman wanted leniency, arguing that the man was a respectable businessman from out of town, that he could make amends to the homeowner directly because he owned a construction company, that he had a good driving record, and that he was very sorry for what he had done. Two full hours after the accident, the officers agreed that the case would not go to court but that the man would have to repair the damage under police supervision and would be given a ticket for drunken driving. The

3. Summer 1973.

amount of the fine would be determined by traffic specialists at police headquarters.[4]

The police, who are seldom surprised about human behavior, are well aware that contrition can be feigned and their good will abused. The police response is suitably cynical. Some kinds of chronic offenders — such as streetwalkers, bar owners who do not close on time, and women who solicit for striptease shows — are allowed to sign formal apolgies precisely in order to create a file of admitted offenses. When the police then do decide to prosecute, the collection of apologies clearly demonstrates that they are habitual offenders and deserve no leniency.

The Japanese recognize that it is difficult in practice to separate discretionary treatment based on a calculation of the genuineness of contrition from treatment based on pure sympathy. But this possibility does not disturb them as it would Americans. With disarming candor Japanese policemen explain the importance of showing sympathy for people enmeshed in the law. Only by letting the "warm blood flow," as they say, will offenders eventually learn to respect both the law and its agents. There are many instances of this. The police discovered that a bicycle being ridden without a light had been stolen. The owner of the cycle, who lived near where the young thief worked, refused to prosecute a "child," though the thief was sixteen years old. Because the boy was very contrite, the police too refused to press the matter. Charges were dropped by the police against a university student caught shoplifting 9,000 yen worth of phonograph records because he had no previous criminal record and was very repentant. A taxi driver parked illegally in front of a small store. The police discovered that because he had many previous violations, notification of this offense would cause his license to be suspended. Already bearing heavy expenses from a recent divorce, the taxi driver was on the brink of financial ruin. The police prevailed on the store owner to write a letter saying he had given permission for the taxi to park there, thus shifting the blame for the offense. Knowing that their sympathetic impulses may get in the way of performing their duties, officers sometimes take steps to protect themselves. For example, chauffeured limousines habitually double-park outside cabarets, waiting for their owners to finish the night's carouse. Near one koban, chauffers were usually

4. Apology figures prominently in a short story written by Einosuke Ito, "The Nightingale," in *Modern Japanese Stories,* ed. Ivan Morris (Rutland, Vermont: Charles Tuttle Co., 1962), pp. 269-71, which is set in a rural village before World War II. A laborer is required to write a letter promising never again to make love to the wife of a chicken thief.

given a fifteen-minute grace period before the police ordered them to move on. Orders were given through a loudspeaker because, said the officers, if they went in person, they would have trouble being stern with the drivers who were only following orders. Though policemen acknowledge that sympathy occasionally causes them to forget duty, they consider the risk worth running in order to establish a personal bond between citizens and the police, subject to the qualification that serious or chronic misconduct is not to be forgiven.

The Japanese language reflects the acceptability of molding law enforcement to individual characteristics. *Giri* and *ninjo* are the significant words for explaining the moral obligations of life. *Giri* refers to duty, the obligations of conscience. *Ninjo*—sometimes translated "fellow-feeling"—refers to sympathy felt by one person for another; it connotes empathetic sensitivity to the needs of the other.[5] A moral person embodies both *giri* and *ninjo*. *Giri* without *ninjo* lacks warmth; *ninjo* without *giri* lacks principle. An exquisite dilemma is created—one repeatedly treated in Japanese literature, drama, and cinema—when *giri* and *ninjo* conflict. In Japan, as in the United States, *ninjo* prompts an individuating response, but unlike the United States, duty—*giri*—does so as well. Though the Japanese acknowledge universalistic standards, *giri* is not a matter of abstract principle. At its core are considerations of dyadic human relationship; that is, reciprocal obligations between specific people or between an individual and a specific group. The importance of this for the police is that by knowing the personal circumstances of an offender, they can draw conclusions about the network of personal obligations in which the individual is lodged. They can judge whether *giri* is likely to constrain the individual, whether, therefore, he is likely to do what he says. *Giri* provides a basis for intellectually individuating, since it provides a way of discussing the sanctioning power of social bonds. This is similar to an American policeman deciding that because an offender is a respectable doctor and dutiful father, he can be excused for a violation because he

5. David W. Plath, *The After Hours* (Berkeley: University of California Press, 1964), p. 85, quotes John Pelzel on *ninjo* as follows: "The idea of *ninjo* seems to be straightforward; it means 'human emotions' of course and by extension 'human nature.' As a proper motivation, it counsels being aware of and reacting sympathetically to the other person as a sentient human being. The emphasis here is on the word 'sentient', which seems to be of primary concern: the other person's capacity, in other words, to feel pleasure and pain. Insofar as one acts in terms of the ideal, one will tend to foresee the consequences of acton upon the individual's capacity to feel pleasure and pain, and will modify behavior to maximize the former and forestall the latter."

would not want to jeopardize his reputation. Americans know that personal relationships can create constraining obligations, but their moral vocabulary does not recognize it explicitly. Japanese police consider personal circumstances openly because their morality— and their language—stresses the primacy of such networks, thereby making the assessment of the consequences of individuation more predictable.

Policemen in the United States also exercise discretion on the basis of demeanor and background of offenders. The difference is that they deny that they do. They pretend that they mechanically apply the law to all offenders, regardless of personal characteristics, leaving punishment entirely up to the courts. To Americans, unequal enforcement on the basis of individual attributes smacks of favoritism, prejudice, or corruption. Though the police do it, recognizing that offenders vary as to the chances of again committing the same offense, they know they run a substantial risk of public censure. The use of discretion has not been legitimated in the United States as it has in Japan. And because its use is hidden, there are few opportunities for policemen to work out even among themselves appropriate grounds for its use.

When the Japanese adapt their behavior to the attitude of an offender, they are reinforcing strong ethical norms that require people to acknowledge guilt. This includes acknowledging responsibility for duties unfulfilled. The great injunction erring Japanese must obey is to say publicly "I'm sorry." A patient in a hospital died three weeks after being transfused mistakenly with blood of the wrong type. While the doctor in charge was absolved of legal responsibility, the incident was not considered settled until the doctor agreed, prompted by a senior official in the public prosecutor's office, to send a letter of apology to the parents.[6] When a military plane was involved in a crash with a commercial aircraft, the Director-General of the Defense Agency resigned after apologizing publicly for failing in supervision. Hikers in the mountains of northern Japan were asked to write out formal apologies if they were caught taking rare alpine plants.[7] An aliens' registration office refused to process a renewal application for an American professor until the professor had apologized in writing for appearing after the

6. Tsuneo Horiuchi, "The Civil Liberties Bureau of the Ministry of Justice and the System of Civil Liberties Commissions," in United Nations, *Effective Realization of Civil and Political Rights at the National Level—Selected Studies* (New York: UN, 1968, ST/TAO HR/33), pp. 74-75.
7. *Japan Times*, 29 August 1972, p. 2. Four thousand three hundred people were warned during late summer; one hundred ten wrote apologies.

expiration date. Another professor who could not produce his passport when asked by the police had to write a letter of apology to the local police station. Three men got caught in an elevator which stopped between floors in a multi-storied bar. The police were called when the men created a scene, shouting and arguing, because the management refused to accept responsibility and apologize.[8] After the massacre of passengers at Lod Airport in Israel in 1972 by radical Japanese youths, the Japanese government published a formal letter of apology to Israel and to the relatives of the victims. To Americans this act appears to be similar to expressions of condolence American presidents automatically send when there has been a natural disaster abroad or a foreign stateman has died. To the Japanese, however, it had a more profound meaning. It was a symbolic act of national atonement. The burden of responsibility may sometimes be too great to be met through apology, as when the father of a radical terrorist hung himself after seeing his son in police custody on television.[9]

An apology is more than an acceptance of personal guilt; it is an undertaking not to offend again. This theme is strikingly confirmed in Japanese folktales, which are an important though little-used indicator of cultural values. Professor Betty Lanham surveyed a selection of popular folktales from the United States and Japan.[10] She found that half the Japanese stories stressed forgiveness for evil behavior acknowledged. In only one popular American folktale was forgiveness asked and given—Cinderella. Even more revealing were the changes that the Japanese wrought in Western folktales when they were translated in Japanese. In a Japanese version of "Goldi-locks and the Three Bears" the story ends with Goldilocks apologizing for her rude behavior and the bears forgiving her and inviting her back. In the American version, Goldilocks runs away, relieved at the narrowness of her escape. In one version of "Little Red Riding Hood" the Japanese have made a change that is almost too good to be true. The wicked wolf captures Little Red Riding Hood and her

8. Summer 1973.
9. *Japan Times*, 29 February 1972, p. 2. The custom of apology has deep roots. Harumi Befu, "Village Autonomy and Articulation with the State," in *Modern Japan*, eds. John W. Hall and Marius B. Jansen (Princeton: Princeton University Press, 1968), p. 310, notes that verbal and written apologies were traditional sanctions employed by villages in Tokugawa Japan.
10. I am indebted to Professor Betty Lanham for bringing this information to my attention. The following discussion is based on her delightful article, written with Masao Shimura, "Folktales Commonly Told American and Japanese Children: Ethical Themes of Omission and Commission," *Journal of American Folklore* (January-March 1967), pp. 33-48.

grandmother, puts them in a sack, and carries them off. Confronted by a hunter responding to their calls for help, the wolf falls on this knees and tearfully asks forgiveness, saying "I won't ever do anything bad again. Please forgive me."[11]

These stories suggest that Japanese and Americans differ profoundly in their views about the mutability of character. The Japanese believe that behavior patterns can be permanently remolded. An act of contrition is not a hollow ritual but an undertaking with respect to the future that can succeed. When policemen accept written apologies — except in the special case of habitual offenders — they do so in order to constrain subsequent behavior. In the United States contrition is not so strongly linked to reform; Americans are skeptical that the past can easily be transcended. It is instructive that in the American version Goldilocks runs away; she never admits her thoughtlessness. Maybe this is why there are so many stories in the United States of offenders who outdistance their past by moving to new communities. They do not apologize and remain; they pay a formal penalty and "start again" by physically going some place else. The Japanese believe that the network of human obligations within which individuals live will produce reformed behavior. The society, in its constituent groups, supports the erring individual in forming new behavior patterns. Apology is the sign that obligations are accepted; forgiveness is the sign that the promise is accepted. Unless character is considered mutable, neither act is meaningful.

If the web of informal human relations are more constraining in Japan than in the United States, more effective in producing reformed behavior, it would be reasonable to expect that recidivism rates would be lower in Japan than in the United States. This is probably the case among offenders as a whole — that is, all who have been discovered committing a criminal offense — but it is not true for persons imprisoned and then released — the usual basis for computing recidivism in the United States. In Japan over the past few years, slightly over 50 percent of all persons released from prison at the end of their sentences committed further offenses within five years. Of persons paroled from prison, about 30 percent committed offenses within five years.[12] The combined rate is about 40 percent.

11. Translation provided by Professor Lanham.
12. Teruo Matsushita, "Crime in Japan — Why Can Japan Enjoy Low Crime Rates?" (Unpublished paper presented at the United Nations and Far East Institute for the Prevention of Crime and the Treatment of Offenders, Tokyo, February 1975), Table 7.

In the United States, considering federal penal institutions only, about 20 percent of discharged prisoners and 30 percent of paroled prisoners have violator warrants issued against them within five years.[13] For state prisons, 12 percent of released prisoners commit major crimes, or have major crimes alleged against them, within two years of release.[14] Since most recidivism occurs within the first year of freedom, the federal and state figures are comparable. About 50 percent of persons sentenced to Japanese prisons have been there before,[15] while in U.S. federal prisons, only 43 percent have had a prior commitment.[16] According to American criteria for judging the effectiveness of a criminal justice system, the Japanese system is even less effective than the American.

The explanation for the paradoxical relation between recidivism and beliefs about the mutability of character — changeable in Japan, unchangeable in the United States — is that formal sanctions against criminal behavior, especially imprisonment, are used much more sparingly in Japan than in the United States. In Japan in 1971 less than 4 percent of persons convicted were given a jail sentence[17] and almost two-thirds of those were suspended.[18] Over 96 percent of persons convicted of a crime were punished only with a fine.[19] Federal district courts in the United States (information on state and local courts was not available) sent 44.7 percent to prison, put 41 percent on probation, and awarded fines to only 6 percent.[20] Recidivism is higher, therefore, in Japan, not because the criminal justice system is not effective, but because it is primarily the habitual offender who is sent to jail. Jails are a last resort in Japan; in the United States they are more commonly a first response.

Shaping official response in accordance with the background and demeanor of offenders, especially sincere repentance, is not unique to the police; it is a characteristic of the Japanese criminal justice system as a whole. Prosecutors, for instance, have almost unlimited discretion with respect to decisions to prosecute. The Code of Criminal Procedure states that prosecutors are to consider "character, age and situation of the offender," as well as "conditions

13. U.S. Department of Justice, *Sourcebook of Criminal Justice Statistics*, 1973 (Washington: Government Printing Office, 1973), p. 456, Tables 6.131 and 6.132.
14. *Ibid.*, p. 458, Table 6.134, for males only.
15. *Summary of the White Paper on Crime, 1973*, p. 17.
16. *Sourcebook on Criminal Justice Statistics, 1973*, p. 373, Table 6.36.
17. *Summary of the White Paper on Crime, 1972*, p. 13, computed from Table 9.
18. *Ibid.*, 1973, p. 13.
19. *Ibid.*, 1972, p. 13.
20. *Sourcebook on Criminal Justice Statistics, 1973*, p. 326, Table 5.33.

subsequent to the commission of the offense."[21] In the past few years, prosecutors have chosen not to prosecute about 40 percent of the suspects submitted to them for commission of serious Penal Code offenses.[22] In about 82 percent of these cases, the decision was based on criminological reasons, not insufficiency of evidence.[23] The more serious the offense, of course, the more likely it is that prosecution will take place. In murder cases, prosecution is more or less mandatory. Appeals against a prosecutor's decision not to prosecute are possible but rarely made.[24] Recently, prosecutors have experimented with granting probationary suspensions of prosecution. Prosecution is suspended for six months, during which reports are received from the probation office about the behavior of the offender. If behavior meets expectations, prosecution is permanently dropped.[25]

Criminological considerations affect prosecution in the United States as well, but it is impossible to tell how much. By and large, American prosecutors are not required to prosecute, even when evidence is sufficient for conviction. Estimates of how many cases are actually dismissed are very impressionistic. A common figure is

---

21. Article 248 reads: "If, after considering the character, age and situation of the offender, the gravity of the offense, the circumstances under which the offense was committed, and the conditions subsequent to the commission of the offense, prosecution is deemed unnecessary, prosecution need not be instituted." Japan, Ministry of Justice, *Criminal Statutes*, Vol. 1.

2 The proportion of cases in which prosecution was not made in 1972 was 14.3 percent for all offenses; 30.6 percent for all Penal Code offenses; 38.4 percent for Penal Code offenses excluding bodily injury or death resulting from professional negligence; 35.4 percent for special law offenses; and 4.1 percent for traffic offenses. *Summary of the White Paper on Crime, 1973*, p. 12. A chart is given covering 1968-1972.

23. *Ibid.,* p. 11. The proportion of cases in which prosecution was declined for criminological reasons has decreased in recent years. In 1958, 38.6 percent of all Penal Code offenses were not prosecuted for these reasons. Atsushi Nagashima, "The Accused and Society: The Administration of Criminal Justice in Japan," in *Law in Japan*, ed. Arthur T. Von Mehren (Cambridge: Harvard University Press, 1963), pp. 299-300.

24. Committees composed of eleven private persons are empowered to hear appeals from a decision not to prosecute and to recommend prosecution if necessary. Law for the Inquest of Prosecution, 1948. Aggrieved persons or third parties may complain to the courts if they are dissatisfied with a prosecutor's decision, and the court can order prosecutions, appointing its own lawyer or prosecutor.

25. A prosecutor who was instrumental in inaugurating this procedure told me that results have been excellent—90 percent of the suspects involved have committed no further offense prior to the expiration of the stated period during which prosecution could be instigated. Conversation, 5 August 1971.

50 percent.[26] If the proportion is so high, and therefore larger than in Japan (50 percent as opposed to 40 percent), it is possible that relative to all offenders the proportion in which criminological considerations play a role in determining prosecution is as great as in Japan.

In both countries the behavior of the offender also influences the severity of the sentences handed down by the courts. Whether there is a significant difference in the operation of this factor between the two countries cannot be determined without comparing statutory provisions against actual sentences and without knowing what was going on in the minds of the judges. It is clear, however, that sentences in general are lighter in Japan than in the United States. Not only are fines awarded more commonly but prison sentences are significantly shorter. In 1971, 94 percent of persons sentenced to prison without labor and 50 percent sentenced to prison with labor served one year or less.[27] Another 40 percent of those sentenced to prison with labor served not more than three years. In the United States in 1971 the average prison sentence given by federal district courts was three and a half years.[28] My impression is that there are fewer mandatory sentences in Japan, thereby increasing the scope for judicial determination.[29] Even in the case of murder, a judge may award a sentence ranging from death to a minimum of three years' imprisonment.[30] There is an interesting exception: patricide is considered so heinous that judges must award either death or life imprisonment.[31] Police and prosecutors make recommendations to judges in Japan about appropriate punishments for particular suspects. Practices vary in the United States. Federal prosecutors have been instructed not to advise judges when sentencing about the background of suspects.[32] One indication that judges are fitting punishments to individual circumstances is the use of suspended and probationary sentences. Compared with U.S. federal judges, the Japanese judiciary appears to award such sentences somewhat more

26. Frank W. Miller, *Prosecution* (Boston: Little, Brown, 1969), Chap. 8. Donald M. McIntyre and David Lippman, "Prosecutors and Early Disposition of Felony Cases," American Bar Association Journal (December 1970), pp. 1154-1159.
27. *Summary of Wite Paper on Crime, 1972*, p. 15.
28. *Sourcebook on Criminal Justice Statistics, 1973*, p. 327, Table 5.34.
29. See provisions of laws pertaining to narcotics offenses, Chap. 6.
30. Article 199, Penal Code.
31. Article 200. The phrase used is "lineal ascendent." The provision applies to killing one's spouse's father as well.
32. Professor Lawrence P. Tiffany, University of Denver Law School, conversation, 1974.

frequently.[33] In both countries defendants who cooperate and confess their guilt are treated more leniently than those who demand trial and are then convicted.[34] Similarly, prior criminal record also influences sentences.[35]

In both Japan and the United States, therefore, prospects for rehabilitation are assessed and allowed to affect the response of the criminal justice system. What is striking about Japan is the extent to which individuation has been accepted explicitly, certainly much more than in the United States where the word "rehabilitation" has an increasingly bad odor among the general populace. In Japan, policemen, prosecutors, and judges openly discuss whether the attitude of an offender and his personal social environment are conducive to improved behavior. The norms governing differentiated responses, whether by policemen or others, are matters of explicit consideration, thereby ensuring that actions of the system are consistent with the public's view of justice.

The legitimation of discretionary uses of authority by policemen enhances their identification with the rest of the criminal justice system. Appropriate to their tasks, they make choices in terms of the same goals and values that shape decisions at higher levels. The police are not aware of being subprofessionals to the extent policemen are in the United States. This is an important reason why relations between police and courts, as well as police and prosecutors, are less hostile in Japan. American policemen bitterly and publicly assail prosecutors and courts for failing to support their

33. In 1970, 57.5 percent of persons convicted were put on probation. Another 14 percent received a suspended sentence or fine. Separate figures are not available for fines and suspended sentences. It is possible that the combined total for probation plus suspended sentences is as high as the Japanese figure. The Japanese figure, however, applies only to suspended *penal* sentences. *Federal Offenders in the United States District Courts, 1971*, p. 11.

34. Japanese evidence comes from the testimony of prosecutors. U.S. data is very clear on this point. *Ibid.*, p. 13. The document cited computes "sentence weights," which is a scale allowing numerical representation of any sentence, whether probation, imprisonment, or fine. Using this scale, the average sentence weight in 1971 for persons pleading guilty was 4.7; persons who were convicted by a court, 6.3; and those convicted by a jury, 13.5.

35. *Ibid.*, p. 17. Persons without criminal record had average sentence weights of 4.4; those with prior criminal records, 12.2. Penal sentences tend to be much less severe in Japan than in the U.S. In 1971, 93.7 percent of all persons sentenced to prison without labor in Japan served one year or less; the remainder, three years or less. Of persons sentenced to imprisonment with labor, 50.1 percent served one year or less; 40.6 percent three years or less; 6.5 five years or less; 2.4 percent ten years or less; and 0.4 percent over ten years. *Summary of the White Paper on Crime*, p. 150. In U.S. federal district courts, the average sentence was three years and nine months in 1971. Twenty-six percent of all sentences were for more than five years. *Federal Offender Datagraphs*, A-18.

efforts to curb crime. In a favorite word, they complain of being "handcuffed." Japanese detectives display none of this. The major impediments to criminal investigations which detectives cite are lack of resources and declining public cooperation. Though they can be pressed into discussing changes of legal procedure that have occurred since World War II that have limited investigatory authority, there is no emotional intensity to the discussion. Criminal investigations have been made more difficult but manageably so. Even though Japanese courts have authority to determine the proper application of police powers, acting in accordance with procedural safeguards very much like those in the United States, the police feel part of the same community of justice.

The Japanese policeman can devote so much more time to considering appropriate treatment because he need devote less time, compared with American police, to determining guilt. The reason for this is that the characteristic stance of a Japanese confronting the police is submissiveness. More than simply being polite or deferential, Japanese are willing to admit guilt and to accept the consequences of their actions. The approved reaction of a suspect in the face of authority is compliance; he must not feign innocence or seek to avoid punishment. In an apt phrase, the suspect is to act "like a carp on the cutting board." The offender places his fate in the hands of society's authoritative agents, cooperating with them in setting the terms of his reconciliation with the community. Japanese policemen who have dealt with American suspects—mostly around military bases—are shocked at their combativeness. Even when Americans are caught redhanded, say policemen, they deny their guilt. They display no contrition and immediately begin constructing a legal defense. They insist on talking to lawyers, remain uncommunicative, and act as if being accused is an infringement of their civil rights.[36] Japanese suspects readily sign interrogation records; Americans never do. From the Japanese viewpoint, Americans are unwilling to accept responsibility for wrongful actions.[37]

Not all Japanese, of course, are submissive before the police. Some people talk back, though more rarely than in the United States, especially if they feel the police have not been respectful enough. When people are angry or frustrated they sometimes scold the police or threaten them with superior authority.[38] Rudeness and verbal

36. Interviews, 1973.
37. The Japanese call a carp that thrashes on the cutting board a "German" carp; presumably it could be called an "American" carp as well.
38. Older policemen recruited during the 1940s say that subservience, measured against those times, is now almost nonexistent.

resistance comes most commonly from hardened street people, such as hoodlums and day-laborers, drunks, and politicized students. The most common insults, apart from omitting "san" in "Omawari-san," are "pori-ko" and "zeikin dorobo."[39] Many other people treat the police as objects of fun. This is most common among young people who have been drinking. For example, a young man suddenly intruded between two strolling police officers; he was bent over as if in pain and holding his crotch. He asked breathlessly if they knew where he could find a toilet. Then he straightened up quickly, laughed at the officer's surprise, and walked away with his friends.

The cooperativeness of the Japanese people with the police and prosecutors is indicated by one stunning fact: over four-fifths of all suspects are handled without arrest on an "at home" basis. The vast majority of suspects cooperate voluntarily in their own prosecution. In 1972 88 percent of all suspects were examined by prosecutors without detention; only 12 percent were actually arrested.[40] The proportion of arrestees to suspects has been declining during the last five years.[41] In the United States, on the other hand, arrest is the beginning of a criminal case; it is the way in which prosecution is instigated. And arrest is tantamount to detention in jail, at least until a judge has heard the charge. It was considered revolutionary several years ago in the United States when the Vera bail project in Manhattan[42] recommended releasing defendants on their own recognizance without requiring bail. In Japan the question of bail rarely arises, since so few people are ever detained. One implication of these figures is that the under-trial and under-investigation jail population relative to the incidence of crime is very low in Japan. Not only are fewer suspects arrested proportionately but not all arrested persons are actually detained: in 1972 only 7.5 percent of all persons examined by prosecutors were detained and four out of five of these were held less than ten days.[43]

The mark of accomplishment for a police force is the number of offenses known to the police in which a suspect is found and sent for

---

39. The literal meaning of *pori-ko* is "policeman-despise"; it is insulting only by custom. *Zeikin dorobo* means "tax robber."
40. *Summary of the White Paper on Crime, 1973*, p. 10.
41. *Ibid.*, p. 11.
42. President's Commission on Law Enforcement and Administration of Justice, *The Challenge of Crime in a Free Society* (Washington: Government Printing Office, 1967), p. 132.
43. *Summary of the White Paper on Crime, 1973*, p. 11. In 1972, 88,579 persons were detained.

prosecution. This is known as the clearance rate. American clearance rates are always indicated by the proportion of crimes in which a person has been arrested—"cleared by arrest." The rate for the United States in 1972 was 22 percent.[44] If arrest figures were used to compute the Japanese clearance rate, the rate would be only 6.5 percent. If, however, the clearance rate is based on the proportion of cases in which a suspect was submitted for prosecution, then the rate in 1972 was 57 percent.[47]

Japanese suspects are more accommodating than American in another respect: they plead guilty more readily. In 1972 94 percent of all offenders sent for prosecution in Japan agreed to a summary judgment, meaning that a court decided their cases on documentary and material evidence without a public hearing or oral defense from the defendant.[46] Because the suspect must agree to the summary procedure, it is similar to a plea of no contest in an American court.[47] In federal district courts in the United States 62 percent of all suspects are disposed of through a pleas of guilty or no contest.[48] In Manhattan between 1963 and 1966 80 percent of all suspects pleaded guilty.[49]

The difference that a complaint population can make in the performance of a criminal justice system can be dramatically demonstrated by pulling together a few facts from each country. In Japan suspects are found by the police in a much larger proportion of offenses than in the United States—57 percent versus 20 percent. In Japan 68 percent of all suspects are prosecuted. This means that prosecution is instituted in 37.4 percent of all offenses known to the police. It is difficult to calculate precisely a similar figure for the United States but a reasonable approximation may be made. For seven catagories of serious crime, the F.B.I. estimates that in the

44. *Crime in the U.S.—1972*, p. 107. The clearance rate for serious crimes against persons was 48.8 percent, and for felonious property crimes, 16.1 percent.
45. The clearance rate of 57 percent applies to all Penal Code offenses except death and bodily injury caused by professional negligence. The clearance rate for all offenses under the Penal Code, including negligence, was 70 percent in 1972. *Summary of the White Paper on Crime, 1973* p. 1.
46. *Ibid.*, p. 11. Of 2,125,552 persons prosecuted in 1972, 111,745 went to formal trial, 2,009,818 through summary order. The sentences under summary order are limited in severity, the heaviest being a fine of Y50,000—about $190.
47. Appeal from a summary court's judgment is allowed but rarely used.
48. *Federal Offenders in the United States District Courts, 1971*, pp. 38-39.
49. James Q. Wilson, "If Every Criminal *Knew* He Would Be Punished If Caught . . ." *New York Times,* Magazine Section, 28, January 1973, p. 9. In a rural county in Wisconsin, the rate was 94 percent, Wilson says.

country as a whole 83 percent of all suspects arrested are prosecuted.[50] Undoubtedly if lesser felonies as well as misdemeanors were included, this proportion would drop considerably, probably below the Japanese figure of 68 percent. In order to be as generous as possible with the United States, let us assume that the proportion of arrested people prosecuted is the same as in Japan. The proportion of offenses in which prosecution is instituted in the United States, then, is 13.4 percent.[51] A larger proportion of prosecuted suspects admit their guilt in Japan than in the United States — 94 percent versus 80 percent, again making a generous estimate for the United States. It follows, therefore, that admissions of guilt are obtained in 35.2 percent of known crimes in Japan as opposed to 10.7 in the United States. Actual convictions as a proportion of known crimes are slightly higher than these percentages since some suspects who do not plead guilty are found guilty by the courts.[52] The Japanese criminal justice system is three times as efficient as the American in matching determinations of guilt to criminal offenses. The dividends from crime are considerably less assured in Japan than in the United States.

Japanese offenders are more willing than American to throw themselves on the mercy of policemen, prosecutors, and judges because reconciliation is considered a more important objective of legal processes than vindication. This is true whether the contest is between an individual and the state — a criminal prosecution — or between two private individuals — a civil action. Private suits between individuals, for example, are much less common in Japan than in the United States.[53] Moreover, Japanese courts have long encouraged conciliation rather than adjudication, so that a high proportion of civil suits are really disguised negotiations.[54] That courts are institutions where one submits rather than where one fights is indicated as well by the small number of lawyers in Japan.

50. *Crime in the U.S.—1972*, p. 35.
51. In order to make these comparisons, it is necessary to shift from figures on the number of offenses to figures on the number of persons arrested and prosecuted. There is, therefore, an implicit assumption that the number of persons arrested and charged is the same for every category of crime. This is not the case. Nonetheless, the comparison between Japan and the U.S. is valid because the assumption fails equally in both countries.
52. The calculation for Japan excludes negligence cases.
53. Dan F. Henderson, "Law and Political Modernization in Japan," in *Political Development in Modern Japan*, ed. Robert E. Ward (Princeton: Princeton University Press, 1968), p. 453, estimated that in 1959 there were fourteen times more suits per capita in California than in Japan. The ratio is twenty-three times greater per capita if suits are excluded whose purpose was reconciliation rather than litigation.
54. *Ibid.*

There are over fifteen times as many lawyers per capita in the United States than in Japan.[55] In Japan there are only twice as many lawyers as there are judges and prosecutors, while in the United States there are almost as many lawyers as policemen.[56] The Japanese view is that truth is not to be discovered through a contest between two more or less equal parties but through the diligence and fairmindedness of the officers of court. Though adversarial features were introduced into the criminal justice system by the American Occupation authorities, the ethos of the system remains inquisitorial. Justice involves more than determining guilt; it involves shaping legal processes to fit particular circumstances and personalities. Japanese judges play an active role in trials clarifying issues and questioning counsel as well as witnesses. They even allow new charges to be framed by prosecutors as the evidence unfolds.[57]

Conflict generally in Japanese society, whether with peers or superiors, is not met with assertiveness, argument, and protestation. Aggrieved individuals "bend like the willow," hoping that unprotesting complaince will generate sympathy and generosity. If this fails, and a dispute must be submitted to outside mediation, such restraint will be read as unusual good faith. Americans are often misled by the Japanese response to conflict. Finding that the Japanese smile when Americans think they should be angry, Americans conclude that no disagreement exists. They then further strain relations by pressing ahead, ignoring, from the Japanese point of view, both the substantive difference and the gesture of trust. Japanese who have lived in the United States report being hurt repeatedly when they tried to meet disagreement in the Japanese way. Adopting a submissive posture, they have found their wishes ignored and their feelings bruised. Americans do not establish respect in others by going the last mile to avoid friction. Rather, they show that they are alert and can act forcefully, that they cannot be taken advantage of. Americans continue to march under the famous colonial flag that shows a coiled snake and the motto "Don't Tread on Me."[58]

Japanese policemen and prosecutors not only expect suspects to confess their misdeeds, they act in such a way as to reinforce that

55. In 1972 there were 9,552 lawyers in Japan. Japan, Ministry of Justice, *Criminal Justice in Japan* (Tokyo: no date), p. 39. In the U.S., there were 342,818 lawyers in 1970. *Statistical Abstract of the United States, 1973*, p. 159.
56. In Japan in 1972 there were 2,681 judges, 2,969 prosecutors (including 898 assistant prosecutors), and 9,552 lawyers. *Criminal Justice in Japan*, p. 39.
57. Nagashima, pp. 315-319.
58. The so-called "Gadsen Flag," after Colonel Christopher Gadsen of South Carolina, and also used by the commander-in-chief of the fledgling American navy.

norm. If submission is judged to be sincere, the appropriate response of persons in authority is to display warmth and understanding and to ease the transition back to rectitude. Repentance, indicating complaince with authority, has the effect of generating *ninjo* in officials, thereby lessening the severity of punishment.[59] Consequently, when a suspect is obdurate, police and prosecutors indicate displeasure; when a suspect cooperates, they feel compelled to be generous. Undoubtedly, therefore, an element of calculation lies behind the compliant behavior of Japanese suspects. They have been raised to expect that submission mitigates punishment. Japanese mothers always teach their children to say "Gomen nasai" — a profound "I'm sorry" — whenever they do wrong, the understanding being that the child who says "Gomen nasai" will not be punished. Though American parents reward honest admissions of error too, they often insist as well on punishment — "to teach them a lesson."[60] So guilt is admitted in Japan for a variety of reasons: because it is a moral imperative, but also because it is a *quid pro quo* for leniency.

In both Japan and the United States the characteristic stance of offenders in the face of authority complements the role-definition of the police. An American accused by a policeman in very likely to respond "Why me?" A Japanese more often says "I'm sorry." The American shows anger, the Japanese shame.[61] An American contests the accusation and tries to humble the policeman; a Japanese accepts the accusation and tries to kindle benevolence. In response, the American policeman is implacable and impersonal; the Japanese policeman is sympathetic and succoring. Both sets of police adopt the tactics of the other only when their initial gambit fails: unable to overawe, American policemen feign personal sympathy;[62] unable to gain submission, Japanese policemen begin to shout.[63]

59. The psychology of this relationship is discussed by L. Takeo Doi, *"Amai:* A Key Concept for Understanding Japanese Personality Structure," in *Japanese Culture,* eds. Robert J. Smith and Richard K. Beardsley (Chicago: Aldine, 1962), pp. 132-39, and Charlotte G. Babcock, "Reflections on Dependency Phenomena as Seen in Nisei in the United States," *ibid.,* pp. 172-185. Babcock notes that persons seeking psychiatric help in Japan easily say to the doctor, "I am in your hands. I need help." American patients take weeks or months to admit their need for help and to acknowledge that what they want is to be cared for.
60. Since we know that Japanese parents do punish, research is needed on the circumstances in which submissiveness mitigates punishment of children.
61. See Richard Halloran, *Japan* (New York: Alfred A. Knopf, 1969), p. 228, on shame as a deterrent to wrongdoing.
62. This is what officers call the "Mutt and Jeff" routine, where one policeman plays a threatening, unsympathetic role, while another plays a warm, accommodating role.
63. The Japanese and Western versions of chess provide an interesting symbol of these differing stances in the face of authority. In Western chess when a piece is

There is a parallel between the importance of contrition in Japanese prosecutions and plea-bargaining in the United States. In both cases the behavior of the suspect diminishes the rigors of the criminal justice process. In Japan confession leads to suspended prosecution or reduced or suspended sentence.[64] Japanese prosecutors are not allowed to reduce the gravity of the charge. In the United States prosecutors encourage offenders to confess to a lesser charge in exchange for dropping prosecution for a more serious offense. Plea-bargaining allows the system to reward cooperation. The result, as in Japan, is to reduce the number of cases that go to trial. But there is a huge moral difference. Plea-bargaining, as the name suggests, is a cost-benefit transaction; it is a mutually advantageous trade between offender and system. It involves no acknowledgment of moral guilt on the part of the offender. Indeed, it obscures guilt because the suspect is confessing to something less than what he actually did. The law connives with him in misrepresenting the nature of his offense.

Suspects who are detained in Japan, a small proportion of the whole, have fewer procedural protections in practice than is the case in the united States. Japanese law allows suspects to be detained up to twenty-three days before a decision to prosecute is made. In effect, they may be detained during investigation.[65] In the United States detention is allowed for only twenty-four hours unless a charge has been filed before a judge. The Japanese police on their own authority may detain a suspect for forty-eight hours; the suspect is then turned over to the public prosecutors who have twenty-four hours to apply to a judge to obtain a remand order. Judges can then authorize as much as twenty days further detention under supervision of the prosecutors before a charge is filed.[66] Japanese law permits release on payment of bail but bail cannot be granted until the nature of the charge is known. Suspects have a right to meet with counsel during the detention period. In practice accesss is limited.[67] Police or prosecutors, depending on the stage of detention, frame rules to regulate meetings between suspects and counsel—when they may be held, how long, and how often. In

---

captured, it is removed from the board; in Japanese chess, when a piece is captured, it joins the other side.

64. As we saw earlier, confession brings lighter sentences in the United States as well. Punishment is more severe for Americans who force cases to trial than for those who confess straightaway.

65. *Criminal Justice in Japan*, p. 8ff.

66. Code of Criminal Procedure, Articles 203-208. Detention can be extended for five more days if the crime committed is very serious.

67. *Ibid.*, Article 39.

general, attorneys are allowed one meeting while the suspect is in police custody and from two to five during the twenty days in prosecutor's custody. If the appropriate official chooses to be unavailable, meetings may be difficult to arrange. Once a confession has been made or a charge filed, visits become unlimited. The time allowed for meetings is short. Though they may last as long as half an hour, the average is about fifteen minutes.[68]

Suspects have a legal right to remain silent in the face of questioning. Moreover, they must be advised of their right to remain silent when they are detained or brought before a prosecutor.[69] Invocation of the right is rare, coming most commonly, according to police officials, from three groups: professional criminals, political persons, and perpetrators of what are called intellectual crimes, such as fraud and embezzlement.

In a country where confession is morally enjoined and the length of time a suspect may be held is very long, the temptation to browbeat unrepentant people would seem to be very great. Moreover, discovery of an involuntary confession is not as damaging to a case as it is in the United States. Not only may the prosecution continue on other grounds but the judge need not throw out the entire confession. He can decide for himself whether specific items in the confession are likely to be true even if other parts are not.[70] Despite these factors in favor of pressing for a confession, most informed observers—lawyers, criminal reporters, law professors, and prosecutors—contend that instances of abuse of persons in custody are rare. Celebrated cases have occurred but the incidence is small, especially when compared with the notorious period before 1945.[71] The suspects that seem to be most vulnerable, according to

68. Interviews wtih attorneys and prosecutors, 1972 and 1973.
69. Code of Criminal Procedure, Book II, passim. The right of protection against self-incrimination is guaranteed by the Constitution, Article 39. The requirement to advise people of their rights has been provided by legislative action.
70. Interviews with attorneys, 1973. At the same time, Article 39 of the Constitution prohibits conviction solely on the basis of confession. This article is not always observed.
71. Chalmers Johnson, *Conspiracy at Matsukawa* (Berkeley: University of California Press, 1971), pp. 259-260, 403; *Japan Times,* 21 January 1973, p. 2; Asahi Shimbun, *The Pacific Rivals* (New York: Weatherhill-Asahi, 1972), p. 151. For discussion of the changes wrought in law by the Occupation, see Supreme Commander for the Allied Powers, "Police and Public Safety," pp. 6, 29-30, in *History of the Nonmilitary Activities of the Occupation of Japan,* Vol. 55. Johnson, pp. 161-162. An evaluation of whether the right to remain silent has become established in Japanese legal practice since 1948 may be found in B.J. George, "The 'Right to Silence' in Japanese Law," in *The Constitution of Japan,* ed. Dan F. Henderson (Seattle: University of Washington Press, 1968).

lawyers, are not the poor, as in the United States, but politically active students. Ideology, not income, structures the misuse of authority.

Because the psychological compulsion to confess is so strong in Japan, the notion of improper pressure is very subtle. Interrogators may provide a cup of tea to a suspect but cannot buy him lunch. The implicit obligation formed by the latter act is considered to be too strong. Offering a cigarette is probably all right, say police interrogators, but they would think twice about it. In one case a confession was judged to be involuntary because, among other things, the chief of the police station had visited the suspect in his bath and undertook to wash his back for him. The court thought this created tremendous pressure on the suspect.[72]

Judging from the testimony of defense attorneys in both countries, it appears that the vulnerable Japanese suspect is handled more considerately in custody by and large than the fortressed American. Certainly public concern with coercion and brutality is much less intense. Of course, appearances may be deceiving. Because Japanese believe submission to authority is appropriate, they may not protest mistreatment as readily, thereby reducing the number of abuses that come to light. Defense attorneys and criminal reporters deny that this is the case but their acuity may be dulled by their expectations. By the same token, the number of instances of coercion in the United States may be exaggerated. Making charges of this kind is part of the game; it is a prized tactic in the adversarial struggle. Assuming, however, that reality is what close observers say it is in both countries, American beliefs about the relationship between procedural safeguards and abuse of suspects are upset. Long detentions without charge and imperfect access by lawyers to clients has not produced rampant abuse. Why not?

First: although confessions have equal value in both systems as the easiest way to win convictions, they are easier to obtain in Japan, given ethical norms, and consequently pressure on suspects need not be as intense. Americans are caught in the paradoxical position of having created a criminal justice system whose ethos makes a virtue of resistance, thereby militating against ready cooperation. In order to obtain compliance, officials are impelled to commit the very abuses the system was designed to prevent. If the objective is to

72. In the celebrated Matsukawa case, on appeal to the Supreme Court. Unlike their American counterparts, Japanese prosecutors cannot promise immunity from prosecution in exchange for confession; this would render a confession involuntary. Interviews with Japanese prosecutors, 1973.

reduce abuse, an ounce of compliance may be worth a pound of defiance. This goes against the American grain, however, where people are taught to insist on their rights. Plea-bargaining, for example, follows an initial denial of a charge. It would not come into play if the first response of a suspect was admission of guilt.

Second: the incidence of misuse of authority is less in Japan than in the United States because custodians of the system accept a fiduciary relationship with suspects. Protection is produced by internalized canons of responsibility operating personalistically between suspect and official. Persons in authority are constrained by their understanding of their role, not by fear of legal checks and balances. Responsibility is a function of institutional norms, not of organizational structure. I showed in chapter 4 that this is true of police behavior; it turns out to be a characteristic of the entire criminal justice system.

The point to underscore is that submissiveness on the part of citizens does not lead necessarily to wholesale misuse of authority even if adversarial protections are weak. On the contrary, absence of adversarial procedures both legitimizes willing cooperation and allows discretion. In Japan contrition and individuation work together to punish the guilty and protect the innocent — not a bad approximation of justice.

Japanese policemen are not viewed by the community simply as agents of law. They possess enormous moral authority. Their role transcends, though it must not contradict, legal prescriptions. A Japanese policeman is more than a specialist in catching criminals and advising about crime prevention. He acts with the aura of a teacher shaping conduct to conform to community standards. There is a space between legality and propriety. Japanese policemen are not afraid to trespass there, their characteristic action being to exhort and admonish. They continually deliver lectures on duty and morality, often in place of making an arrest or issuing a citation. For instance, a young man caught driving considerably above the speed limit was let go with a warning after the patrolman, no older than the driver, lectured him quietly in front of his friends about protecting the lives of people riding with him. A middle-aged man who had pushed his way into a neighbor's house to rebuke the son for dating his niece was admonished by a senior patrolman for playing the role of policeman. A teenage boy who omitted the "Sumimasen" — "Pardon me for bothering you" — in talking to a policeman was given a lecture on manners. A drunk was told to "act like a Japanese man" rather than like a derelict. A street-tough was asked rhetorically what kind of a Japanese he was if he was ashamed to admit his occupation.

The moral authority of the police derives from their affiliation with government generally. The prestige of government servants is very high, and police are accepted as part of this establishment. The function of government, according to Japanese political culture, is to lead, shape, and tutor. Government is viewed as an in-dwelling function of society; it is inseparable from the existence of community. In Anglo-Saxon countries, on the other hand, government and society are distinct. Governement is created by decision of communities; its authority rests on the adequacy of representation and adherence to fundamental principles. In the United States, law has authority only so long as it is just. By extension, agents of government are to be obeyed only when they reflect the will of the people. American policemen have the authority of manmade law; Japanese policemen have the authority of unspoken moral consensus. Government is more exalted in Japan because it is not considered an artifact, a creation of human design.

Admonitions are effective constraints on behavior in Japan because the opinions of policemen are weighty with community censure. Policemen need rely less on explicit sanctions; it is sufficient to indicate that a person has gone beyond the pale. Japanese visitors to the United States are often surprised at the explicitness with which threats of punishment are spelled out: fines for the return of library books, for walking on the grass, for littering, for parking illegally. Through Japanese eyes Americans appear as penalty-calculating machines, computing the risks of illegal actions. In Japan prohibitions are stated publicly but penalties are hidden. The threat of exclusion from the community, not the severity of formal punishment, is the basis of conformity. An individual's sense of well-being, indeed his very identity, depends on his place within groups — family, workplace, school, neighborhood, and nation.[73] Standing alone is intolerable, a lesson first implanted in childhood. Observers of Japanese culture have noted that youngsters are punished by being put outside the house; American children are punished by being kept in.[74] American mothers chase their children around the block to get them to come home; Japanese mothers are chased by their children so as not to be left behind. Children are rarely left with babysitters.[75] Safety consists of being within the family circle; outside are strangers, uncertainty, dread.[76]

73. Benedict, p. 288: "All his life ostracism is more dreaded than violence. He is allergic to threats of ridicule and rejection, even when he merely conjures them up in his mind."
74. Vogel, Chap. 12.
75. *Ibid.*
76. Benedict, Chap. 12.

The feeling that security consists in acceptance is transferred from the family to other groups, allowing them to discipline members through the fear of exclusion. This accounts for the ability of the police to discipline their own members so effectively.[77] By enwrapping the officer in family-like solicitude, the organization raises the psychological costs of expulsion. Similarly, a Japanese accepts the authority of law as he would the customs of his family.[78] The policeman is analogous to an elder brother who cautions against offending the family. In both situations, the specter of separation is raised.[79] Wrongdoing impinges directly on the individual's sense of security. As a result, Japanese have a heightened "sense of the fatefulness of their antisocial impulses."[80]

The primary purpose of the Japanese criminal justice system, therefore, unlike the American, is not to exact punishment. Punishment is used neither retributively nor as a deterrent. It is symbolic, indicating exclusion. In psychological terms, the system relies on positive rather than negative reinforcement, emphasizing loving acceptance in exchange for genuine repentance. An analogue of what the Japanese policeman wants the offender to feel is the tearful relief of a child when confession of wrongdoing to his parents results in a gentle laugh and a warm hug. In relation to American policemen, Japanese officers want to be known for the warmth of their care rather than the strictness of their enforcement.

Awareness that they are a moral rather than just a legal force makes Japanese policemen sensitive to the intangible effects of what they do. They do not need to be told that their actions influence attitudes toward law, government, democracy, and ethical conduct.

77. See discussion in Chap. 4
78. R.P. Dore, *City Life in Japan* (Berkeley: University of California Press, 1958), pp. 91-96.
79. *Ibid.*, Chap. 24. Dore suggests, in a subtle and intriguing chapter, that particularistic loyalties of individuals to families and small communities have been transferred to new groups in the years since 1868. The same kinds of loyalties are now attached to modern groups, which are much larger in scale. Economic development in Japan has not shattered the mechanisms by which social control is maintained. This suggests, referring to the United States, that informal sanctions are attenuated not because of industrialization but because of a traditional insistance on individualism.
80. For this excellent phrase, I am indebted to Christie W. Kiefer, "The Psychological Inter-dependence of Family, School, and Bureaucracy in Japan," *American Anthropologist* (February 1970), p. 69. Great material cost is also involved in being excluded in Japan because occupational mobility is quite low. A worker commonly stays with the same employer throughout his working life. Occupational mobility is thus intertwined with penitence, rehabilitation within groups, and the forcefulness of informal sanctions.

They recognize that how they do something is as important as what they do. Knowing they are more than legal instruments, they accept the obligation of moral tutors to be upright in word and deed. By contrast, American police officers are ambivalent about claiming a social role for themselves apart from the prescriptions of law. They are curiously self-denying. They want to believe they have moral authority yet shrink from the responsibilitlies entailed. Blamed so much as it is, they pretend to be no more than technicians mechanically applying the law. They seek to protect respect by acting as if their role was very circumscribed. Since it is not in fact, their pretense leads to neglect of their more diffuse responsibilities.

The reaction of the average Japanese to the police, laden as they are with moral authority, is complex.[81] The police appear to be awesome but approachable. There is no indication that people hesitate to go to a koban for assistance.[82] Even student radicals who show reflexive hostility in organized groups do not hesitate privately to go into a koban. As the Japanese say they show "two faces" to the police. At the same time, many Japanese testify that they are wary of the police, especially if the terms of meeting are set up by the police rather than themselves. The police have enormous latent authority. A senior patrolman of twenty-four years service confessed to me that he felt anxious when he had to go into a police station in plainclothes where he was not already known. Japanese, like people all over the world, are defensive in the face of authority. But this senior patrolman's delightful revelation shows another factor that may have special importance among Japanese. They lack a sense of personal efficacy in bureaucratic situations.[83] Personal introductions are essential in approaching anybody. Japanese act confidently only within what have been described as "frames," settings in which relationships among participants are mutually understood and accepted.[84] Japanese have more trouble than Americans in entering

81. Public opinion surveys about crime and the police have been conducted periodically since 1951 by the Office of the Prime Minister. The latest, on which these conclusions are based, was done in June 1972.
82. In the 1972 poll, in answer to a question about rapport with policemen, 40 percent of respondents said they did feel rapport; 45 percent said it was average; and 7 percent said they felt none. Eighty-six percent said they knew where the local koban was located and 41 percent recognized the faces of local policemen. Only 6 percent said they would not cooperate by giving the police information, either voluntarily or when asked. Of those who had contact with the police during the previous year, 51 percent said police behavior was good, 43 percent said average, and only a handful were dissatisfied.
83. Vogel, pp. 99-100.
84. Chie Nakane, *Japanese Society* (Berkeley: University of California Press, 1970), Chap. 1.

novel situations and demanding treatment of a certain sort because
they have a right to it. Efficacy is thought to be a function of status
and personal contacts. This explains why name cards are immediately exchanged between newly introduced people in Japan. They
facilitate placing people in "frames," allowing adustment of status
relationships. The senior patrolman was apprehensive because he
was not on familiar interpersonal ground.[85] The insecurity of the
Japanese in impersonal circumstances suggests another reason why
the koban, as a system of police deployment is so appealing to
Japanese. By making the police familiar in neighborhoods, it
increases their approachability. It offsets psychological distance,
thereby reducing anxiety, by creating a setting which is intimate,
permanent, and small in scale. Its significance must be seen not just
in terms of deployment economies but in terms of Japanese attitudes
toward interpersonal relations.

The discussion of this chapter has shown that the behavior
of the police is related in subtle ways to general patterns of value
and behavior. Because analysis has been far-ranging, a summary
is in order. Police behavior meshes in particular with views about
the mutability of character, nature of government, utility of
various kinds of sanctions, and the role of authority. The aspects of
police behavior and culture that have been discussed are listed in
Chart 1. Each aspect constitutes a dimension of variation, and the
position of Japan and the United States with respect to each has
been characterized.

CHART 1

Variables	Japan	United States
I. Police		
1. Discretion	Legitimated	Suspect
2. Authority	Moral	Legal
3. Enforcement	Individuated	Categorized
4. Relations with rest of criminal justice system	Collegial	Antagonistic
II. Sanctioning process		
1. Sanctions	Informal, not explicit	Formal, explicit
2. Outcomes	Repentance	Punishment

85. Halloran, pp. 87-88, notes that officials in one ministry will not go directly to
their counterparts in another, but will first go to a friend and ask him to arrange a
meeting.

Variables	Japan	United States
3. Approved behavior	Confession	Plea-bargaining
4. Agency	Community	Government
III. The individual		
1. Stance before authority	Submissive	Combative
2. Demeanor	Embarrassment	Anger
3. Character	Mutable	Immutable
IV. Political culture		
View of government	Organic	Artifactural

Though the chart suggests it, Japan and the United States are not the obverse of one another. Dichotomization exaggerates differences; variation is actually a matter of degree. The crucial point is not that countries differ. Of course they do. What is instructive is the patterns in the variation peculiar to each country. Variation along one dimension reinforces, or undermines, variation along another dimension. The articulations of police behavior, or any other feature, conform to as well as support the configuration of other parts. Criminal justice systems are not made of interchangeable parts.

8. Violence

In February 1972 the police launched "Operational Steamroller" against radical youths who had perpetrated a series of terrorist attacks. In addition to leading violent demonstrations in which molotov cocktails had been used, the radicals had placed a bomb in a koban wounding several officers, sent another bomb concealed in the base of a Christmas tree to a Tokyo police koban which exploded and cut off the legs of one man, and killed the wife of a high ranking police officer with a homemade bomb sent through the mail. Part of "Operation Steamroller" was concentrated in the snowy mountains of central Japan where several radical hideouts had been reported. It immediately netted several youths and drove others, trying to escape, through the forests. After a long chase, five of these took shelter in an expensive villa near the border of Gumma and Nagano Prefectures, taking hostage the wife of the caretaker. This was the beginning of an extraordinary police action—the ten-day seige of Asama-Sanso.[1]

The villa was three stories tall and built down-slope with the main entrance on the top floor. The least exposed route of approach was along a narrow road and driveway leading to this entrance. After surrounding the villa, the police made several attempts to rush the top floor but were forced back by gunfire. Several officers were wounded. The primary concern of the police, as well as the public, was for the safety of the woman hostage. They knew the youths were desperate and feared that a concerted attack would cause them to kill her. The radicals refused to let the woman be seen or talk, so that as the days went by the police had no way of knowing what her physical condition was, even whether she was still alive. This became a particularly important consideration after the fourth day, when, after long deliberation, power was cut off to the villa. Since temperatures were subzero, living conditions within the villa deteriorated sharply. The police managed to attach listening devices to

1. The incident is named after the villa which was besieged. It was located in Minamikaruizawa, Nagano Prefecture, and belonged to the Kawai Musical Company. My account of the siege is based on reports in the *Japan Times* and interviews with several police officers, including the chief of the Gumma Prefecture and a commander of the riot police sent from Tokyo.

the walls of the villa but were unable to distinguish individual voices. They even considered analyzing urine from the villa in order to determine the sex of the occupants but could not gain access to the sewer line.

The siege was covered live by television, so that the entire nation had firsthand knowledge of the tactical situation moment by moment. Suggestions from the public for gaining entrance to the villa without harming the hostage poured into the police head-quarters. Injection of sleeping drugs into the water supply was rejected because it provided too much warning to the captors. Also rejected was a suggestion for lifting the roof off by helicopter. But the police were far from helpless. Earthen breastworks were slowly extended toward the front door. Every day armored cars and water-cannon trucks made forays to the entrance of the top floor and poured tear gas, smoke, and thousands of gallons of water into the villa.[2] They employed psychological tactics under the expert guid-ance of two professors brought from Tokyo. The husband of the hostage and mothers of two of the radicals made impassioned appeals by means of a loudspeaker. From time to time tapes were played that imitated the sounds of massed preparations for attack. At night, in order to deprive the captors of sleep, noise was broadcast continually and at full volume — sirens, chainsaws, trains, motorcycles, and the shouts of demonstrators.

By the tenth day, hope for the safe release of the hostage was abandoned and the police resolved on a frontal attack. Early in the morning a large crane equipped with a heavy concrete wrecking ball was driven up to the front of the villa. It had been hurriedly armor-plated over night. Methodically it began to batter down the walls of the top floor. Given strict orders not to use their pistols, a crack team of policemen was ordered to the assault. They were supported by 1,200 other policemen, ten armored cars, and four water-cannon trucks. Watched live on television by an avid nation, the police obtained entrance about eleven o'clock. Room by room the police moved through the house. After an hour and a half, a police officer was killed, shot by one of the radicals. Only then was an order issued allowing the police to use firearms within the villa. The fighting continued throughout the day, from one story to the next. Finally, at six in the evening, with the upper floors occupied by the police and holes being knocked in the walls of the first floor by the wrecking ball, the radicals surrendered. Though the police lost a

2. Japanese police use the CN variety of tear gas, which is not as effective as the CS type used by American police.

second officer and fifteen were wounded, not one of the radicals was injured and the woman hostage was found alive and unharmed.

To Americans the patience and ingenuity shown by the Japanese police at Asama-Sanso is incredible. The radicals were known to be ruthless, fanatical killers. They had been involved in terrorist attacks on the police; they were using their mountain hideouts to manufacure explosives; and they had wounded several officers by gunfire during the siege. Still, the police refused to use firearms until, in the final battle, after a siege of ten days, a police officer was killed.

This amazing incident demonstrates how extremely reluctant the Japanese police are to use firearms. Though all uniformed patrol officers carry .38 caliber revolvers, they are hardly ever used. Officers of twenty-five and thiry years' experience have never drawn their pistols from the holster. Only a handful of officers have ever discharged them except in practice. Moreover, policemen assigned to traffic regulation are expressly ordered to leave their weapons at the police station. More surprising still, so too are riot police. Plainclothes detectives, except in desperate situations, work without firearms. Arms are not carried by officers off duty but are left in the police station, locked in a safe.

The contrast with police practice in the United States could not be more stark. In New York City in 1970, over 600 officers fired their pistols in earnest. The toll from these gun battles was 7 policemen killed, 242 wounded, and 50 offenders killed, 212 wounded.[3] There are no national figures on the use of weapons by the police, partly because most forces are reluctant to publicize them. It is known, however, that each year during the 1950s and 1960s over 200 people were killed as a result of police intervention. In the late 1960s the figure was rising beyond 300.[4] Not all of these are due to gunfire but it is safe to say most are. Though only a minority of officers actually kill someone during their careers, most learn quickly to use pistols for warning, threatening, and protecting. Firearms are not the last resort of the American police; they are often the first. When hijacking of commercial aircraft threatened to become epidemic, the first response of the federal government,

---

3. Robert Daley, *Target Blue* (New York: Delacorte Press, 1971), p. 93; Andy Logan, "Around City Hall: A Hail of Bullets," *The New Yorker* (24 March 1973), p. 80.

4. Sam Chapman, ed., *Police Patrol Readings* (Springfield, Ill.: Charles C. Thomas, 1970), p. 463, from information collected by the Public Health Service, Department of Health, Education, and Welfare, for the years 1950-1967 and printed in *Vital Statistics in the United States*, Mortality, Part A.

acting on the advice of experienced police officials, was to put armed guards in plainclothes in the confined space of aircraft cabins. Within a few days of the Asama-Sanso incident, F.B.I. agents shot out the tires of a hijacked airplane gathering speed for takeoff. The bloody quelling on an inmate rebellion at Attica prison in New York State was unprecedented only in scale, not in the tactics employed.

Possession of a revolver is an essential part of being an American policeman, not necessarily because it is used that often but because of its symbolic value. Even more than the badge, it sets an officer apart from ordinary citizens. Rules about always being armed are strict; even off-duty policemen are required to carry their pistols. Around police facilities, the individual with a pistol on his belt has official status, even though he may be in plainclothes.[5] A pistol for an American policeman is not just an implement, occasionally important for self-defense; it is a visible sign of authority. It is significant that police authority in the United States is associated with being deadly; it is not so in Japan.

In place of firearms the Japanese police emphasize hand-to-hand combat. To qualify for appointment as a police officer, candidates must obtain "black belt" status in judo or its equivalent in kendo by the end of training in police school.[6] Many police achieve even higher degrees of proficiency: 60 percent of all officers earn one of the ten rankings within the top bracket of judo and 55 percent do the same in kendo. All officers are required to practice "art of arrest" which combines the skills of judo and kendo. Dressed in judo costumes, boxing gloves, and helmets, and sometimes using police batons, policemen fight one another in a free-for-all, no holds barred. The object is to subdue the other. Physical conditioning is a fundamental part of life in the police. It shows in their physical appearance—a fat policeman is hard to find. Beer-bellies are definitely taboo. Each station as well as police headquarters sets aside a large room for judo and kendo practice. Twice a year there are judo and kendo tournaments among the stations and head-quarters sections. In mid-summer each prefecture holds a tourna-ment to determine the champion station, administrative section, and riot company in both judo and kendo. Banners and trophies won in these competitions are prominently displayed in police

5. Daley, p. 99ff, is excellent on the mystique of the gun among American policemen. He notes that when a policeman in New York is accused of a crime, he is suspended and his gun is taken away. Such men, who work as clerks and messengers, are derisively known as the "Rubber Gun Squad."
6. Kendo is a popular sport derived from sword fighting. See footnote 50, Chap. 4.

facilities. The police are enormously proud of their self-defense prowess, especially of their perennial high ranking in national championships and their contribution to Japan's Olympic judo teams.

The tradition of hand-to-hand self-defense goes back to the foundation of the modern police during the Meiji Era. Samurai were prohibited from wearing swords and, unemployed as a result of the abolition of feudal estates, flocked to join the police. They brought with them the pride of the traditional warrior class and the skills of fencing—with real swords at that time—and jujitsu.[7] These origins account for the feeling within the police, shared by the public as well, that the use of guns is unfair, even cowardly. A "real man" fights hand-to-hand. Today, when policemen are attacked with knives or swords, they first try to disarm their opponent by using the nightstick. Senior officers have to urge their men to use their pistols more freely and not take undue risks.[8] Firearms are never to be used to stop the escape of a fleeing felon.[9]

The average Japanese policeman is smaller in stature relative to the general population than the average American policeman. A Japanese officer must be five feet three inches tall (160 centimeters) and 119 pounds in weight (54 kilograms); the average Japanese man is about five feet seven inches tall and weighs 130 pounds.[10] While the Japanese minima for recruitment of policemen are below the average for males generally in the population, police minima in the

7. Baron Kanetake Oura, "The Police of Japan," in Count Shigenobu Okima, *Fifty Years of New Japan* (London: Smith, Edder and Co., 1909), Vol. 2, pp. 292-293; Shuichi Sugai, "The Japanese Police System" in *Five Studies in Japanese Politics*, ed. Robert E. Ward (Ann Arbor: University of Michigan Press, 1957), p. 4; and E. H. Norman, *Japan's Emergence as a Modern State* (New York: Institute of Pacific Relations, 1940), p. 83.

8. Plainclothes policemen as well as some uniformed officers assigned to patrol cars carry an expandable club called a *tokusha-keibo* in place of a nightstick. It is worn on the belt and elongates at the flick of the wrist from seven to fifteen inches. Made of metal and quite heavy, it is a very effective weapon at close range.

9. The reluctance of the police to use guns in self-defense is in part a legal requirement. The law penalizes anyone for acts of self-defense in which the injury done is greater than that averted. Penal Code, Article 37. The police are subject to this provision except under conditions expressly set forth under the Police Duties Execution Law, Article 7.

10. Informaton on the size of Japanese men has been provided by the Consulate-General of Japan, San Francisco. The data are for males sixteen years old in 1972. Since growth is not complete at this age, I felt justified in adding a little bit. This information is sufficient to support the point since standards of physical size for policemen are under the average even for sixteen year olds, which is not the case in the United States.

United States tend to coincide with the average for all males. Until the early 1970s, when height requirements began to drop in many American police forces, the average minimum height was five feet eight or nine inches.[11] Since the average American man is five feet eight inches tall, policemen, by-and-large, are bigger than most men with whom they must deal.[12] Because weight varies with height, it follows that even without weight minima, policemen will also be bulkier than most men. It seems odd that the Japanese police, who stress hand-to-hand fighting, should recruit officers smaller in relation to the population among whom they work than American police forces, which encourage more free use of the pistol. There are probably two reasons for this peculiarity. First, an American policeman is supposed to be a "take charge guy," in the language of the police. Police authority in the United States must be visibly imposing. Second, guns are not the functional equivalent of physical bulk. Guns give an illusion of total security, but in fact they cannot be employed conscientiously in all situations where force is required. They are too deadly. Relying so much on the gun, American policemen have neglected training in hand-to-hand combat. When, therefore, they do have to fight, physical size is very important; they have to subdue their opponent by sheer heft. It is interesting to speculate that recruitment of smaller police officers in the United States might encourage development of hand-to-hand techniques and eventually lead to less reliance on guns. This may be one effect of increased recruitment of women as police officers.

Not only do Japanese policemen use guns less often than American policemen, they are involved in fewer instances of "police brutality" — excessive use of physical force.[13] There are several reasons for this.

First, because Japanese officers are rigorously trained in hand-to-hand combat, they are more discriminating in the use of physical force. They are able to draw on a greater variety of techniques for restraining and subduing violent people.

Second, excessive use of force most commonly involves people who have a marginal position in society, dwelling on the fringes of

11. Private correspondence with the Executive Director of the National Association of State Directors of Law Enforcement Training, 1974.

12. U.S. Department of Health, Education, and Welfare, Public Health Service, "Weight, Height, and Selected Body Dimensions of Adults, United States—1960-1962," in *Vital and Health Statistics* (Washington: GPO, SEries 11, number 8), pp. 26-27. This is the latest information available.

13. For the testimony of observers and figures on the number of complaints on this score, see Chapters 1 and 4.

respectability. This explains why police brutality in the United States occurs most frequently against racial minorities, homosexuals, derelicts, and hoodlums.[14] Japan has hardly any racial or ethnic minorities. Sexual deviance is viewed tolerantly and sexual molestation is rare.[15] The group that is most consistently subjected to excessive force, according to both police and civilian observers, is radical students, especially in connection with public demonstrations. In other words, marginality in Japan is almost solely a matter of ideology.

Third, a great deal of brutality results from anger triggered by displays of disrespect.[16] This is true in Japan as well as in the United States. In Japan, however, the amount of overt disrespect appears to be much less than in the United States. Police contacts with citizens are less confrontational; their penetration of the community is more routine and low-key.[17] It is significant that Japanese officers single out drunks as the primary offenders in this respect; apparently alcohol is needed to lower customary inhibitions against affronting a policeman. Japanese policemen are less brutal, in short, because there are fewer provocations.

Fourth, Japanese policemen appear to be less sensitive to expressions of disrespect than their American counterparts. American officers, in my experience, are less able than Japanese to absorb abuse calmly; they are easier to provoke. This is a curious conclusion since it is Japanese society that is portrayed as paying exaggerated attention to deference and respect. The capacity of policemen to withstand abuse is related, I suspect, to general levels of regard in which policemen are held. An American policeman defends his honor more swiftly because he perceives it as less secure. His self-esteem is more brittle than a Japanese officer's. If police brutality is related to public regard, then an element of circularity enters the relationship. Lowered public regard reduces police self-esteem, thereby making brutality more likely. But increased brutality lowers public regard, and so the pattern is given an additional spin.

14. Paul Chevigny, *Police Power* (New York: Random House, 1969), Chap. 7; Michael Banton, *The Policeman in the Community* (New York: Basic Books, 1964), p. 171.
15. See Chapter 6
16. Chevigny, Chap. 3; Banton, p. 171; Albert J. Reiss, Jr., *The Police and the Public* (New Haven: Yale University Press, 1971), p. 149.
17. George L. Kirkham, "A Professor's 'Street Lessons'," *F.B.I. Law Enforcement Bulletin* (March 1974), p. 7, discusses the hostility and abuse that policemen draw by the mere fact of being policemen.

Fifth, reserve and physical restraint are highly valued in Japanese society. Overt conflict is to be avoided even at the cost of severe emotional repression. A Japanese policeman who forebears to use physical force not only remains undamaged in his self-esteem, he believes he is more respected for doing so. By contrast, American policemen believe they cannot allow a challenge to go unmet. Backing down is cowardly.[18]

Sixth, demonstration of physical superiority is more important to American than Japanese policemen. American policemen act out physical strength in ways Japanese officers never do. Though Japanese policemen are skilled in hand-to-hand combat and maintain excellent condition, they hardly ever engage in physical posturing. They do not throw fake punches at one another, arm wrestle, or feint attacks as American policemen so commonly do. They do not move on the street with the swagger and heft of American policemen.[19] This is not to suggest that Japanese officers do not esteem manliness, rather that they do not display it in attitudes divorced from serious use of physical skills. Reserve is again the key: concealed prowess is more impressive to the Japanese than vaunted prowess. To some extent, therefore, American policemen are overbearing because they believe it is expected of them. This may explain the finding in a recent study that women patrol officers had significantly fewer incidents of violent arrests than male officers.[20] Between a female police officer and a male offender the thought of proving themselves through physical strength simply does not arise.[21]

18. Wambaugh, pp. 17-18, portrays American policemen as believing they must prove themselves physically in order to win respect. One character—a policeman— says: "A beat cop has to be big or he'll be fighting all the time. Sometimes a tough, feisty little cop resents it because he can't walk a foot beat, but the fact is that most people don't fear a little guy and a little guy'd just have to prove himself all the time, and sooner or later somebody'd take that nightstick off him and shove it up his ass." Studies have shown that short policemen fight more often and are more violent than tall officers. Hans Toch, "Reducing Violence in the Criminal Justice System" (Speech delivered to the Northwest Conference on Violence and Criminal Justice, 7 December 1973), p. 4.

19. See Chapter 3.

20. Peter Bloch, *Policewomen on Patrol* (Washington: The Police Foundation, 1973).

21. In an excellent study of factors contributing to violence in the police, Hans Toch (p. 5) lists three factors: (a) allowance rules—norms within the police that ensure that an officer will not be reported by a colleague; (b) work norms, having to do with the status of a police officer, such as "you only give an order once," "wise guys need to be taught a lesson," "clobber people who are disrespectful"; and (c) norms in specialized subgroups of the police, such as tactical and stake-out squads,

The fastidiousness of the Japanese police with respect to the use of force is enormously facilitated by social context. Japan is an almost totally disarmed society. Registration is required for all firearms, knives, and swords.[22] No handguns are permitted in private hands, even registered, with the exception of people who participate in international shooting competitions.[23] In effect, the prohibition against handguns in private hands is total because people who do compete internationally—some seven or eight persons—are members of the police or the Self-Defense Forces.[24] Shotguns and small-caliber rifles are permitted for hunting. There were thirty-seven thousand registered rifles and about six hundred thousand registered shotguns in 1971.[25] In the United States there are at a conservative estimate 100 million guns in private hands, at least 25 million of them handguns.[26] The latent demand for firearms in Japan appears to be very small. Only a handful of cases of illegal possession occur each year—on the average about six hundred involving pistols and nine hundred involving long-guns.[27] The number of violations for illegal possession of swords and knives is larger but still small: about eight thousand violations a year, with an equal number of persons arrested and weapons seized.[28]

The tradition of a disarmed society is almost four hundred years old. Severe restrictions on private ownership of guns, swords, and

---

whose pride is based on being tougher and stronger than anyone else. The last two factors are much less evident among Japanese policemen. Reserve is highly prized and the norms of specialized squads, such as the riot police, are—as we shall see below—that excessive force is to be eschewed regardless of provocation.

22. This includes rivet guns, rope-discharging guns, and signal guns for athletic games. Law Controlling Possession, Etc., of Fire-arms and Swords, Article 3, clause 8 (Law No. 6, March 1958). Swords and knives over six inches in length or with blades that automatically extend by mechanical action are prohibited except under permit.

23. Article 4.

24. The "Self-Defense Forces" are Japan's military.

25. Figures provided by the National Police Agency in a mimeographed paper entitled "Gun, Rifle, and Sword Control in Japan." Permits for owning weapons are issued by prefectural Public Safety Commissions. The maximum penalty provided for violation of the gun law is seven years in prison.

26. National Commission on the Causes and Prevention of Violence, *Firearms and Violence in American Life* (Washington: Government Printing Office, 1970), p. 6. Estimates are for 1968. A Harris Poll conducted for the Commission in 1968 found that half the households in the U.S. had some sort of firearm.

27. "Gun, Rifle, and Sword Control in Japan."

28. *Ibid.* In 1971 there were about fifteen thousand registered swords and knives in private hands.

knives began with the famous "Sword Hunting Order" of Toyotomi Hideyoshi in 1588.[29] The only exception was made for samurai, the traditional warrior class who formed about 7 percent of the population. In 1876 this last vestige of a right to own weapons privately was eliminated, causing great bitterness among the samurai for whom the wearing of swords was a distinctive mark of identity. A last great sword hunt was ordered by the American Occupation authorities in 1945-1946, a part of their plan to shatter the martial traditions of Japan. Today there is not the slightest movement for a relaxation of the weapons' law.

The use of firearms in crime in Japan is negligible. Each year less than 150 crimes involve guns.[30] Out of approximately 80,000 serious offenses committed in Tokyo in 1971,[31] only *sixteen* involved the use of handguns.[32] In the United States, on the other hand, about 65 percent of all murders (11,500 instances)[33] are committed with firearms; 25 percent of all aggravated assaults (91,000 instances); and 41 percent of all robberies (154,000 instances).[34] The uncertainty, anxiety, and honest fear that American policemen experience in making street contacts or responding to summonses for assistance are totally unfamiliar to the Japanese police. Less than five officers are killed feloniously each year, and hardly ever by firearms. In the United States over a hundred officers are killed each year, three-quarters of them by handguns.[35]

The killing of a policeman causes a good deal more shock and outrage in Japan than in the United States. In part this is because police deaths are simply more common in the United States; emotion has been blunted by familiarity. It is also traceable to a basic difference in solicitude felt for the police by the people of each country, a difference that may be directly related to guns. Americans accept the killing of police officers by guns as an occupational

29. *Ibid.*, p. 1.
30. Committee on Comprehensive Countermeasures, *Interim Report* (Tokyo: National Police Agency, 1970), p. 55. In 1970, 140; in 1969, 99; in 1968, 99.
31. Murder, nonnegligent manslaughter, robbery, forcible rape, burglary, and assault.
32. Yorihika Kumasaka, Robert J. Smith, and Hitoshi Aiba, "Crimes in New York and Tokyo: Sociological Perspectives" (Unpublished paper, 1972), pp. 4-5.
33. These figures are approximate because they are the product of a percentage calculation.
34. *Crime in the U.S.—1971*, pp. 8, 12, 15. For further information see *Firearms and Violence in American LIfe*, Chap. 7.
35. Between 1967 and 1971, 428 officers were killed by firearms. F.B.I., "Law Enforcement Officers Killed in the Line of Duty," p. 2.

hazard, understood by anyone who joins the police. Americans apply implicit rules of fairness to judgments about armed confrontations between police and criminals. Some deaths are considered outrageous, but others are not. As long as the criminal does not take unfair advantage—an ambush, for example—casualties are lamentable but not unacceptable. In Japan, though, where private possession of guns is illicit by long tradition, any armed killing of a policeman is shocking. Death by firearms is not a risk policemen should be asked to face.

It is clearly unrealistic to expect any police force to disarm if the populace at large is allowed to possess substantial quantities of firearms.[36] At the same time, willingness of the police to use firearms may affect the way guns are viewed by society. Specifically, the fact that police accept the inevitability of armed confrontations with offenders may reduce pressure for more stringent gun-control laws. Consider, for instance, what would happen if American police officials publicly announced their commitment to strict gun-control legislation and then announced they would disarm themselves, as an example of how safe society really is most of the time. The immediate reaction, of course, would be astonishment and incredulity. The long-run effect would be to make the killing of policemen wanton acts. If policemen were unarmed and then killed, the implicit norms of fairness would be violated. They wouldn't have a chance. The public would have greater difficulty than now in denying responsibility for protecting police officers. Support for strict enforcement of penalties against guns in crime would stiffen, as would pressure for gun-control legislation. Guns in police hands and guns in private hands are related. But there is more symmetry in the relationship that is usually recognized. The police will feel compelled to be armed as long as much of the populace is. But the populace may not limit arms ownership without persistent encouragement from the police, especially willingness to sacrifice some of the appearance of self-reliance. The police probably possess more initiative than they are willing to exercise.

Opponents of gun-control legislation in the United States generally couch their arguments in terms of self-defense, the necessity for private citizens to be able to fend off actual attacks or deter

---

36. T.A. Critchley, *The Conquest of Violence: Order and Liberty in Britain* (London: Constable, 1970), p. 8, argues that the "Bobby" is disarmed today because he was created in 1929 when British society was generally without firearms. If he had been created in Tudor times, Critchley argues, he would be armed today.

potential ones. Though Americans are less willing than the Japanese to share policing responsibilities with the police,[37] they argue for possession of arms in exactly the same terms as policemen. They argue as if they were as exposed to danger as policemen. As in the vigilante tradition, every man in the United States thinks of himself as his own policeman. Paradoxically, while they delegate responsibility for maintaining social order to the police, they refuse to allow the police to monopolize force so that they might be effective in discharging it. Rather than seeking to diminish the violence of crime by prohibiting the possession of weapons, Americans insist on maintaining the option of fighting fire with fire, guns with guns. They seem to recognize that police are necessary but fear both their efficiency and their inefficiency, and so create a situation in which the level of violence in any criminal activity is increased.

Though policemen most of the time do not face great danger, the possibility is a real one in the United States and it dominates perceptions of what a policeman must be prepared to do. The possibility of armed confrontation shapes training, patrol preoccupations, and operating procedures. It also shapes the relationship between citizen and policeman by generating mutual apprehension. The policeman can never forget that the individual he contacts may be armed and dangerous; the citizen can never forget that the police is armed and may consider the citizen dangerous. Such expectations are not universal in the world. The Japanese do not have them, nor the British. It is not the way things have to be.

It is exceedingly doubtful that the United States will cease to be unique among modern industrial societies with respect to the private possession of firearms; it is also very unlikely that the police will play a formative role by way of example in changing public opinion on the issue. If these predictions come true, Americans must recognize that they are locked into a particular pattern of relationships between police and society. Though they may deplore it, gun possession by private citizens increases the danger to the police, diminishes the solicitude with which the police are regarded, enhances mutual dread, and makes any contact between policeman and citizen more confrontational than it might otherwise be. Though Americans may like to pretend otherwise, guns have consequences.

The picture of Japan as an unusually peaceable society which rarely threatens the safety of policemen is flawed in a very persistent

37. See Chap. 5.

and serious way. Collective expressions of defiance — riots, protests, demonstrations — are common and fierce. Thousands and occasionally hundreds of thousands of people have gathered to indicate disenchantment with government policy. Snake-dancing mobs have disrupted traffic, occupied railway stations, destroyed property, and burned trucks and automobiles. Buildings have been forcibly occupied, officials held hostage, and terror tactics employed against the police. Revision of the U.S.-Japan Security Treaty in 1960 and restoration of diplomatic relations with South Korea caused months of turmoil. In 1968, when student violence was increasing sharply, there were thirty-nine major incidents involving over half a million people and resulting in the arrest of almost four thousand; in 1969 there were eighty-eight incidents involving a million two-hundred thousand persons resulting in the arrest of almost eight thousand.[38] A year later there were over five thousand separate riotous incidents or demonstrations for which 329,000 police had to be mobilized.[39] In short, the kind of events that so disturbed Americans during the anti-Vietnam War movement have been a fixture of postwar politics in Japan. In the glare of burning gasoline, the gloom of smoke, and the stench of tear gas, the Japanese police have had to cope repeatedly with what amount to small well-organized wars.

When the police deploy to handle riots and demonstrations they deliberately disarm themselves. Rather than breaking out new and more deadly forms of weaponry, as American police do, they take off their pistols and leave them in the police station. They do carry nightsticks, which are worn on the belt unless explicit orders for their use are given.[40] Though the battles fought by police and demonstrators have been ferocious, involving rocks, wooden clubs, and molotov cocktails, only 4 demonstrators have been killed in over twenty years, 3 of them through inadvertent actions of their colleagues.[41] The police have had 9 killed since 1967 and many injured.[42] In the United States many more people have been killed

38. Tokyo Metropolitan Police Department, Kidotai, Second Mobile Unit, *990 Days of Turmoil* (Privately printed, 1971). This volume of pictures and commentary is devoted to incidents of riotous demonstration between 8 November 1967 and 23 June 1970.
39. Data furnished by the National Police Agency, 1971.
40. In extremely dangerous situations, special squads may be equipped with rifles or pistols, as at Asama-Sanso or Narita Airport, but these occasions are rare.
41. Bill Hosokawa, "Japan's Patient Riot Police," *Reader's Digest* (January 1971), pp. 82-86. Confirmed by letters with police officials. One demonstrator was trampled by the crowd, another was run over by a police vehicle stolen by a confederate, and another died of burns from a molotov cocktail.
42. Private letter quoting N.P.A. data from 1967 to the fall of 1973.

in a much shorter period of time. Between 1967 and 1973, 233 persons were killed in civil disturbances, not all by police action.[43]

In place of guns, Japanese police handle riotous crowds with substantial bodies of elaborately trained, highly disciplined men operating with massed precision and supported by specialized equipment. During protest marches riot police three and four deep will force demonstrators against the guardrails separating sidewalk and roadway. A file of police will match each file of protestors, linking arms with them so as to maintain contact. At intersections the demonstrators are prevented from straying from the approved line of march by a corridor of riot police, the front lines holding aluminum shields four feet high. When demonstrators are milling, surging back and forth, the police stand shoulder to shoulder, three and four deep, and move left, right, forward, and backward on command, pushing with their hands to bar passage. Night demonstrations are illuminated by huge xenon lights mounted on extensible mobile towers. Riot police commanders watch the scene from elevated platforms on top of sophisticated communications vehicles. In the shadows of side streets wait riot-troop transporters mounted with water cannon. If a demonstration becomes violent, riot police move against the crowd in solid ranks fronted by glinting shields. Nets on high poles are held in front of the advancing ranks to catch missiles thrown from the crowd. At a signal the nets are lifted high in the air and riot police charge forward uttering a terrifying war-whoop. If tear gas must be used, the ranks part to allow special squads to pass forward and disperse the mob. During a slow advance the police shelter behind steel-mesh screens attached to small tractors. Barricades can be made out of the oblong vans used to transport the riot police. Sallies are made from behind them under cover of jets of water, smoke, or tear gas.

Riot police are elaborately outfitted in midnight blue combat uniforms set off by white gloves and scarves. The basic uniform is an American-style combat field jacket worn with baggy paratrooper trousers tucked into high-top combat boots. The jacket covers several pieces of body-armor: a corselet hanging from the waist, an aluminum plate down the backbone, and small shoulder pads. Armored gauntlets are worn over the jacket shaped to fit forearms and the back of the hands. To protect their heads riot policemen wear plastic helmets with a flaring padded skirt down the back of the neck. A clear plastic faceplate is hinged to the top of the helmet

43. The proportion killed by the police is not known. *Statistical Abstract of the United States*, 1973, p. 148.

so that it can be swung on top when not in use. The armored uniform weighs 14.5 pounds and the individual aluminum shield about 12 pounds. A policeman must be in excellent condition to operate effectively for long periods of time. Altogether the visual effect of uniform and equipment is somber and awesome. The police look like automata out of a science-fiction movie.

Riot operations have a decidedly medieval quality about them. Shield-equipped riot police are the equivalent of infantry, while behind them are massed artillery in the form of water cannon and smoke-dispensers mounted on trucks. Mechanized cavalry are provided by armored cars, carrying water cannons, and personnel carriers. Trucks with folding booms are used as mobile siege towers to shoot water or tear gas into occupied buildings. The long transport vans have been constructed with doors in the middle of square-cut front and rear so that they can be parked end to end to form protected tunnels for penetrating occupied buildings. The resemblance to premodern warfare is not simply a matter of equipment. Demonstrators and police operate in close-order formations marshalled by commanders with whistles and portable loudspeakers. Skirmish lines and defensive squares are formed. Both sides send units out in flanking movements and make charges and countercharges. Demonstrators tend to be fleeter of foot than the police, like barbarian tribesmen against armored knights. They dress in jeans and T-shirts, sometimes light jackets, protected only by brightly colored helmet liners marked with the symbols of their group. Towels, usually moistened, are worn over mouth and nostrils. Leaders on both sides, say police experts, study manuals on medieval warfare. Police and demonstrators train extensively in order to maintain in battle the compacted bulk that gives confrontations their deadly earnestness. Over the dull roar of a mob shrill the high-pitched whistles of opposing commanders, sounding like the trilling of demented birds. Several hundred people locked in a dense mass generate enormous momentum; they become a ponderous human battering-ram, irresistible unless opposed by an equal mass and dangerous to policeman, partisan, or spectator who falls in the way. When these ranks are fronted with squared lances several feet long, they crash against the massed shields of the police with tremendous force.

Riot tactics and equipment, on both sides, have undergone a process of evolution. The uniform of riot policemen originally consisted of fatigue clothes and army helmets. The visored helmet was not introduced until the mid-1960s. The tactic of "sandwiching" demonstrators against curb-guardrails was perfected about the same time. Student demonstrators wore helmets for the first time in 1966.[44] Offensive arms among demonstrators at first were only stones and concrete ripped up from the street plus ordinary sticks. By the late 1960s the sticks had become heavy squared staves and bamboo lances several feet long. Gasoline-filled bottles — molotov cocktails — were thrown at police for the first time in 1967. In 1970 there was an even more ominous escalation in weaponry: several homemade bombs were used against riot-police formations and a few demonstrators began to carry light homemade pistols, what Americans would call "zip-guns." Just as the intervention of gunpowder shattered conventional tactics in Europe several centuries ago, so the introduction of guns and explosives threatened to revolutionize contemporary agitational confrontations. The implicit tactical agreement that had existed throughout the 1950s and 1960s, whereby serious injuries had been minimized, seemed on the verge of being destroyed. The mood among police officials was somber indeed. They began to armor-plate their vehicles, as well as the individual aluminum shields, and develop defensive tactics against bombs. But the radicals, sensing perhaps the unpredictability of "modernizing" traditonal weaponry, pulled back from the escalation. Since late 1972 the former agreement on armament appears to have been reestablished. How brittle it is remains to be seen. The continued existence of relatively stable rules of the game, especially in the face of gunpowder, highlights the stylized quality of confrontations between police and protestors. Confrontations, though potentially deadly, are not normless. Police and protestors recognize limits; they are bound by an unspoken code that constrains both sides.

The disciplined nonlethal response of the police to riots and demonstrations has been made possible by the establishment of permanent companies of policemen specially selected and trained for riot duty. These units are known as the "Kidotai."[45] Created in response to the May Day riots of 1952, the Kidotai now number approximately 10,000 men throughout the country. The largest contingent — 5,200 — is in Tokyo.[46] Recruits to the Kidotai are selected from regular police personnel with one year active experience. They must be physically strong, adept in judo or kendo, and poised under pressure. Riot work is not popular and though some men volunteer, most are selected. Because of the physical demands,

44. Information furnished by the Tokyo Metropolitan Police Department, 1973.
45. Pronounced "key-doe-tie."
46. National Police Agency, *The Police of Japan,* 1971, p. 59.

Kidotai personnel tend to be young. It would be unusual to assign a man to the rank-and-file of the Kidotai after the age of thirty. There are also "reserve" riot police composed of officers assigned to police stations who have already served in the Kidotai or who have received riot-training in a series of short courses. In this way the strength of the permanent companies may be increased in an emergency by about one-third. In American terms, the Japanese police are their own National Guard, though they are much more extensively trained for riot work than the National Guard. Except for a few "tactical" squads in large cities, American police mobilize entirely from reserves. And, unlike the Japanese, they form comparatively untried units; they are not fitted into seasoned, tightly knit formations. If the Japanese police are unable to restore order, civil authorities may ask for help from the Self-Defense Forces. There has never been an occasion to do so.

Kidotai units live a self-contained existence very much like life in a military cantonment. Each unit, which is composed of four hundred men, has its own administrative offices, drill fields, maintenance facilities, kitchen and dining hall, gymnasium, barber shop, store, and bachelor officers' dormitory. Each unit maintains its own transport and support vehicles, including water cannon.[47] Training is constant, focusing on physical conditioning, close-order drills, and command exercises. Calisthenics and a three kilometer run (about 1.8 miles) are mandatory each day. So well-conditioned do the men become and so extensive is judo and kendo training that Kidotai units are not allowed to compete against ordinary police personnel. Mock battles are staged complete with molotov cocktails and simulated explosives in which policemen assume the role of demonstrators. Command officers participate in war games in the field as well as at their bases. Tactical problems are posed on large maps and counters are moved in accordance with orders received over two-way radios from various levels of command personnel. A military atmosphere is more pronounced in the Kidotai than the regular police: salutes are snappier, dress code more rigidly enforced, and rank differentiations more formal. Ceremonies punctuate the routine. Personnel sent out on assignment are applauded as they leave the cantonment and senior officers are formally welcomed to the mess hall at meal time. Commanders say that it takes recruits as much as half a year to adapt to the discipline and punctilio of Kidotai life. Because

47. Tokyo also has a "Special-Duty Vehicle Unit," formed in 1969, which acts in support of foot-Kidotai units.

demonstrations are episodic, life in the riot police is largely a matter of drill and training. Boredom is a considerable problem for commanders; they must think of ways of enlivening the routine so the men will not go stale. Most units hold regular classes designed to prepare men for promotion examinations. These classes are a powerful inducement, especially for young patrolmen, to serve a tour with the Kidotai. Because of the physical demands, discipline, and boredom most men stay in the riot police for only two or three years. Commanders view regular infusions of new recruits as beneficial since it prevents the Kidotai from becoming too ingrown and the men too long out of touch with ordinary police work. Riot policemen are encouraged to think of themselves as regular police officers — which they must be before they join — called upon temporarily to do a specialized job.

The Kidotai perform other duties besides dealing with crowds. They are trained in rescue work and giving assistance during natural disasters. They guard embassies, government buildings, jails, and visiting dignitaries. If the need arises, they are assigned to supplement police station personnel in carrying out routine work. For example, they may be asked to patrol areas where particularly vicious crimes have occurred, to set up traffic control points, and to gather intelligence on radical groups.[48]

The ability of the riot police to cope with provocative demonstrations without recourse to firearms is the product of tight discipline, close supervision, and group support. A riot policeman never faces a mob alone; he is always surrounded by friends, usually as many as seventy, which is the complement of the standard company.[49] Kidotai training stresses group action, especially the importance of defending one's fellows. Individual action is anathema. Riot policemen always work under the direction of familiar leaders. Supervisory officers are distributed throughout the formations. Each squad of nine men is commanded by a sergeant, and even in the three-men kumi one man is designated as the leader. Each Kidotai member carries a breast-pocket radio receiver with an earpiece built into his helmet, so that commands may be given simultaneously to everyone even amid the din of a demonstration. Commanding

48. In 1971 somewhat over one-fifth of the duty-time of Kidotai units throughout Japan was occupied in these ways. Information furnished by the National Police Agency.
49. A Kidotai unit of 400 men is composed of four companies, each with 70 men; each company has three platoons, each platoon three squads and each squad three kumi. The balance of the personnel are assigned to support functions. A kumi is a three-man unit. It is used independently only for reconnaisance.

officers continually assess the balance between experienced and inexperienced officers in each unit. Even in a kumi, at least one experienced man must be present as a stiffener.[50]

Kidotai commanders continually try to instill pride not in fierceness, which is real enough, but in poise under stress. The primary injunction for the Kidotai is the avoidance of injury on both sides. Nonetheless, cases of excessive use of force occasionally do arise. Sometimes individuals are transferred to other work because their tempers are too quick. Discipline is tried to the breaking point when men who are hot, tired, and often hungry, are forced to remain passive in the face of abusive taunts and physical attacks. When such units are finally allowed to charge, the release of pent up emotion can submerge sound judgment about how hard to strike members of the crowd. The command dilemmas for senior officers are acute. If units have been responsive to command and restrained under provocations, it is hard for a commander to discipline his men too severely unless excesses are particularly serious. After all, the rules of the game are known to both sides. Kidotai members harbor deeper resentment against some antagonists than others. Feelings about radical students are especially intense, partly because the causes the students espouse seem to policemen to be excessively abstract. A trade union demonstration is at least directed toward issues of immediate human wellbeing. Kidotai also know from long experience that students are more violent than others. And there may be some class hostility between Kidotai and students. While both are about the same age, their prospects in life are very different. The students are Japan's elite-in-the-making; they have the kind of educational opportunities every policeman wishes he had but few will ever obtain.

By remaining restrained in the face of violent demonstrations and terrorist bombing attacks, the police have succeeded in shifting the cloak of innocence from the radicals to themselves. The police are no longer viewed as repressors but as victims of radical ferocity. Live television coverage of two incidents helped considerably—the Asama-Sanso siege and the occupation of Yasuda Hall at Tokyo University in 1969. Public support for police activity against demonstrators and against radicals generally is acutally higher now than before the cresendo of agitational activity in the late 1960s and

50. The neglect of group support in riot situations in the United States has been noted by former police chief James Ahern, *Police in Trouble* (New York: Hawthorne Books Inc., 1972), Chap. 2. The innovations in crowd control made in New Haven by Chief Ahern and his staff in preparation for the May Day events in 1970 followed very closely the Japanese experience, though fortuitously.

early 1970s.[51] Since 1968 the press has become noticeably more critical of student demonstrations.[52] Kidotai commanders say that their men used to hide their affiliation but now proudly admit it; they are even given free drinks in bars. The opprobrium of being the aggressor has shifted to the radical side. A vivid indication of this are the signs mounted twelve feet tall in front of Tokyo police stations designated them as "Headquarters for the Control of Radical Left-Wing Groups." The police are able to solicit information publicly to help them deal with the radicals.[53] Police relations with the student community remain touchy, however, more so in Tokyo than elsewhere. Some university campuses are for all intents and purposes off-limits to uniformed patrolmen. If serious crimes occur there requiring investigation, plainclothesmen are sent, and even they often seek authorization from university officials. Wire mesh has been hung down the face of a university building in Tokyo adajacent to a police station to prevent students from pelting the courtyard with debris. Some kobans keep buckets of water handy to smother incendiary bombs; all are alert for intruders with packages. In Tokyo all police stations as well as administrative buildings have guards posted at the entrances.

The response of the Japanese police to violence contains an interesting lesson with respect to the relation between tactics and hardware. In Japan choices about tactics have been made prior to choices about hardware. For example, the police have decided to minimize casualties in riots. They have disarmed their riot police and developed ingenious formations, drills, and equipment to contain riotous demonstrations. In the United States, hardward determines tactics. If the American police had been called to Asama-Sanso, is it likely they would have waited ten days before storming the villa? And when they did, would they have used a wrecking ball? The existence of certain kinds of equipment, especially if they are econmical and overwhelming in power, can stifle

51. Public Opinion (*Gekkan Seron Chosa*), (December 1972). In the June 1972 public opinion poll, only 3 percent of the sample thought the police too active against radicals; 77 percent thought they were doing right and could be even more vigorous. With respect to the kidotai, only 5 percent criticized them for being too hard on demonstrators, compared to 7 percent who felt that way in 1969. Thirty-four percent thought the Kidotai were performing exactly as they should; 11 percent thought they needed to be tougher.
52. Richard Halloran, *Japan* (New York: Alfred A. Knopf, 1969), p. 127.
53. One reason that Japanese radicals have been cropping up with increasing frequency abroad may be that the climate has become too uncongenial for them at home. A cooperative public and diligent police have created a new Japanese export — radical youth.

the search for alternative approaches. For American policemen, the shortest distance to most solutions is through existing technology.

Two items of hardware in particular have played an unusually formative role in the development of American police tactics — the revolver and the automobile. A gun is indispensable to American policemen. A disarmed policeman is almost a contradiction in terms. The American attachment to the gun regardless of need is beautifully demonstrated by the policy pursued by the Occupation authorities in Japan after World War II. An explicit goal of the Occupation was to create an assertive self-reliant population that could not be overawed by authoritarian government. Nonetheless, General MacArthur, over the objections of the Japanese themselves, ordered all policemen to carry pistols for the first time in history.[54] Though the American authorities said they were dedicated to the establishment of democratic institutions in Japan, they put instruments of deadly force into the hands of the police. They destroyed the grip of the military on national life, but not the monopoly of force possessed by the government. Occupation officals must have reasoned that since the United States was democratic and its police were armed, democracy and arms were not incompatible.[55] The episode demonstrates an important lesson in the relations among nations: advice given by one country to another about social development is likely to be affected more by what is done at home than what is required abroad.

The automobile is the second item of hardware that has shaped American police procedures more than Japanese. The Japanese, disdaining the economies of the patrol car, kept a vision of the social function of police posts. They realized that there were dividends in approachability, trust, and cooperation to be gained through kobans. American police operations have become totally dependent on patrol cars, and the importance of neighborhood contacts through beat patrolmen and "store-front" police posts is having to be rediscovered.

54. SCAP, "Police and Public Safety," pp. 59-61. See also Harry Emerson Wildes, "The Postwar Japanese Police," *Journal of Criminal Law, Criminology, and Police Science* (January-February 1953), p. 660. The order was made in 1946. In 1948, discovering that few policemen had become armed in fact, American military authorities undertook to supply weapons and ammunition.

55. In fairness to SCAP it should be noted that a study in 1947 showed that violence from firearms was increasing. Casualties among the police in 1947 were over twice as high as just before the surrender and six times as high as in prewar years. At the same time, the Japanese police authorities did not recommend being armed and thought the American move unwise. SCAP, "Police and Public Safety," p. 60.

In general, Americans are readier than Japanese to adopt exclusively technological solutions to police problems. Their search for solutions begins rather than ends with examination of equipment. The standard advice that American police consultants give abroad is that equipment must be modernized.[56] A foreign police force is thought to be primitive if it does not have automatic data-processing machines, patrol cars, radios, and the latest forensic equipment. Since the United States is one of the world's most advanced industrial nations, it follows that there is little for American policemen to learn abroad. American consultants tend to ignore the human procedures for dealing with people, or they dismiss them as being culturally unique—what works for them wouldn't work for us. The tendency of American policemen to regard hardware as a short-cut out of most difficulties may be more than an occupational peculiarity. It may be a matter of national temperment. Many scholar have noted that the Japanese succeeded in preserving various primary social structures despite headlong industrialization over the past century.[57] This may be one reason why crime rates are not rising as rapidly as in other industrial nations. Though the Japanese are technologically progressive, they appear—certainly in the realm of police activity—to have less faith in technology's creations than Americans.

In confronting rising levels of interpersonal violence, nations behave in very different ways—characteristically different ways. Americans, for example, are peculiarly passive in terms of an organized collective response. The threat of violence is met individually, a private act of self-defense. One reason for the failure of Americans to search for the social roots of contemporary violence is the popular notion that the present is the inevitable result of a unique process of historical development. The West, the "frontier tradition," are seen as the source of current difficulties. It is interesting that Rapp Brown's famous statement that violence is as American as apple pie was accepted so easily. It became dogma overnight, assisted to some extent by a national commission on violence.[58] Blaming the past is comforting because it relieves people of responsibility for what they have become. The past is unchangeable

56. For example, William H. Parker, *Report to the Ministry of Home Affairs of the Government of India Through the United States A.I.D. Mission to India* (typescript, *circa* 1964). At the time, Parker was Chief of the Los Angeles Police Department.
57. R.P. Dore, *City Life in Japan* (Berkeley: University of California Press, 1958), Chap. 24.
58. President's Commission on the Causes and Prevention of Violence.

and inescapable. But blaming the past for present-day violence is a terrible oversimplification. Again Japan provides a fascinating comparison. Japanese history is every bit as bloodsoaked as American and its present tainted by violent traditions. For centuries justice was meted out on the basis of class; until a hundred years ago a samurai had the right to cut down with a sword any peasant who insulted him. Executions for crime were quick and brutal. There was and still is a cult of the sword similar to that of the gun in the United States. Martial values and regimen, which Americans tend to deprecate, have been extolled in Japan for generations. Political assassinations have been far more common in Japanese history than American. Since 1945 seven political leaders have been killed or injured in terrorist attacks.[59] Over thirty-five plans for assassination have become known to the police each of the last fifteen years, most being stopped in very early stages.[60] Both countries fought civil wars at approximately the same time. Though the bloodletting was less extensive in the Japanese case, the parochial loyalties overcome were probably more intense. Samurai dramas are a staple of Japanese television as westerns are in the United States. The sword-wielding warrior, especially if he has turned outlaw, fascinates popular culture.[61] Violence on television, on which many American ills are blamed, appears to be as prevalent in Japan as in the United States.[62] Guns fascinate in Japan as they do in the United States. Toy guns are popular items in department stores and replicas of modern pistols have sold widely in recent years. Indeed, they are so exact that sale has been banned.[63]

59. Information provided by the National Police Agency.

60. *Ibid.*

61. George A. De Vos and Keiichi Mizushima, "Organization and Social Function of Japanese Gangs: HIstorical Development and Modern Parallels," in *Aspects of Social Change in Modern Japan*, ed. R. P. Dore (Princeton: Princeton University Press, 1967), p. 319, believe that outlaws in both countries are "symbols of unfettered masculinity and freedom of initiative, even violence, with societies in which outlets are less directly available than most."

62. Albert Axelbank, *Black Star Over Japan* (London: Allen and Unwin, 1972), pp. 21-22, refers to a study by a member of the Diet in 1971 reporting that between eight and nine o'clock in the evening one Sunday, forty-two persons had been either stabbed or cut. In three hours, starting at 6 P.M., there were 509 beatings, shootings, and fights. If this seems a lot, it is partly attributable to the greater number of TV channels than is usually the case in the United States.

63. The law became effective 1 October 1971. Dealers complied with the letter of the law by painting the guns gold to detract from verisimilitude and blocking the barrels. However, repainting and minor adjustments make the replicas functional, and several cases have come to police notice.

Generalizations about the amount of violence in a nation's past and contemporary attachment of people to that portion of the past are necessarily very impressionistic. But both aspects are sufficiently similar between the United States and Japan to raise doubts about whether the amount of violence in the American past should be considered an important cause of today's crime rates. The United States has a violent past and high crime rates in the present; Japan has a violent past and low crime rates in the present. Japan has a violent past and within living men's memories political assassination was epidemic. The United States has a violent past and political assassination is rare. The point that these comparisons make is that violence assumes many forms. It is a category that can be differentiated. Thus martial arts are not incompatible with gun control; denigration of the soldier is not incompatible with gun cults. Legitimation of suicide is not assoiciated with a high incidence of murder. Television violence does not inevitably contaminate a nation's children. If the United States has high crime rates today, it is not because the past was violent but because it was violent in particular ways. Similarly, if Japan has low crime rates today, it is because social sanctions today effectively contain major forms of criminal violence, not because Japan did not have violence in its past.

Just as societies get to like and to consider normal their own kinds of political rights and institutions, so they get to like and consider normal their own kinds of violence. The fact that a nation has had a violent past, in some sense, should not be used to excuse violent crime in the present. What must be done is to determine the particular sinuosities of a country's culture that encourage some forms of violence and discourage others.

In meeting the challenge of violence between persons, American police institutions are hampered by a faith in hardware and a belief that change is impossible apart from radical reform in the larger society. American policemen deny themselves an active role in shaping society, befitting their conception of the proper role of agents of representative government, and they fail to perceive the consequences of technological choices. They often contend they are victims of circumstances beyond their control. If they are, it is because they have surrendered to them. They are, after all, American.

9.The Nation and the Police

A police force is more than an organization; it is an institution. It exists within a larger human community whose customary views about what is appropriate shape what the organization does. These views constitute a police force's normative environment, and they vary from society to society. So do the mechanisms whereby a community imposes its vision on the police. In some places the community regulates certain aspects of police behavior directly; in others only diffuse social controls operate. This too is a matter of institutional tradition. Policemen themselves are children of the community. They share inherited views about what is proper for police to do, though their views are sometimes modified as a result of experience within the organization. In order to understand why a police force behaves in distinctive ways, it is essential to examine what the community by tradition expects the police to be. In short, what are the traditions of a community with respect to the relations of the police with the community?

The institutional traditions of the police in Japan and the United States differ substantially with respect to three key features of any social organization—namely, its role, structure, and mode of external regulation. I shall examine each of these in turn, searching for what is distinctive in the institutional constraints on the police in each country.

The role which the Japanese police are expected to play in society is much more ramified and less well defined than the American. While fundamental to the role of both is maintenance of order and the curbing of deviance, they have contasting relations to processes of explicit social change. The Japanese police are expected to assist actively in inculcating values entailed by the community's vision of what it wants to be. They have a teaching function as well as a legal brief. Japanese police have a positive orientation toward the polity. American police, on the other hand, have a negative orientation. They are not viewed as an active agency shaping social development. At best their function is prophylactic, to maintain conditions suitable to the performance of formative acts by others. A diffuse role in politics is anathema; the only civic lesson they can reinforce is the importance of remaining passively within the injunctions of law, in effect, of being apolitical.

There have been two formative periods in the development of the modern Japanese police — the Meiji Restoration, especially the years 1872 to 1889, and the Allied Occupation, 1945-1952. In both periods, police development was informed by a clear vision of political objectives. Meiji statesmen saw the police as an instrument for creating a new nation. Along with schools, courts, and military, the police were to be used to mold feudal Japan into a strong nation respected in the world. In addition to maintaining law and order, the police were to embody national ideals and instruct the people in the new political vision.[1] Speeches of police officials at the time are filled with words like "spirit," "dedication," and "virtue."[2] American police forces, assuming modern form also in the nineteenth century, were created to deal with quite specific law enforcement problems — urban riots, drunkenness, especially among immigrant groups, hooliganism, prostitution, and gambling. State police forces too, which began to be developed in the early twentieth century, were not created as part of a new political dispensation but to enforce state laws that local communities were neglecting.[3] Instruction in civic lessons has historically been left to school teachers and to politicians. All that Americans expected of their police was vigorous and honest enforcement of the law.

The Allied Occupation after World War II also reformed the Japanese police in accordance with an explicit political vision. Like the Meiji statesmen before them, Occupation officials were determined to change the political orientation of the Japanese people and they saw the police as an instrument for this purpose. The police were to be one of several demonstration projects in democracy.

1. Shuichi Sugai, "The Japanese Police System," in Robert E. Ward (ed.), *Five Studies in Japanese Politics* (Ann Arbor: University of MIchigan Press, 1957), p. 2.
2. When the Imperial Rescript on Education was issued in 1890 — a kind of loyalty oath setting forth the basic standards of citizenship — some leaders thought it was unnecessary to include the phrase "respect the Constitution and obey the laws." This was assumed to be so obvious as not to need mentioning. Roger F. Hackett, *Yamagata Arimoto in the Rise of Modern Japan, 1838-1922* (Cambridge: Harvard University Press, 1971), p. 132ff. Japanese leaders during the Meiji period believed that obedience to law followed from inculcation of a basic orientation toward national objects, especially the Emperor. Contrast this with the importance of oaths in American life pledging loyalty to the law and constitution. Americans are preoccupied with compliance, Japanese with the commitment from which compliance follows.
3. Bruce Smith, *Police Systems in the United States* (New York: Harper and Row, second edition, 1960), pp. 147-154.

They had to be nonauthoritarian in manner, responsive to public opinion, restrained by constitutional rights, and accountable to local communities.[4] In contrast, efforts to reform the police in the United States have always been prompted by particular shortcomings of the police, either inefficient enforcement, especially of vice laws, or impropriety, such as corruption and brutality. It is one of history's delightful ironies that American officials during the Occupation, some of them experienced policemen, undertook to reshape Japanese police institutions with a sensitivity to general political objectives that had never been reflected in police reform in the United States. They became aware that policemen are more than enforcement technicians, that the actions of policemen can affect the moral basis of political community.

In Japan, determination of the character of the police has preceded specification of tasks; in the United States specification of tasks has preceded concern with character. American policemen fulfill their responsibilities when they bring people into compliance with law; Japanese policemen seek more than compliance, they seek acceptance of the community's moral values. They are not merely the law's enforcers; they are teachers in the virtue of the law. The Japanese police have been given a moral mandate, based on recognition of their importance in shaping the polity; American policemen have been given legal instructions, and have been enjoined from straying behind the law.

The structures of contemporary police organization in Japan and the United States also reflect distinctive historical traditions. Japan has a national police system, coordinated by the central government and standardized in operations. The United States has a radically decentralized system with little standardization and a marked lack of coordination. The Japanese police were created by an act of central initiative designed to consolidate national government.[5] They were formed from the top down — more accurately, the center out. By 1874 police affairs in every prefecture except Tokyo were directed by governors appointed by the central government. A Police Bureau in the Ministry of Home Affairs coordinated police affairs nationally.[6] The Tokyo police became subordinate to the

---

4. In the words of SCAP, "Police and Public Safety," p. 5, "These were not purely police problems, however, being but phases of the major occupation objective of a government responsible to the will of the people."
5. E.H. Norman, *Japan's Emergence as a Modern State* (New York: Institute of Pacific Relations, 1940), p. 118; Hackett, Chaps. 2 and 3; Ruth Benedict, *The Chrysanthemum and the Sword* (Boston: Houghten Miffin Co, 1946), Chap. 4.
6. The Bureau was originally lodged in the Ministry of Justice, 1872, but was transferred to the Home Ministry in 1874.

Home Ministry in 1886, superceding control by a semiautonomous local board.[7] The central government paid the salaries of all policemen above the rank of Inspector and subsidized part of general expenditure.[8] Where the Japanese system is national by design, the American system is national by default. American police forces were created by action of autonomous local communities. Policing was considered an indispensable part of local government. Later state and national forces — such as state patrols and the Federal Bureau of Investigation — were established to supplement the law enforcement capabilities of local communities. In all cases police organizations sprang from existing units of government. They represented the elaboration of any government's function — namely, enforcement — not a decision to reorganize government in new structures.

Today in Japan command of police operations is vested in prefectural organizations. This makes forty-six police forces in Japan proper, plus Okinawa. The central government has no operational forces of its own; it can direct prefectural police operations only where there has been a declared state of national emergency.[9] The National Police Agency, which is located in Tokyo and is part of the national government, is entirely a staff organization devoted to planning, coordination, and supervision. It maintains a variety of facilities for the use of prefectural forces, such as criminal files, forensic laboratories, communications networks, and advanced training schools.

Though the National Police Agency cannot direct field operations, it has considerable power to shape police conduct and procedures. The National Police Agency's influence is exerted in several ways. First, it sets the curricula for all police schools, including recruit training schools run by each prefecture. The N.P.A. maintains its own schools for training supervisory officers — sergeants and above. These are located in Tokyo and seven regional centers.[10]

Second, though the size of prefectural police forces is determined by local ordinance, they must meet minimum standards established

7. Baron Kanetake Oura, "The Police of Japan," in Count Shigenobu Okuma, *Fifty Years of New Japan* (London: Smith, Elder and Co., 1905), pp. 282-283; Hidenori Nakahara, "The Japanese Police," *Journal of Criminal Law, Criminology, and Police Science* (November-December 1955), pp. 583-584.
8. Nakahara, pp. 583-584, and Sugai, pp. 1-4.
9. The Police Law, Articles 71-75.
10. In another irony of the Occupation, there were no coordinated national training schemes for the police prior to 1947. The Occupation standardized police training to ensure that education of policemen was conformable to democratic precepts throughout Japan. SCAP, "Police and Public Safety," p. 56.

by the central government. This ensures that coverage is roughly the same from place to place.

Third, wage rates for policemen in each prefecture must conform to standards established by the National Police Agency. The N.P.A. sets levels around which prefectural salaries may fluctuate. They vary within a range of about 15 percent.[11]

Fourth, the national government makes financial contributions to prefectures to cover several catagories of expenses connected with police operations. The national government is required by law to pay for all police schools, communications equipment, facilities for criminal identification and data collection, and the purchase and maintenance of all vehicles, boats, and arms. It must also pay for operations related to national public safety. By decision of the central government, national funds are used to defray half of all construction costs and, in the case of several very poor prefectures, contributions are made to local police salaries.

Fifth, all officers with the rank of senior superintendent and above, wherever they may be stationed, are designated as national government employees and are paid out of central funds. They constitute a national corps of police administrators that may be rotated among the prefectures as the National Police Agency directs. There are two routes into this administrative elite. One is by promotion from the rank of patrolman within a prefectural force. Most of these men continue to serve in the force to which they were recruited. The second is by direct appointment to the National Police Agency on the basis of having passed the national advanced public service examination.[12] These officers are paid by the central government throughout their careers except when they are on deputation to a prefectural force. They belong to what is called the "elite course." The top posts in most prefectures are reserved for them, with the result that the senior personnel are, by and large, not local men.[13]

Japan has succeeded in standardizing performance while decentralizing command. In the United States, on the other hand, there is a greater number of autonomous commands relative to population

---

11. Information furnished by the National Police Agency.
12. They are recruited at the rank of assistant inspector but are very quickly promoted.
13. The practice of central appointment of senior personnel in the prefectures did not begin with the Police Law, 1954. The old Home Ministry appointed chiefs of police in every prefecture. The National Police Agency is merely following the tradition, with the important modification that local public safety commissions may now veto appointments. The Police Law, Article 50.

and geographical extent, and the quality of policing varies enormously. Americans are so strongly attached to vigorous local
government that attempts at standardization, even on a state basis,
have met strong resistance. Most states have some law setting forth
standards of police operations. They tend not to be very effective.
Most deal only with standards for recruitment and provide no
mechanism for supervision.[14] Standardization on a national basis, as
in Japan, would be impractical given significant differences in scale.
Japan is about the size of California; prefectures are the equivalent
of American counties.The Japanese model is more appropriate to
the states rather than the nation as a whole.

The size of police jurisdictions in Japan and therefore the scale of
force organization is much more rational than in the United States.
Japan did not patch together a system of police coverage out of
intensely jealous local government units. Impelled by a vision of a
strong centralized government, Meiji statesmen were guided by
administrative convenience. The average Japanese police force —
one in each prefecture — contains on the average five thousand
officers and covers about 2.5 million people. In the United States,
there are about twenty-five thousand police forces, each containing
on the average about eighteen officers and covering eighty-four
hundred persons.[15] There are no overlapping jurisdictions in Japan,
unlike the United States where city, county, and state police forces
may have concurrent jurisdiction.

The costs of policing are affected by the scale of organization. It
would be reasonable to expect that the Japanese have achieved lower
unit costs in providing coverage because of economies of sale of

14. Supervision by the state exists in Texas, Florida, and California. Interview with
James Sterling, Professional Standards Division, International Association of Chiefs
of Police, March 1974.

15. The number of enforcement agencies in the U.S. is a matter of dispute. For
years people have quoted Bruce Smith's figure from *Police Systems in the United
States* of 40,000. There is no justification for it. A survey by the Law Enforcement
Assistance Administration in 1970 found 14,901 police agencies in states, counties,
municipalities, and townships of over 1000 persons. Fourteen thousand of them
were run by local levels of government. LEAA, *Criminal Justice Agencies in
Pennsylvania* (Washington: Law Enforcement Assistnace Administration, no date),
Foreword. The President's Commission on Law Enforcement and Administration
of Justice, *Task Force Report: Police* (Washington: Government Printing Office,
1967), p. 7, found 25,000 police agencies in the mid-1960s with jurisdictions
covering less than 1000 people. More recent estimates, LEAA, p. 1, places this
figure at about 10,000. I have chosen the figure 25,000, which is roughly 14,901
plus 10,000. The number of police personnel in the United States as of 21 June 1973
was 459,492 according to information from the Government Division, Criminal
Justice Branch, U.S. Bureau of the Census. The *Statistical Abstract of the United
States, 1973*, p. 252, gives total fulltime police officers as 472,066 in 1971.

police forces and the absence of overlapping jurisdiction. This is not in fact the case. Per capita costs of a unit of policing are almost identical in Japan and the United States. In 1973 there was one policeman for every 585 persons in Japan and one for every 445 in the United Sates.[16] There was 31 percent more policemen per capita in the United States than in Japan.[17] The per capita costs of policing in Japan were $23.60 and in the United States $28.60[18] Americans paid 21 percent more per capita for police coverage. Thus Americans paid 21 percent more and got 31 percent more coverage per capita. Though these figures are approximations, at least for the United States, and exchange rates fluctuate substantially, it is fair to conclude that unit costs of coverage are about the same in both countries.

The Japanese, however, devote a larger share of national resources to policing than Americans do. They spend 0.92 percent of their Gross National Product on police, as opposed to 0.52 percent in the United States.[19] In per capita terms as well, the burden is greater on the Japanese: police costs consumed 1.2 percent of per capita national income in 1972, as opposed to 0.64 percent in the United States.[20]

So far, the measure of police output has been quantitative — the number of policemen per unit of population. If the quality of performance is considered — proportion of arrests to offenses, incidence of police corruption, cordiality of police-public relations — then the Japanese are getting a much better return than are Americans. At equal unit costs, Japanese are obtaining a far superior performance. At the same time, if Americans spent as much on the police proportional to their wealth as the Japanese, qualitative gains in performance could undoubtedly be made. Almost twice as much money would be available for police purposes and, if patterns of expenditure remained the same, there would be twice as many policemen. Most observers agree that adding personnel does reduce crime and raise arrest rates. There is an important

16. Computed using figure of 472,000 officers for the U.S.
17. Per capita figures: Japan, for every person there are 0.0017 police officers; United States, for every person, 0.0022 police officers.
18. Total budget for the police in Japan was Y670,900 million. Information furnished by the National Police Agency. Total expenditure on police in the U.S. was just over $6 billion. *Statistical Abstract of the United States, 1973*, p. 250; statement by the Executive Director of the National Commission on Criminal Justice Standards and Goals, *Denver Post*, 1 October 1973, p. 8.
19. *Statistical Handbook of Japan, 1972*, p. 105: Gross National Product, Y70.9 trillion. *Statistical Abstract of the United States, 1973*, p. 319: Gross National Product, $1,151.8 billion.
20. Per capita national income in Japan was Y551,200; in the U.S., $4450. *Ibid.*

implication of this discussion: a unit of police coverage produces substantially different results in the two countries. The United States, with more policemen per capita, achieves lower qualitative performance. This suggests that differences in return from a unit of coverage are attributable to nonpolice factors. If this is true, there may be sharply declining returns from employment of additional police manpower after a certain point. It is possible that no amount of investment in the police in the United States will produce results as good as the Japanese.[21]

The third difference in institutional traditon has to do with the way control is exerted by the community over the police. In the United States, the police, like any government agency, are accountable to elected political bodies. Americans fear creation of police organizations that are immune from inspection and direction by elected representatives of the people. Politicians supervise the police directly. The disadvantages of this has been that politicians can be self-serving and irresponsible. American history is littered with cases of politicians using the police as a base of power or obtaining special favors from them in exchange for promotions and raises in pay. Reform efforts over the past one hundred years have tried to achieve political accountability while avoiding partisan intrusion. A variety of formal arrangements have been tried: direct election of senior police officers, supervision by elected bodies, appointment of nonpartisan regulating committees, state supervision of local forces, and appointment of senior officers by elected executive officials.[22] Today most police chiefs are appointed by an executive officer, usually an elected official, subject to confirmation by a representative assembly. Police forces are linked directly to politicians at the apex of the police hierarchy.

In Japan police officials are not accountable directly to politicians and never have been. From the Meiji Restoration until 1945 immediate supervision over the police was exercised by bureaucrats. Prefectural chiefs of police reported to governors appointed by the central government. National police affairs were coordinated through the Ministry of Home Affairs. The only politician involved was the Home Minister, quite removed from direct contact with uniformed officers. The Occupation abolished the powerful Home Ministry but kept a protective layer between police and elected

21. In mathematical terms, the relation between increases in police investment and performance may be asymptotic. The location of the asymptote is a function of cultural variables.
22. Smith, Chap. 7; James F. Richardson, *The New York Police* (New York: Oxford University Press, 1970), Chap. 9.

officials — the public safety commissions.[23] Public safety commissions are composed of three to five members depending on the size of the prefecture; members are appointed for fixed terms by the governor with the approval of the legislature.[24] Public safety commissions are hybrids, neither bureaucratic nor political, like regulatory agencies in the United States. Elected politicians are ineligible for appointment as are persons who have served in the police or the prosecutor's service within the preceding five years.[25] A national public safety commission appointed by the Prime Minister and confirmed by the national legislature is responsible through the National Police Agency for overall direction and coordination.[26] The public safety commissions have exclusive authority over the discipline and dismissal of all police officers.[27] Prefectural chiefs are appointed and dismissed through coordinated action by local and national public safety commissions. Because Tokyo is the capital, it has a unique position in the system; the consent of the Prime Minister is required for a change in its chief of police.[28]

Public safety commissions are not the only device for attenuating political pressure on the police. Mandated national standards for pay and size of local forces reduce dependence on local legislatures. Top administrative positions are filled with officers recruited nationally, paid by the central government, and nominated by the national public safety commission. Local control can be exerted only through the prefectural public safety commission which must be nonpartisan in composition. Prefectural forces are sufficiently large that personnel can be rotated through positions every two years. Officers cannot become too intimately involved with local communities. Because promotions are determined by the police

23. Contrary to what many Japanese think, the idea of public safety commissions does not appear to have originated with Americans. It came from the Katayama government in 1946 which suggested a three-member national public safety commission. SCAP, "Police and Public Safety," Chaps. 2 and 3. There are appointed public safety commissions in some cities in the U.S., but they are not the rule.

24. The Police Law, Article 39. Commission members may be reappointed indefinitely.

25. There must be a balance among political party affiliations represented on a commission. The Police Law, Articles 9(3), 9(4), 41(3), 41(4), 41(5).

26. The National Public Safety Commission is composed of five members plus a chairman who is a Minister of State and therefore a cabinet official. This is the closest contact between police and politician that is allowed.

27. The Police Law, Article 55(4).

28. *Ibid.*, Articles 48, 49, 50.

organization itself, subject to approval by public safety commissions, there is nothing a local politican can do for a police officer.
He controls neither money nor the prospects for advancement.
Japanese policemen can afford to be confident and even con-
descending in their relations with politicians.

Japanese and Americans want their police to be responsive to
community sentiment without becoming unprinicipled. Reflecting
different political traditions, they have chosen contrasting institutional arrangements for accomplishing this. Americans distrust
bureaucratic government and consider close supervision by politicians indispensable to liberty. Japanese readily accept bureaucratic
government and consider intrusions by politicians dangerous to
liberty because they are self-serving. Cultivation of the police by
politicians is viewed as inappropriate and undesirable. Prime
Minister Tanaka was strongly censured by the press when he
addressed a national meeting of prefectural chiefs of police.[29] The
visit was not regarded as a gesture of public support, a fillip to
morale, as it would have been in the United States, but as a possible
first step in compromising the political neutrality of the police.

The Japanese strategy for achieving a responsible police force is to
insulate them from specific community pressures, fix upon them
responsibility for their own conduct, and consistently demand high
standards of performance. In practice external checks upon the
police, such as public safety commissions, come into play only when
the police fail to meet their responsibilities. The public safety
commissions are restraints in reserve, as are the press, courts, and
bar. Initiative belongs to the police; nonpolice persons, especially
politicians, merely ratify. In the United States, on the other hand,
responsible conduct is sought through a delicate formal balancing
of power between the police and external, primarily political,
institutions. External supervision is active; it is a first line of defense
against the misuse of police authority. Accountability to nonpolice
institutions is considered more important than the development of
police initiative. Self-regulation cannot be trusted; it requires too
much independence. The result is that American police have not
developed the kind of pride in self-discipline found among Japanese
police. American politicians, on the other hand, are loath to
develop coherent policies for the police lest they be accused of
undue intervention in police matters. Americans insist on external
control but have had sufficient experience to know that very often it
can be uninformed, partisan, venal, and demoralizing to the police.

29. 1973.

So politicians confine themselves to spasmodic and righteous criticism in the name of democracy and the police demonstrate responsibility by denying initiative. No one is consistently in charge and everyone has a bad conscience.[30]

There has been a great deal of talk in the United States in recent years about establishing what are called "professional" police forces. This means encouraging police organizations to admit that police work is judgmental, to begin to discuss criteria for regulating discretion, to advise the community in the requirements of civility, and to develop pride in meaningful self-regulation. The goals are admirable — and very Japanese — but the movement goes against the American grain. Because Americans fear self-regulating bureaucracies, they cannot allow the police the kind of independence accorded to doctors, lawyers, and ministers. It is an article of faith that civil servants must be amenable to direction by elected representatives. This is doubly true for those who possess raw power. The slogan "Support your local police" — genuinely intended to encourage the police and bolster morale — contains a fine irony. Insistence on small jurisdictions in the name of responsiveness ensures that police forces will be vulnerable to political penetration, thereby weakening initiative, and insufficiently large to provide attractive careers to ambitious and talented persons. The only pride such police officers can feel is in their authority. Local control and professionalism are not compatible.

Summarizing the discussion so far, there are the following differences between the institutional traditions of the Japanese and American police. Police in Japan, though required not to act contrary to law, assume diffuse social responsibilities and regulate themselves in accordance with standards of propriety shared with the community, except where there are clear indications they are unable to do so. American police are created to perform carefully specified tasks; the only legitimate impingement of the police on the community is what is detailed in law. The best guarantee that this mandate is not exceeded is direct and vigorous supervision by elected officials.

The American tradition is distinctive, certainly compared with Japan, and it has affected contemporary police practices in several ways. First, because only mandated actions are legitimate, the

30. Cyril D. Robinson, "The Mayor and the Police — A Look at the Political Role of the Police in Society" (Unpublished manuscript, 1970); James F. Ahern, *Police in Trouble* (New York: Hawthorne Books, Inc., 1972), p. 140; James Q. Wilson, *Varieties of Police Behavior* (Cambridge: Harvard University Press, 1968), pp. 234-235.

police are relatively insensitive to social effects flowing from authorized actions. Their denial of wider and more subtle impingement is self-protecting: police cannot be accused of failing to meet responsibilities they do not have. Second, operational requirements for performing particular tasks are the primary determinants of police behavior and organization. Tactical decisions shape strategy. Performance goals are defined primarily in terms of completing specific jobs, such as making arrests, regulating traffic, clearing drunks from the street, and solving sensational crimes. Preoccupied with concrete tasks, the police neglect development of an ethic supportive of underlying political and moral principles not specifically enjoined by law. Third, relying so extensively on external checks to ensure right behavior, police are not encouraged to develop a binding self-enforced disciplinary code. Discipline is accepted grudgingly, as an external demand, rather than pridefully as a condition of membership in a unique institution.

The fundamental argument of this book is that police institutions are shaped by social context. Policemen do not stand in isolation; they reflect the society. The variety of circumstances that help to mold the police is very great. In searching for the roots of contrasting Japanese and American police practices, we have seen the importance of factors such as the following: social homogeniety, occupational mobility, the role of groups in developing personal identity, faith in technology, regulation of firearms, sexual morality, deference to authority, and political philosophy. One implication of the conclusion that police behavior and social context are inextricably linked is that police practices cannot be exported successfully from one country to another. Because Japan has such an enviable record of police efficiency and propriety, it is tempting to advocate importation to the United States of a variety of Japanese practices—stratified recruitment, neighborhood police posts, disarmed riot policemen, enhanced police discretion, and civilian auxiliaries. But police practices are not interchangeable parts. Some will fit a different social context, others will not. There is no cultural inhibition in the United States against expanding the duration of police training to a year, as the Japanese have done, or setting up counselling offices. There are enormous impediments, however, to disarming policemen and conducting residential surveys. Discovery that the international market for police practices may be limited does not vitiate the importance of examining foreign experience in the police field, though it does mean that trade will not be on a cash-and-carry basis. The most important reason for studying foreign experience is to learn to recognize the character of our own institutions. Recognizing what we are is essential for planning what we might become.

A second implicaton of the discovery of the importance of social context is that police reform cannot be directed exclusively at policemen. Take the case of police brutality. Excessive and unjustified use of force is related to such factors as the presence in a population of categories of people considered marginal to customary morality; to low levels of public respect for policemen which impel them to defend their self-esteem in physical ways; and to popular attachment to firearms that raises the intensity of apprehension in any police-citizen contact and makes experimentation by the police with nonlethal force more dangerous.[31] Or consider the difficulties of changing the way policemen act on the street. How they move, stand, and talk is affected by popular resentment of police in personal affairs, by the unwillingness of the public to share policing tasks, by the tradition of thinking of policemen as legal instruments rather than agents of moral authority, and by the belief that justice is obtained by assertion rather than submission. The same sobering lesson — that society may have to change as well as the criminals — applies to the treatment of crime. Searching for an explanation for remarkably different crime rates in Japan and the United States, it is a mistake to write off as fortuitous the fact that Japanese, compared with Americans, are less combative in confrontations with authority; that offenders against the law are expected to accept the community's terms for resocialization rather than insisting on legal innocence and bargaining for mitigation of punishment; that individual character is thought to be mutable, responsive to informal sanctions of proximate groups; that government intervention in social life is more acceptable; and that individuals feel a moral obligation to assist actively in preserving moral consensus in the community. If social context is crucial for understanding how the police behave, it is unlikely to be less important for understanding criminal deviance, since deviance is the pretext for creating the police in the first place.

Recognition of the importance of environment on police practice does not mean that police agencies are powerless to change by their own initiative. Nor does it mean that improvement is impossible without the total transformation of society. Despairing acceptance of the status quo is no more justified than uncritical faith in the prospects for change. What is needed is discerning analysis. There are three steps in estimating whether reform is possible. The first

31. See Chap. 8.

step is to specify in practical terms the features that are to change. Police institutions are complex; activities must be disaggregated if they are to be studied intelligently. Rather than talking generally about reforming the police, discussion should focus on deployment, anonymity of personnel, nonenforcement contacts, use of weapons, complaint procedures, individuation of treatment, counselling, and so forth. There is not a single problem of respect for the police; there are a host of them. People evaluate the police differently depending on the situation; the same criteria for judgment do not apply at all times. Improvement of regard requires a variety of tactics depending on the activity involved, the situation, and the portion of the public contacted.

Having specified in practical terms what is to be changed, the second step in analysis is to discover whether the crucial constraints exist within the police organization or outside it. There are three possibilites, not just two as one might think. First, the police may have total control, lacking only the will or imagination to do differently. For example, few people would care very much if the police wanted to recruit at two rank levels in order to provide a higher proportion of officers with educational skills appropriate for staffing senior executive positions. Similarly, the police are free to experiment with nonlethal uses of force if they wish; the public cannot compel them to use firearms. Second, the police may not have effective control over what they do and changes in practice will require community support. For example, if the police want to increase the amount of formal training required of recruits, additional funds would have to be appropriated. Again, if police patrolling is deemed inadequate for preventing crime, then the public must consider shouldering more of the burden of policing or allowing penetration by the police in novel ways. Third, changes in police practice may require cooperation from the community but the police can be instrumental in generating that response. Policemen need not always stand helpless before social constraints. They have demonstrated effective political capabilites already that need not be confined to defensive trade-unionism. For instance, the police could make a major contribution to transforming the public's view of the utility of firearms for private protection. Or they could encourage the growth of community spirit in residential neighborhoods by helping to develop an expanded role for private citizens in crime prevention.

Only after determining what specific aspects of police activity must change and where the impediments to change lie can an assessment be made of the difficulties of bringing it about. This is the final step, one that can now be made intelligently. Some reforms will be easy—matters of convenience to be achieved by resolute decision. Some will be unthinkable—resting on the encrusted reefs of tradition and culture. And some will be possible but difficult, requiring concerted effort by police and public over long periods of time.

Perhaps the greatest impediment to change in the American police is perspective. Americans have a narrow vision of the police. They are unaccustomed to seeing the police as social actors; they see them only as enforcement technicians. Because Americans are anxious about the creation of governmental authority, the great injunction they lay on the police is to fight crime within the letter of the law. They do not demand that they fight crime within the law in particular ways that reinforce the values that undergird democratic life. Legality and efficiency in enforcement do not exhaust the contributions police make to society. Can American perspectives on the police be broadened? It is doubtful. Political tradition as well as contemporary scandals combine to make the police protectively self-denying and the public loath to trust them further. The dilemma of the police in the United States can be posed in a single question: how can esteem be kindled for a role most people accept only as an unpleasant necessity?

Index

Accountability, 67-70, 80-82, 191-194 passim; legislative control, 69; mechanisms, 77-78, 82. *See also* Discipline
Adultery, 118
Alcohol. *See* Drinking
Allied Occupation, 185-186
Apology, 134-136. *See* Authority
Arrest: police procedure, 19; cleared by, 146-147. *See also* Law
Asakusa, 107
Asama-Sanso incident, 160-162
Assassination. *See* Violence
Athletics, 73-74, 163-164. *See also* Police, physical training
Authority, 66-67, 138ff, 145ff, 149

Board of Health, 110-111
Brutality. *See* Misbehavior
Burakumin, 86

Cho-kai, 93ff
Chuzaisho. See *Koban*
Complaints. *See* Misbehavior
Confession, 151-153. *See also* Criminal justice system
Corruption. *See* Misbehavior
Counselling, 87-89
Courts. *See* Criminal justice system
Crime: rates compared, 5-6; underreporting, 7-8; trends, 7; quality of life, 9; causes of, 9-11, 155-156, 181-183, 196. *See also* Firearms, Narcotics, Violence
Crime Prevention, 89-91, 99-100. *See also* Crime Prevention Associations
Crime Prevention Associations: functions, 91-93; patrols, 92; organization, 93-94; "contact points," 93-94; National Federation of, 94-95; finances, 94-95; membership, 94-95; leadership of, 96; development, 96-97; relations with police, 97-99 passim
Criminal justice system: philosophy of, 140, 149; prosecution, 141-143; guilty pleas, 147, 151; efficiency of, 147-148; lawyers, 148-149; arrest, 151-152; rights of suspects, 151-154. *See also* Sentences
Customs: sleeping, 23, n. 15; privacy, 45; civic responsibility, 100-101; sexual, 117-122 passim; marriage and divorce, 118; attitudes toward technology, 181

Demonstrations. *See* Violence
Detectives, 19
Deviance. *See* Crime
Discipline, internal, 62-64 passim; superiors' responsibility, 64-65; mechanisms for, 65-66, 70-72, 78-80.
Discretion, police, 39-41, 88-89, 134-138 passim
Drinking: customs, 75-76; laws, 104ff; arrests for, 104; police attitude toward, 105; types of establishments, 106, 108-109; Tiger Boxes, 108; hours for, 109-111. *See also* Entertainment
Drug addiction. *See* Narcotics

Entertainment: areas, 29ff, 106-108; prices, 30, 109; hostesses, 30, 120-121
Entrapment, 114
Expense accounts, 109

Family Affairs Counselling Office, 88
Firearms: in crime, 11, 169; numbers, 168; regulations, 168-169; attitudes toward, 170-171, 182; effect on police work, 171; in riots, 175. *See also* Police, casualties and armament
Folktales, 139-140
Force: police tradition, 164; by policewomen, 167. *See also* Police, use of force; Police, physical training
Fraud. *See* Entertainment, Prostitution
Friends of the Police Association, 99

Gambling, 95, 111-112
Gangsters, 129
Ginza, 107
Giri, 112
Go, 112
Government: informal, 93; moral authority, 155-156

Han. See *Government, informal*
Homosexuality, 122
Hostesses. *See* Entertainment
Human Rights Bureau, 3, 68-69

Juvenile delinquency, 107, n. 17

Kabukicho, 107

199